1992

# The Iraqi Revolution of 1958

# The Iraqi Revolution of 1958

## *The Old Social Classes Revisited*

Edited by

Robert A. Fernea and Wm. Roger Louis

I. B. Tauris & Co. Ltd.
*Publishers*
London · New York

Sponsored by the Center for Middle Eastern
Studies, University of Texas at Austin

Published in 1991 by
I.B.Tauris & Co Ltd
110 Gloucester Avenue
London NW1 8JA

175 Fifth Avenue
New York
NY 10010

In the United States of America
and Canada distributed by
St Martin's Press
175 Fifth Avenue
New York
NY 10010

Sponsored by the Center for
Middle Eastern Studies,
University of Texas at Austin

A catalogue record for this book is available from the British Library.
ISBN 1–85043–318–6

Library of Congress Cataloging-in-Publication Number: 90–063392

Printed and bound in Great Britain by
Butler & Tanner Ltd, Frome and London

# Contents

# Foreword

ALBERT HOURANI

The occupation of Kuwait by Iraq, and the reaction to it in the Middle East and throughout the world, have opened a new phase in Iraqi history. It is too early to say how the crisis will develop, how it will change the nature of Iraq, and how it will affect the other countries involved in the conflict. The subject of this book is another sudden event that changed the history of Iraq, the revolution of 1958. The book is based on papers delivered at a conference held in 1989 and revised before the events of August 1990. Far from dealing with what might now seem to be the ancient history of 1958, it throws light on the process of change which led to the present crisis. Hanna Batatu's book on social and political change, *The Old Social Classes and the Revolutionary Movements of Iraq*, formed the starting point of the conference and of the present volume; in his concluding chapter here Batatu expresses the belief that 'it is in moments of great upheaval that societies may best be studied'. It may be that a study of the revolution of 1958 will help to explain certain aspects of Iraq as it is today.

The revolution of 1958 revealed the fragility of the structure that had been created during the period of the British mandate and which continued in that of ultimate British control which followed it. The basis of the structure was the continuing British presence: the air-bases, the advisers in government departments, and the control of the country's most important economic asset, its oil. On this foundation new political institutions had been erected: the monarchy, the government, the parliament, the civil service, and the army. Fragile as they were, such institutions, it was hoped, would provide a framework within which power could be acquired, exercised, transferred, and even limited, and within which an Iraqi nation could grow. The destruction of the monarchy and the end of British influence in 1958 opened the way to a struggle for power between groups linked by interest and kinship. The result was a power that could be exercised without restrictions except those imposed by fear of conspiracy or assassination, and, as has now been seen, could try to extend its limits beyond the frontiers of the state.

The institutions which had existed before 1958 had not in fact served to create a national political society in the full sense. The forty years between the withdrawal of Ottoman rule in 1918 and the revolution of 1958 had been too short a time for three Ottoman provinces, with populations mixed in ethnic origin and religious allegiance, and a countryside scarcely subjected to the authority of the urban government, to coalesce into a national society. The dynamic force essential for the creation of a nation could not be provided by a royal family which was still half-foreign, a ruling group which did not represent all the social forces of the country, a machinery of civil and military control still in the process of being formed, and behind them all a foreign and resented presence.

By the 1950s there was developing a political culture which could not find expression through the institutions of the state. There was a larger educated class which drew its categories of explanation from pan-Arabism or Marxism, or a mixture of the two. A growing mass of the urban poor in Baghdad and Mosul was expressing its needs in terms of these new ideologies or in those of a just Islamic society.

Those who observed the revolution of 1958 at close quarters have borne witness to the explosion of new ideas and the social forces they represented. The sense, so common at moments of great upheaval, was that everything was now possible. This proved to be a false dawn. The communists, after a short period when they were in the ascendant, saw their power destroyed. The vision of pan-Arabism was dissolved, in the struggle for influence between Gamal Abdel Nasser, who embodied it, and Abdel Karim Qasim, who had come to power in Iraq partly on a wave of enthusiasm for it. The Baathist regime, which emerged as the victor in the struggle for power, had an official ideology of pan-Arabism, but its two decades of rule may also have helped to create a special Iraqi nationalism. With the passing of one generation to another, what was artificial came to appear natural. The extension of government control, national education, economic development, and the common experience of a long war, may all have created an Iraqi nation.                    *December 1990*

# Preface

In March 1989 the Center for Middle Eastern Studies at the University of Texas at Austin sponsored a symposium on the Iraqi Revolution of 1958. Hanna Batatu's *The Old Social Classes and the Revolutionary Movements of Iraq* provided the theme. Each of the participants was asked to reassess the Iraqi Revolution while reflecting on Batatu's interpretation. The papers have been subsequently rewritten in light of the conference discussion and edited for the present volume.

We wish to thank Professor Majid Khadduri for his guidance at an early stage of the project. We benefited from Isam al-Khafaji's presentation in the conference. We are grateful especially to Hanna Batatu for allowing his work to be used as a catalyst, for participating in the conference debate, and for contributing the concluding chapter. We acknowledge support from the Center for Middle Eastern Studies, the College of Liberal Arts, the Office of Graduate Studies, the Department of Anthropology, the Department of Government, the Department of History, the Lyndon B. Johnson School of Public Affairs and the Faculty Seminar on British Studies. We are exceedingly indebted to the Director of the Center for Middle Eastern Studies, Ian Manners, and to William A. Braisted, Annes McCann–Baker and Marjorie Payne for their help. We extend our thanks above all to Dr Robert W. Stookey, a retired Foreign Service Officer and Research Associate at the Center, for his assistance in preparing the book for publication.

# Contributors

**Frederick W. Axelgard** (Ph.D. The Fletcher School of Law and Diplomacy) directs an office in the State Department's Bureau of Politico–Military Affairs. He was formerly a Senior Fellow in Middle Eastern Studies at the Center for Strategic and International Affairs. His works include *A New Iraq?* and *Iraq in Transition*. His doctoral research focused on US–Iraqi relations before the Iraqi revolution of 1958.

**Hanna Batatu** (Ph.D. Harvard University) is Professor of Arab Studies, Georgetown University. He was previously Professor of Politics at the American University of Beirut. He is the author of *The Old Social Classes and the Revolutionary Movements of Iraq: A Study of Iraq's Old Landed and Commercial Classes and of its Communists, Ba'thists, and Free Officers.*

**Norman Daniel** (Ph.D. Edinburgh University) served in the British Council from 1947 to 1979, mainly in the Arab countries. He was in Iraq in 1958. In retirement he stayed on in Egypt. His work, primarily medievalist, extends to neo-colonialism. He is the author of *Islam and the West; Islam, Europe and Empire; The Cultural Barrier; The Arabs and Medieval Europe* and *Heroes and Saracens.*

**Marion Farouk-Sluglett** (Dr. Phil. Humboldt University, Berlin) is Lecturer in Politics, Department of Political Theory and Government, University College of Swansea. She has taught at University College, Dublin, and held research fellowships at the Universities of Durham and Leiden. She is co-author of *Iraq since 1958: from Revolution to Dictatorship*.

**Robert A. Fernea** (Ph.D. University of Chicago) is Professor of Anthropology and a former Director of the Center for Middle Eastern Studies at the University of Texas. He is a member of the Executive Board of the Society for Cultural Anthropology. He is the author of *Shaykh and Effendi, Nubians in Egypt* and, with Elizabeth Fernea, *The Arab World: Personal Encounters*.

**Rashid I. Khalidi** (D.Phil. Oxford) is Associate Director of the Center for Middle Eastern Studies and an Associate Professor of History, University of Chicago. He has taught at the Lebanese University, the American University of Beirut, and Columbia University. He is the author of *British Policy toward Syria and Palestine* and *Under Siege: PLO Decision-Making during the 1985 War*. He is the co-editor of *Palestine and the Gulf* and *The Origins of Arab Nationalism*.

**Wm. Roger Louis** (D.Litt. Oxford) holds the Kerr Chair in English History and Culture at the University of Texas and is a Supernumerary Fellow of St Antony's College, Oxford. With James A. Bill he has edited *Musaddiq, Iranian Nationalism, and Oil*, and, with Roger Owen, *Suez 1956: The Crisis and its Consequences*. He was Chichele Lecturer at All Souls College, Oxford, in 1990.

**Roger Owen** (D.Phil. Oxford) is a Fellow and former Director of the Middle East Centre, St Antony's College, Oxford, and a Lecturer in the Recent Economic History of the Middle East. He is the author of *Cotton and the Egyptian Economy* and *The Middle East in the World Economy, 1800–1914*. He is co-editor of *Studies in the Theory of Imperialism* and *Suez 1956*. In 1990 he was Visiting Professor of Economic History at the University of Texas.

**Peter Sluglett** (D.Phil. Oxford) is Lecturer in Modern Middle Eastern History, University of Durham. He is the author of *Britain in Iraq 1914–1932* and co-author of *Iraq since 1958: from Revolution to Dictatorship*. He has also co-edited two volumes of studies on Middle Eastern cities.

**Joe Stork** (M.A. Columbia University) is the Editor of *Middle East Report* and the co-founder of the Middle East Research and

Information Project (MERIP). He is the author of *Middle East Oil and the Energy Crisis*, and his essay on class and political power in Iraq recently appeared in Berch Berberoglu, ed., *Power and Stability in the Middle East.*

**Nicholas G. Thacher** (M.A. Princeton) is a retired Foreign Service Officer who was political officer at the American Embassy in Baghdad, 1956–58. He later served as Minister Counselor and Deputy Chief of Mission in Tehran, and, in his final post, as Ambassador to Saudi Arabia.

**Abdul-Salaam Yousif** (Ph.D. University of Iowa) is Adjunct Professor, National University, San Diego. He was previously Lecturer at the University of California, San Diego. He has published scholarly articles on Iraqi literature and culture. His Ph.D. dissertation was entitled 'Vanguardist Cultural Practices: The Formation of an Alternative Cultural Hegemony in Iraq and Chile, 1930–1970'.

**Sami Zubaida** (M.A. Leicester University) is Senior Lecturer in Sociology at Birkbeck College, University of London. He is the author of *Islam, the People and the State: Essays on Political Ideas and Movements in the Middle East*, and co-editor of *Popular Culture, Mass Culture and Social Life in the Middle East.*

# Introduction

The Iraqi Revolution of July 1958 was a landmark in the history of the Middle East. It overthrew an existing social order, one that had been shaped by the British after the First World War in a region that had already been subjected to foreign domination under the Turks. The upheaval had political and economic consequences that persist to the present day. On the eve of the Revolution, Iraq was ruled by an elite consisting of the monarchy, merchants and property owners. Many of the latter included tribal shaikhs, lawyers, politicians, newspaper publishers and high-ranking civil servants. This orchestra of complementary interests was directed largely by the British, although they received help from the Americans, whose influence had been felt in Iraq since the Second World War. The British were committed to the well-being of the Iraq Petroleum Company, which they largely owned and controlled. 'Common sense' – the widely accepted views of foreign observers at the time – recognized that the country had problems, but believed that they could be dealt with through the oil revenue channelled into the Iraq Development Board, which included British and American advisers. Iraqi self-interest seemed to coincide with British economic and strategic self-interest. The Americans, who had begun to wage the cold war, also regarded Iraq as an anti-Soviet outpost. 'Common sense' again seemed to indicate that the Iraqis would respond in the same way as the British and Americans to the dangers of the cold war. On 14 July, 1958, however, a revolt of young officers led by Brigadier Abdel Karim Qasim broke out in the Royal Iraqi Army and quickly developed into a revolution that overthrew local elites and eliminated foreign influence. The British lost their air bases and, eventually, their oil revenues. The Americans lost the political and military influence of the Baghdad Pact, which they had helped to construct but had never joined. At least in its direct manifestations, Western imperialism ended and Iraqi public life turned in new directions.

Two decades later, in 1978, a book on the 1958 Revolution was published which represented a milestone in the study and interpretation of the subject. It was begun initially as part of a Ph.D. dissertation at Harvard by a young scholar of Palestinian origins, Hanna Batatu. It was published by the Princeton University Press as *The Old Social Classes and the Revolutionary Movements of Iraq* and comprises nearly 1,300 pages of descriptive analysis of both the pre- and post-revolutionary distributions of wealth and power in Iraq. Before and after the 1958 Revolution Batatu had the opportunity to pursue his research in the police files of the Iraqi government. Based on interviews and government documents as well as secret police dossiers, the book describes and analyses the old pre-revolutionary order and argues that the roots of the post-revolutionary political struggles may be seen in society prior to 1958. Batatu's probing study of class differences in Iraqi society also encompasses an analysis of the ethnic and religious groups in the national population. He identifies the men who made Iraqi history in the context of the complex differences in wealth, power and communal identity. Accounts of their struggles for power and control of the state form the central focus of the work. *The Old Social Classes* reveals the social structures of a Middle Eastern country during a period of radical change, a period in which the Revolution of 1958 is of central importance.

As stated in the Preface, in March 1989 the Center for Middle Eastern Studies at the University of Texas at Austin convened a symposium on the Revolution of 1958 with Batatu's work as the centrepiece. Each of the participants was asked to reappraise the Iraqi Revolution bearing Batatu's arguments in mind. The resulting chapters reveal how a moment of history can be constituted and contested in various disciplines and professions, including anthropology, economics, history, literature and sociology, as well as diplomacy. What emerges is an intersection of diverse understandings cultivated according to different training and personal convictions. In the comments that follow, we view the chapters comparatively and against the background of Western 'common sense' expectations that made the 1958 Revolution and the events that followed so surprising to so many observers.

No one living in Iraq at the time of the Revolution could have been unaware that the royal government headed by Prime Minister Nuri Said was highly unpopular among intellectuals and Communists, but the latter were assumed to be under the control of the police and probably no one was prepared for the cheering crowds which swept through the streets of Baghdad on 14 July 1958. It was part of this crowd which caught and killed Nuri Said on the next day as he fled down an alley, covered with a woman's cloak. According to Norman Daniel, a British Council representative in Baghdad at the time, the crowds were angered by British imperialism and ardent for Gamal Abdel Nasser's pan-Arab nationalism rather than enthusiastic about any of the individuals or institutions in Iraq. The 'cheerful spontaneity' and mood of 'release and liberation' which Daniel felt in the crowd fuelled a strong drive to liberate Iraq from the shackles of British imperialism, a motivation which Daniel assesses in relation to the urge to overturn the 'alien' monarchy and the 'parasitic' shaikhs. Using the French Revolution as an historical counterpoint (he reminds us that it also broke out on 14 July), Daniel sees the Baghdad crowds as evidence of basic changes in the Iraqi 'state of mind'. Daniel's chapter is thus a study in perception and opinion. Only by taking into account the spirit of the times can we hope to understand the events of 1958 as they were perceived by contemporaries.

Was it this Iraqi 'state of mind' that escaped the attention of British and American diplomats and intelligence personnel? Daniel had no diplomatic responsibility, but, like many foreigners in Iraq at the time who were in regular contact with Iraqis, he was well aware of the growing loss of confidence in the government of Nuri Said. Batatu provides a wealth of evidence and commentary about the conditions in Iraq related to the government's lack of popular support. Foreigners could travel practically everywhere in Iraq with far less restriction than has ever since been the case and, it appears in retrospect, one would have had to be blind not to have seen the abject poverty in the country. Why then did the officials of Britain and the United States seem so totally surprised and unprepared when the 1958 Revolution broke out? The 'common sense' shared by outsiders assumed that both the British and American governments had plans well in place to secure a new footing in Iraq if trouble occurred. Four of the contributors to the present volume – Norman Daniel, Roger Louis, Nicholas Thacher and Frederick Axelgard – see the Revolution as a rebuff to British and American policies towards Iraq in the preceding period. These chapters help us to understand why no such plans actually existed.

Nicholas Thacher was an American Foreign Service Officer in Baghdad in 1958. One can see from his chapter that global policies, and their implicit ideology, coloured American official opinion about conditions in Iraq. American policy was presumably based on information and assessments passed to the State Department from the American Embassy in Baghdad. The Ambassador, Waldemar J. Gallman, actually referred to the Baghdad crowd as 'hoodlums', which suggests that any awareness of the Iraqi 'state of mind' may have been limited in Baghdad as well as in Washington. The 'pacto-mania' that charaterized the 'cold warriors' of the State Department contributed to a mentality that was disinclined to believe that Iraq was an unstable ally. This was certainly the attitude of the Secretary of State, John Foster Dulles. Moreover, American officials who gave warning about deepening Iraqi resentment towards Zionism were often disparaged in Washington as 'State Department Arabists'. The theme that emerges from Thacher's chapter is that the Western powers could have supported the Middle Eastern states more informally, with measures less counter-productive than those of the Baghdad Pact, which Iraqis generally felt was designed to sustain British imperialism and the grip of the governing elite.

The British, above all, upheld the view that Iraq was an important battlefield of the cold war and that Nuri Said could help secure Western aims. How did the British assess the strengths and weaknesses of the Iraqi government before the Revolution? Roger Louis, on the basis of newly accessible archival evidence in London, quotes the British Ambassador to Iraq, Sir Michael Wright, as saying that Nuri was 'a sincere patriot working according to his own lights for the betterment of all Iraqis'. The British, of course, were also interested in the 'betterment of all Iraqis', especially if it coincided with British self-interest, but they, as well as Nuri Said, miscalculated on the time it would take for the oil revenues invested in capital projects to benefit the common people. They also misjudged the sentiment against the Baghdad Pact, which isolated Iraq from most of the other Arab states. After the Suez crisis of 1956, the British were certainly aware that the identification of Britain with Israel would exacerbate the anti-Zionist and consequently the anti-British sentiment in Iraq, but Sir Michael Wright continued to believe that Iraq was not in a revolutionary situation. Some of the political reporting from the British Embassy in Baghdad was much closer to the mark. Sam Falle, the Oriental Counsellor, observed that 'unemployment, widespread poverty and actual hunger' were prevalent in many parts of the country. This was a clear warning but it was not heeded. Veteran British hands in Baghdad were heard to comment that Nuri Pasha was a clever fox who, better than anyone else, knew how to keep things in hand. This was the 'common sense' of the 'old guard', some of whom had been following the country's politics since its creation at the end of the First World War.

The United States was historically less involved in Iraq, and thus at first sight it is difficult to see why American policies were as dogmatic as the British. America was not so deeply associated with the status quo, yet Frederick Axelgard, probing the course and motives of American policy on the basis of recently released records, finds that the United States played an active part in backing the British at critical times in the last year of the Iraqi monarchy, thereby contributing to the unwillingness of the Nuri Said regime to address the social and political inequities that led to the Revolution. Axelgard records American officials as stating that the British alliance with the ruling elite was resented by Iraqis generally and that it undermined the stability of the country. Yet American policy generally remained subordinate to that of the British. Axelgard's chapter suggests that a bad case of short-sightedness in Washington and Baghdad complemented the deaf ears of 'pacto-mania' suggested by Thacher. There was also a preoccupation with local Communists, as Norman Daniel mentions, along with incorrect assumptions about the loyalty of the Royal Iraqi Army. Thacher helps to explain the mythology of 'common sense' among Western observers before 1958 which assumed that the British in Iraq were the experienced 'professionals'.

Since the officers of the Royal Iraqi Army were well treated by Nuri Said, they were widely believed to be strongly in support of the status quo before 1958. Nevertheless, the Revolution was instigated and led by a small band among their number. Batatu suggests that it was largely the Iraqi Communist Party (ICP) that covertly moulded public sentiment against the monarchist government. What was apparently not known was how extensive the network of Communist cells had become. Secret membership among newly educated Iraqis throughout the country provided the basis for political indoctrination extending well beyond party membership. It is thus not surprising that the Iraqi Communist Party played an active, often decisive, part in the political life of the country after the Revolution. The question of who would wield political power – the revolutionary army officers and their nationalist allies, or the Communists – quickly became the vital issue. In the end the Communists were decimated. This was a time when the Soviet Union was believed to be the protecting patron of Communist parties throughout the world; 'common sense' thus suggested that having such a party in power in other countries was a principal aim of the Soviet Union. For many observers of Iraq, the failure of the Russians to act decisively in support of the Iraqi Communists after the 1958 Revolution was indeed puzzling. In the midst of the cold war, the Russians were widely believed to desire world domination. Why was it that they missed the opportunity to maintain and strengthen a Communist party which had developed considerable political capital before the 1958 Revolution and seemed to be on the verge of ruling the country in the months that followed? While Batatu deals extensively with the Iraqi Communist Party in *The Old Social Classes*, Soviet policy towards the ICP remains in the background of his discussion.

Joe Stork's chapter takes up the issue of Soviet–Iraqi relations and points out that one of the key developments in Soviet policy occurred well before the Iraqi Revolution. In May 1948 the Soviet Union recognized the new state of Israel. In doing so Moscow may have overestimated the strength of the Jewish left as a future ally, but in any case the Soviets were consistent in their policy towards Israel and it weakened the Communist movement in Iraq. Only after Stalin's death did the Iraqi Communists receive Soviet encouragement, and then at a time when nationalists and Communists were united against the Baghdad Pact and after Nasser had emerged as a pan-Arab leader. The Iraqi alliance between Communists and nationalists collapsed soon after the Revolution. 'Sole Leader' (as he was termed) Abdel Karim Qasim was determined to remain independent from Nasser's Egypt and was equally determined to prevail over the Iraqi Communist Party. As a result, one of the mortal struggles between Arab Communists and Arab nationalists was fought in Iraq. Abandoned by its popular following, its leadership executed in large numbers, the Iraqi Communist Party was forced to go underground. Though Stork does not give a definitive answer to the question of why the Soviets abandoned the Iraqi Communists to their own fate, it appears that the Russians had other priorities and were, perhaps, unwilling to sponsor a group they could not with any certainty control. Or perhaps they were less adventurous and less ideologically governed by the desire to expand the Communist world than was imagined at the time. In fact the Russian leadership had little trouble in accommodating the Egyptian and the Iraqi governments that persecuted, imprisoned and executed local Communists. Stork shows how Iraq in more recent times, in the confrontation with Iran, succeeded in gaining the support not only of the major Arab states but of the Soviet Union and the United States as well.

To the remarkable lack of American and British understanding of pre-revolutionary conditions in Iraq – and the apparent Russian indifference to the persecution of Iraqi Communists after the Revolution – must be added the failure of the Revolution to contribute to the cause of Arab unity. This is yet another affront to the 'common sense' of the period, for by 1958 Arab nationalism and Arab unity were major forces in the Middle East. The withdrawal of the British, French and Israeli forces after their attempt to reoccupy the Suez Canal zone raised Nasser's popularity to new heights as the principal leader in the Arab world. His hopes for pan-Arab unity under his leadership were widely discussed in all Arab countries, not least pre-revolutionary Iraq. Arab unity seemed to be the popular will, the Iraqi 'state of mind', as described by Norman Daniel. Yet in the weeks that followed the Revolution there was a serious deterioration and finally open hostility between the revolutionary Iraqi leadership and Egypt's Nasser. Unity between the two countries became a fantasy – another collapse of commonly held expectations.

Rashid Khalidi is concerned with the impact of the Iraqi Revolution on the rest of the Arab world. The 1952 Free Officers' *coup d'état* in Egypt had appeared to signify a breakthrough in the development of the pan-Arab movement. The Egyptian Free Officers toppled the monarchy and assailed the 'feudal' ruling class, thus setting a pattern for other Arab countries. Nasser called for unity over 'Radio Cairo', and he could be heard on the new pocket transistors that had spread throughout the Middle East. The tide seemed to be turning in the direction of an Arab world unified under Nasser's leadership. Qasim, however, pursued an exclusively Iraqi nationalism and came into head-on collision with Nasser. Qasim's resolute independence, in Khalidi's view, marked the end of the Arab 'age of innocence' regarding pan-Arab unity. Apparent historical parallels between the two countries did not dissipate centuries-old distance between Mesopotamia and the Nile Valley. Khalidi carries forward Batatu's argument by demonstrating how the aftermath of the Revolution led to conflict between the particular nationalism in Iraq and the regional nationalism of Nasser.

Nevertheless, according to Peter Sluglett and Marion Farouk–Sluglett, pan-Arabism did form the core of the beliefs of the small group of officers who overthrew the Nuri Said regime and who ran the country in the weeks following the Revolution. Another area of agreement among the officers was the opposition to the British, and still another was the intention to overthrow the ruling dynasty. To understand the collapse of this consensus it is useful to study the question of power in assessing the relative importance of the ingredients of the Revolution. In the 1950s the opposition to the government was largely dominated by the Iraqi Communists, but neither they nor anyone else appears to have had a blueprint for the future beyond abolition of the old regime, which would be followed by general social reforms. Interest in Arab unity disappeared as the question of power and its uses suddenly confronted the post-revolutionary leadership. Here the authors pursue one of Batatu's themes by investigating the 'traditional' urban middle class active in commerce, services and small-scale manufacture. By concentrating on this part of Iraqi society, which has largely been overlooked in favour of the extremes of rich and poor, the authors describe the social and political transformation taking place at the time of the Revolution.

Robert Fernea is interested in the same transformation but in a different context – that of a tribal community south of Baghdad. He is concerned with the pre-revolutionary struggle for hegemony between state and tribe; not the struggle between pro- and anti-revolutionists, but between national and communal forces of power and control. By what criteria and by whose authority were judgments to be rendered, disputes mediated, crimes defined and punished, and resources allocated? What were the respective claims of the state and of local practices? By the early 1950s most rural Iraqis were obliged to turn to state institutions for such things as identity cards, military service, land registration, certification of birth and death, and, to a limited extent, schooling and medical care. In regions dependent on irrigation, water rights were a matter of long-standing and often contentious importance. Fernea suggests that implicit local resistance to the authority of the state was embedded in the culture of communities such as Daghara, where the shaikh was the central figure of local political practices. Batatu in *The Old Social Classes*, stresses that many large, often absentee, landowners were shaikhs who had privatized tribal property and become part of the wealthy, propertied class. Fernea, however, writes about a shaikh who remained an active part of the tribal culture that Batatu acknowledges still prevailed in much of rural Iraq as late as 1958. In the ostensibly friendly relations between the shaikh and the government adminis-trators, the loyalties and identities of the local community were at stake. By 1958 the sense of Iraqi national identity was still much less significant for most of the rural population than was allegiance to a local social group.

Why was there no popular enthusiasm for 'king and country', no sense of well-being associated with the status quo among most Iraqis? Why did the 'colonial state' created by the British fail so completely? Roger Owen begins his chapter by noting that Hanna Batatu in *The Old Social Classes* did use British archival sources that might have allowed him to inquire into the nature of the quasi-colonial state created by the British. He examines one of Batatu's central propositions: that in the 1920s and 1930s the socially-dominant landed classes vied with each other for power, prestige and property, and that in the 1940s and 1950s they combined to defend the existing social order. What part did the British play in the social and economic balance by forging the formal institutions of the state? Above all, the British were concerned with what might be called paternalistic administrative control: the supervision of finance and security, the management of tribal areas, control over elections and influence in the development agencies. Before the end of the mandate in 1932, the British took effective steps to ensure the preservation of their influence in the country after independence, including the installation of a significant British element in the Iraqi civil service. Nevertheless they left behind an unstable government in which ministers succeeded one another with unsettling frequency.

Owen analyses the central function of the independent Iraqi state before 1958 in taxation, security forces and the politics of development. He concludes that government policy benefited the tribal shaikhs, contributed to the improverishment of the masses and, perhaps most importantly, inhibited the development of loyalty to the state. The legacy of British colonial policies eventually had the opposite of the intended effect by stimulating revolutionary change. The colonial institutions that were installed on the basis of the prevailing 'common sense' in the 1920s collapsed in the 1950s. This outcome may appear to be inevitable in retrospect, but it was not a widely acceptable Western view at the time of the Revolution. People of good will looked for 'governmental reforms' and 'better development programmes' that would lessen the distance between the rich and the poor and would provide a degree of democratic government. But, judging from Owen's analysis, the Iraqi government was from its inception almost as alien a set of institutions as it had been during the Ottoman and British regimes.

What *was* popular in the urban-based Iraqi culture of the revolutionary period? Roger Owen sees the culture of colonial imperialism embedded in the structure and operations of pre-revolutionary Iraqi government. Abdul-Salaam Yousif finds the origins of the revolution in the urban popular culture of the period. The monarchical regime exercised censorship by controlling radio and television, but its hold over the press, the educational system and the publishing world was far from total. Pan-Arab ideology permeated school texts in a variety of guises. Critical reviews as well as books of fiction and poetry protested against economic and social inequities, including the seclusion of women. Literary work as well as political debate reflected strife among revolutionary forces. Anti-government poetry by urban poets spread throughout the country by word of mouth and clandestine publications. After the Second World War there was a sharp increase in the import of European and American books, but literary developments in Iraq were also influenced by Communist ideology of the period. Newly educated Iraqis constituted a market for new ideas. Recent graduates of local or foreign schools, as well as literate, urbanized Iraqis, challenged the older, Turkish-influenced generation of which Nuri Pasha was a prime example. The government authorities took drastic measures to halt the subversive tide by banning publications and by imposing fines and prison terms. Publications had to be conservative in tone or allegorical in style if they were to express serious criticism of the government. It was the underground literary movement that reflected the revolutionary spirit of the majority of Iraqis. Abdul-Salaam Yousif sees the July 1958 Revolution as being greeted by a jubilant explosion of relief as well as a sense of liberation – the same qualities Norman Daniel saw in the revolutionary crowds on Baghdad streets. The first months of the Revolution witnessed a resurgence of music, poetry and drama in which women played a prominent part. The Qasim regime, however, soon instituted a crack-down on literary works that reflected the sprit of pan-Arabism or Communism. Public expression and participation in a popular culture of political ideas and ideals declined drastically, especially after the persecution and exile of many intellectuals in the 1960s. Ultimately, this chapter demonstrates an intense cultural turbulence from the 1940s to the early 1960s among the slowly-forming group of Iraqis with Western educations or the Iraqi counterpart. The ferment of ideas constituted an Iraqi cultural renaissance and was a decisive political catalyst.

Abdul-Salaam Yousif points to the revolutionary period as one of national involvement in Iraqi popular cultural expression. In *The Old Social Classes*, Batatu finds the Revolution of 1958 to be a time of collective struggle in which communal, regional, religious and tribal differences were reconciled in a moment of 'progress of Iraq towards national coherence'. Sami Zubaida, however, argues from a different vantage-point. He maintains that, before and after the Revolution, each part of Iraqi society had a different view of the 'national entity', in other words, a distinct outlook on what constituted the Iraqi nation. Zubaida's sociological analysis inquires into the nature of the Iraqi state as well as the remarkably diverse society that was divided along religious, tribal, ethnic and regional lines. In the years following the Revolution, however, there was a transformation. Zubaida describes how a clique of army officers belonging to exclusive kinship groups or 'clans' consolidated their control and dominated the government using the banner of Baathist ideology. With the advantage of soaring oil revenues, the new regime imposed a far more repressive system of rule than that of the monarchy and Nuri Said. By this analysis, it was Iraq under Qasim that came closer than ever before, or after, to acquiring a genuine national identity. It was in the Qasim period following the Revolution, for example, that Iraqi nationalism came to be publicly welcomed in the place of pan-Arab nationalism. Zubaida argues that at that time 'traditional and communalist interests could function politically only through support for the ideological parties', regardless of whether or not Iraqi communal groups agreed with the party ideology.

Communal struggles in Mosul in 1959, and subsequently in Kirkuk, in the same year, contributed to the downfall of the Qasim regime. Administrative control by means of bloody repression replaced the comparatively open field of political opportunity that had characterized the months after 14 July 1958. After the ascendancy of the Baath Party ten years later with its 'clan' leadership, the lines of social and ideological conflict as well as the balance of political forces were transformed by the destruction of alternative bases of power. The bounty of the oil revenues assisted the Baath in the implementation of direct methods of domination. These resources also enabled the regime to pursue development plans and welfare programmes that greatly improved the material standard of living for most Iraqis. The Iranian Revolution and the subsequent war have apparently succeeded in directing the political orientation of the Iraqi Shia minority towards national identity. The end of the war has provided opportunity to destroy armed resistance among the Iraqi Kurds. The potential for future social and political upheaval may be immense, but fear of a ruthless regime with modern instruments of control at its disposal holds political discontent in check. This is a far cry from the populist politics of the Qasim regime, when the population was briefly motivated by ideologically unifying political forces.

From the collective analysis of this book, what conclusions can be drawn about continuing themes in Iraqi history? In the absence of unrestricted research in Iraq itself, any conclusions would involve an unfortunate return to 'common sense'. It does seem clear, however, that a popular will for genuine independence does not necessarily provide a sustaining political environment for the national 'community in embryo' that Hanna Batatu saw in the 1958 Revolution and in earlier Iraqi uprisings. 'Common sense' that is influenced, perhaps, by democratic principles, once led many Westerners to believe that a newly educated middle class might prevail against the re-establishment of a repressive state. This of course did not happen in Iraq after 1958. But since then there has been a long period of urbanization and Iraqis have together fought a sustained and bloody war and are today in a crisis confrontation with most of the external world. Have these experiences finally moulded a spectrum of common interests and identity that will one day be shown to have transcended communal differences? Do the people of contemporary Mesopotamia now consider themselves to be Iraqis in a way that transcends other identities? There is no longer a Western 'common sense' with ready answers to these questions.

Hanna Batatu in the concluding chapter reflects on the Revolution and comments on the other contributions. In a sense his reflections are autobiographical. He recalls the works that influenced him while writing *The Old Social Classes*: Alexis de Tocqueville, Peter Geyl, Max Weber, Karl Marx. His remarks help one to see his own work within the larger historical interpretation of revolutionary upheaval, especially of the American, French and Russian Revolutions. Together with the essays of the other contributors, Batatu's concluding comment makes the Iraqi Revolution of 1958 more comprehensible in its regional and international as well as its national manifestations.

Robert A. Fernea
Wm. Roger Louis

# 1

# Contemporary Perceptions of the Revolution in Iraq on 14 July 1958

NORMAN DANIEL

## Opinion

At the time of the 14 July Revolution, whether on the day itself, in the period leading up to it, or in its immediate aftermath, most Iraqi perceptions of the event were strongly felt, but negatively defined; the general attitude was conditioned by apprehension of what the British might try to do, and by an over-assessment of what they *could* do. Any study of the subject must be dominated by Hanna Batatu's *The Old Social Classes*, and, in order to confirm its own claims, must quarry Batatu's many lodes of information. What I am saying does not conflict, and often interlocks, with his main themes, which do not, however, include the history of opinion as such. He records some fluctuations of opinion, and the rise and fall of parties (such as which Baghdad districts came out for the Communist Party) or the formation of groups (such as the growth of the Free Officers' movement), but he cannot cover every point in detail. An exception is his lengthy treatment of tactical changes in Communist politics within the leadership. He has less to say about why popular support for the Party was erratic; sometimes he seems to assume that the support of 'the masses' needs no explanation, and to minimize any other political commitment.[1] He tabulates social origins which are a major source of motivation. He has managed to combine social history, history of the Revolution and a history of the Iraqi Communist Party, and he would surely claim that enough is enough. He may well have a valid point, and I shall not attempt anything of the kind either; but I should like to see whether I can

1

recapture to any extent the state of mind of Iraqis on around 14 July, and see how far that will contribute a footnote to the analysis of forces and events. I should stress that, stimulated by Batatu's book, I am simply reporting the impression that the Revolution made on a foreign resident, and that this chapter is a contribution to the history of perceptions. How in fact did Iraqis assess their own revolution at the time?

Hanna Batatu, widely read in the history of revolutions, nails his colours to the mast in his statement that his is 'an analysis that draws essentially upon the insights of Karl Marx and Max Weber'.[2] A simple social analysis that recognized some economic and environmental factors was current, however, earlier than nineteenth-century philosophy and was even anticipated in the Middle Ages. A rather primitive form of such an analysis prevailed in Iraq in the 1950s among both the Iraqis and the British. It was a common perception that power in Iraq was based on three interests: the monarchy, the British and the tribal shaikhs. This crude analysis is valid within its limits and conformable to the argument of the *The Old Social Classes*.

Many of the British refused to take sufficiently seriously the thinking of Iraqis. The British regarded a possible revolution with dismay, but did not find it unthinkable, although their ambassador believed that the growing expenditure on development had probably assured security.[3] My view of Iraqi attitudes dominant at the time is based on the opinions of a wide range of outspoken citizens. It is a question that raises the problem of what intellectuals are, and how important; in the Arab world, especially, they are often self-conscious and take for granted that they carry a special responsibility for political leadership. In political activism in the 1920s, 1930s and 1940s, Arab students and some teachers were ahead of the world, which caught up with the possibilities for effective student action only in the 1960s. 'Student', 'revolutionary' and 'intellectual' are compatible terms but not coterminous. Leadership seems to be more of a class matter. Analysis of the Islamic *Jihad* or the *Takfir wa Higra* in the 1980s,[4] as of Batatu's Iraq in the 1950s, seems to show that there is a revolutionary epicentre somewhere in the lower middle class. I doubt if we can plot the social class of revolutionaries more exactly than to say that they have enough material advantages to give them energy and initiative, but few enough to stimulate ambition. They want opportunities for their wasted talents, especially in government. Those who are not vocal need intellectual spokesmen.

It is more obvious who is an intellectual than who is not, and there is no hard line to draw. Intellectuals may not be clubbable, but neither are they always eccentric or solitary; they share the common human condition. All are liable to emotional thinking and are influenced by general trends. Intellectuals are not necessarily original; the best definition that I know is that they are articulate. Some believe that because they articulate thoughts they originate them, and this is possible, but it is also possible that often they simply express the thoughts of the ordinary people among whom they live. To articulate is an honourable function not to be despised, but perhaps intellectuals may simply throw ideas back to the less articulate 'masses', amongst whom these ideas, in more nebulous form, may have originated and coalesced.[5] The Iraqi Revolution was not led by intellectuals – there was no Sieyès, no St Just, no Marat even (unless it were Fadil Abbas al-Mahdawi), and no Jefferson either – but the ideas which the leaders voiced were those that the intellectuals had been airing, and a nation had taken for granted, for a long time. Over years there is a groundswell of opinion which carries everyone along, and it is my contention the views everyone held, the intellectuals verbalized.

Why did the British ignore them? It is not the job of an embassy to report the views only of the rulers. Professional diplomats must gather knowledge without policy and bias; the place for these is after the facts are in. This is quite distinct from the secret information work of spies (unsuitably lodged in embassies whose functions they usurp if they interpret public affairs). Bias, however, militated against professional judgement. It seems that the British and the Hashemite regime, and likewise the Americans, were sensitive to the danger of organized Communism. I would suggest that they were oversensitive, because it caused them to confuse quite distinct varieties of opposition and to ignore the general climate of unorganized non-party opinion. It was as though the imperialists had themselves been reading too much Marx when they should have been reading Tocqueville.[6] They believed more readily in 'agitators' than in the solid disapproval of the ordinary active and busy middle classes. They were happy to be disliked in a good cause, and they failed to make sure that, even by their own standards, their cause was still good.

In 1958 no one doubted that the British dominated the scene. This was the last time that the way the British perceived or were perceived by the Arabs would be of any particular significance: we had come to the climacteric. The Suez aggression was still fresh in everyone's mind and seemed to presage a new intervention in Iraq on the model of 1941; it turned out that Suez was actually the last effort of men whom the world had at last passed by. Most recently there had been the enormously unpopular Baghdad Pact, which opposed the United Arab Republic and brought Iraq firmly into the cold war, thus, as Batatu says, alienating everyone, nationalists, Communists and isolationists.[7] Iraqis lacked Egyptian political experience, Rashid Ali al-Gailani was no Zaghlul, and there had never been anything like the 'Wafd' Party, but something important and relevant had recently happened. The enormous popularity of Gamal Abdel Nasser, his prestige in the entire world, derived from the fact that he had called the imperialists' bluff in the face of the Suez aggression; it was the great achievement of his life. It had transpired that Western power, Britain at least, which in 1956 could still consider itself powerful, really was a paper tiger. What happened next was not quite what people expected. The Suez adventure had raised to power in London a great opportunist and realist, Harold Macmillan, the Prime Minister, who would only attempt what he knew he could do, who knew how and when to cut his losses, and who was not interested in playing at empire any more. Like a schoolmaster in charge of his class, he would not ask it to do anything that he could not enforce.

Although old-style imperialism was dead, no one was sure that it was not shamming. It took time to dislodge the British bogey, which had been almost an obsession, from people's minds. Barely four months after the Revolution, I was assured by an Iraqi whom I had never met before – we sat next to each other in an aeroplane – that the British were behind Abdel Karim Qasim, and had engineered his coup. This could be credible only on the assumption that anything that succeeded must have been arranged by the British. My interlocutor offered no evidence, he just 'knew', and he saw no need for evidence, because he 'knew' I knew. I do not have much idea how this process was thought to work. I imagine that it was supposed (as is still fairly common) that the embassies of great powers are mostly composed of secret agents handing out slush money under cover of various ostensible functions. Since then the CIA has been widely held responsible for many such American operations and the greater openness of American politics has confirmed that many of these rumours were true. The British policy of official silence did nothing to discourage similar beliefs about British operations in the period of imperial afterglow declining into imperial impotence.

One relic of colonialism was that the British put their confidence in people who called themselves their friends, when sometimes a better word would be 'client' or even 'sycophant', so that the regime cut itself off from the public, and the public in turn was alienated from decision-making. These 'friends' were neither responsible, nor responsive, to public opinion. The British, for their part, unaccountably failed to realize that foreign intrusion makes the adrenalin surge wherever there is either patriotism or ambition. The regime seemed to everyone an alien imposition, and for the left it also corresponded to the classic Marxist–Leninist analysis of monopolistic capitalist exploitation of colonial power. There was more to it than that, of course, but the cap could be made to fit.

The British themselves thought of the regime as 'friendly' rather than as dependent. They showed great confidence in Nuri Pasha;[8] he might need encouragement on the side of development, but he could be relied on absolutely to rule efficiently in the traditional manner. When the public hanging of Fahd and two of his colleagues in the Communist Party was criticized as brutality, some experienced old colonialist would be sure to shrug and say that Nuri knew best how to manage his own people.[9] In their patronizing way the British left governing to him and his various understudies, but Iraqi opinion was that whatever happened should ultimately be attributed to the British, who upheld the regime through the monarchy; willing the end they willed the means. Perhaps this was true, but it was an exaggeration and an over-simplification.

Of the three social forces with which we started, the British, the monarchy and the tribal shaikhs, two were alien to all the people and the third was parasitic. The tribal shaikhs were poor developers whose self-interest was unenlightened and who had survived from an age before Iraq was a nation.[10] They would boast that they could always 'send in the tribes' to subdue an insurrectionary city population.[11] This was fantasy, but the landlords, though anachronistic, were at least indigenous. This was not true of either Britain or the monarchy, both of which were relative newcomers and had overstayed. No profound sentiment existed for the monarchy and none for the British either of course. It is not extravagant to say that the royal family were viewed as immigrants. The British had been longer in Iraq than they had: Batatu discusses British commercial interests in Iraq in the nineteenth century and earlier,[12] but these did not amount to a great deal for Britain, ranking vastly smaller than those in India or even Egypt. Iraq was a small country in population and rather unproductive until the development of the oil industry. If the British had shallow roots, however, the Hashemites had none at all.[13] Iraqis who thought about it (as most Iraqis did) could see that, apart from any incalculable foreign intervention, only the army kept the regime in power. I doubt if at that time they could have perceived that the British attachment to the monarchy or to some of the old social classes was a sign of weakness rather than of colonial cunning.

All saw the inefficiency of the system, but I am not sure how many drew the conclusion that it would be easy to get rid of. It was a real puzzle that the British should have chosen to operate through an inappropriate monarchical institution. Not only was monarchy a British importation historically, it was also a British notion philosophically, one that could be grafted easily enough on to a Turkish sultanate, but that Arabs felt was foreign to all their traditions. Iraqis had reason to ask also why Britain had arbitrarily imposed a monarchy after the model of George III rather than of George VI.[14] Also, of course, to wonder why they had imposed a monarchy at all? The Hashemites tried to conform to a northern model (for example, with their fox-and-jackal hounds), but they never corresponded to any Islamic ideal. They might better have taken up falconry. Even their Hashemite descent was questioned. Abdulillah, the Regent, does not seem ever to have attracted general respect, or the King any personal feeling at all. Nuri Pasha, although in anti-colonialist jargon a 'lackey', did earn respect; I think that the personality of this great minister was more to the fore in most minds than Batatu's book suggests. It was as if Nuri belonged to an older regime, to the last days of Ottoman rule, and he was recognized as an international figure by the Islamic world, though not willingly by Abdel Nasser's generation. The Hashemites, established successfully in Amman, where they were appreciably less foreign, in Iraq might as well have been Tatar il-Khans for all the local appeal they had. Moreover, they had arived there under the aegis of (in Iraqi eyes) the arch-spy T. E. Lawrence. The weakness of the British was the weakness of the regime.

Whatever is most foreign tends to recede from view and may be less irksome than something less foreign, but close to, and seen and heard constantly. A case in point is the mentality of the 1950s, when the British 'colonialists' may, I think, have been resented less in themselves than for the flavour they gave the dynasty – or 'lackeys'. The old politicians were believed simply, and not in all cases correctly, to be getting rich on pay-offs; after the Revolution the People's Court was more successful in proving harsh administration than corruption. In 1958 the intelligentsia, living mostly around the seat of government or the other big cities, remote from the few development projects and surrounded in Baghdad by poor immigrants from the south, could see only the classic face of cruelty and corruption, and that, they saw, was foreign. The local face of both of these was yet to come (and does not concern us here).

We need to recall how much the climate of world opinion has changed since 1958. The retreat of the Europeans from empire had only begun, and old-style colonialism still existed across Africa. Non-alignment still had far to go to correct the diplomatic balance (the Revolution immediately announced that it adhered to Bandung). The USSR had not yet blotted its carefully nurtured copybook, alienating opinion even in Iraq itself; the United States, which at the time of Suez had taken a stand acceptable in the Arab world, was to revert in Viet-Nam to the quasi-imperial tradition of 'Manifest Destiny', and to lose world approval. This would be replaced by something more realistic, but realism was not yet acceptable to the United States – or to Europe – and neither was it the mode of thought current in Iraq. Behind much of the confusion in those last days of colonialism was an irrational romantic hope of finding somewhere a disinterested international patron who would guarantee independence for nothing; no one quite understood that every country acts solely in what it conceives (often wrongly of course) to be its own interests. When dependent countries first achieve national freedom, and begin to encounter problems of realpolitik, any hopes they had of an easy solution fade.

The new Iraq would prove wary of the ill-formulated anticipation of autarchy that some among the nations 'rightly struggling to be free' attempted. The concept of foreign aid for development as we know it now, when newly freed nations would invite neo-colonialist investment, had not yet become a commonplace of the Third World. Today most countries in this predicament hope to control foreign aid by keeping it competitive. Iraq has been insulated by its oil from the worst effects of this generally lowered level of expectation but not from the new realism of hard-headed open markets. To go back to 1958 is to return, not to an age of innocence, but to one of inexperience.

Most people then were preoccupied by the present and had thought very little about the future. Members of the Communist and Baath parties thought that they knew where they were going, but most of the older intellectuals, lawyers and other professional men and academics were not party affiliates. Hanna Batatu is forced by the nature of his source material, however critically he treats it, to emphasize the role of the parties.[15] Lenin proved himself a better judge of a revolutionary situation than Marx, but we should not generalize from his experience. The spontaneous climate of opinion is an important component of the opportunity to act, and a revolutionary situation is not an absolute, an unrepeatable opportunity that needs that needs an innate talent, like a dowser's, to be recognized. Even for theorists of the dialectic of history, that is a misreading. There is no one time when a revolution *must* take place, there are just times when it can.[16]

In July 1958 the nation awaited only the catalyst, and it was the army, not one of the parties, that effected 'the will of the people', which is a grandiloquent phrase, but it means only 'what most people wanted'. The forces of change, when they were tested, proved stronger than the forces in power, and the strongest of the forces for change was the general consent. The British had served a useful last purpose, in provoking that deep resentment from which the Revolution sprang, and not, as it turned out, to the immediate benefit of any organized party, but to that of a liberator uncommitted to party or even to policy. Qasim personified the undecided state of a nation agreed about the old regime but with little notion about the future.

Any fantasies of life in a freed nation gave place to realities of rivalries and disagreement. Not among members of the parties, but among the public, divisive Communist or nationalist sympathies had been eclipsed by the common distaste for the old regime. Now any outsider found that people of different sympathies would no longer mix. Few intellectuals had no political inclination at all, or at least no observable preference, and for many their inclinations might now harden into positive commitment. Some would fall foul of political violence and even begin to migrate. The exemplar of uncertainty remained Abdel Karim himself, and it is this that makes him unique among the rulers of Iraq and his period of rule so interesting.

As is clear from Batatu's book, Qasim was a man of sound moral purpose and possessed a political appetite that grew with what it fed on. He was far more committed to the public good than had been any of his old regime predecessors. 'Sons of the people', cites Batatu, 'I am Abdel Karim Qasim and stronger and more resolute for the sake of the poor.'[17] His manipulation of the political balance – 'I am above trends and inclinations'[18] – may have been no more than a matter of political survival, or simply of survival *per se*, but it is fair to regard him as a Cromwell, as an adventitious monarch entering a vacuum and looking for political principles by which to govern and for ministers and methods to enable him to do it well. He wanted it thought, and even wanted to think himself, that he had acted alone: 'I had no partners when I exploded the volcanoes of violence.'[19] Undeniably paternalist, he was at least home-grown, and perhaps we should attribute his reluctance to commit himself, at home or abroad, to the object lesson left him by the hereditary monarchy. He was the 'sole leader', as Nuri had never been, and there was now no sole patron such as Britain. All that was left when Qasim had turned the old regime out was a vacant place in which he was a little lost. He was not only the exemplar of 'centrism' but its architect too. Batatu quotes a politbureau member, Zaki Khairi, on Communist policy: 'Qasim was looked upon not as the leader of the bourgeois class but as a military individual of diverse inclinations.'[20] I am not sure that this is correct Leninism but it is a good, short description of Qasim and it pinpoints not only the tactical problem facing the Communist Party but also the quandary of men of all shades of opinion, disconcerted by these individual diverse – even vacillating – inclinations. The bourgeois class did not count on him to lead them and he came to feel a justified 'sense of isolation'.[21] Like a despot of ancient Greece, he in fact traded his natural lifetime for five exciting, abruptly terminated, years of cheering crowds.

What were the ideas of the masses? Batatu gives excellent information about the Communist leadership, but to say that 'a thrill of hope greeted their rise to great influence' in 'poor and strictly laboring places' in Baghdad seems more a pious assumption than proof from evidence. Perhaps it was so, and perhaps not. Party influence on the people, before the parties came into the open, is hard to measure, and even afterwards it is hard to interpret popular reactions. Batatu thinks that in the months after the Revolution the Communists inspired 'such fear as prevails in revolutionary times' in nationalist and well-to-do districts, but does not consider that any of the poor felt intimidated by the party. Many no doubt were motivated more by hope than fear, but it would be difficult to find evidence now and it must remain presumptive. If there was hard inside evidence of authentic political commitment among the people wearing *dishdashas* in Baghdad, however that may suggest a curiously appropriate parallel to the *sans-culottes*, Batatu would have found it. There was probably a combination of motives and fluctuations of opinion among working people, as there was to my knowledge, among the professional classes, to whom at one time 'the party seemed unbeatable'.

Batatu fully admits the phenomenon of 'July 14 Communists', 'Communists of the flood-tide' and 'time-servers, bandwagon climbers'.[22] I believe that this was true of the 'masses' as well as of the bourgeois, but they discovered *civisme* for the first time and were able to participate actively in revolution through the People's Resistance Force. This, as Batatu shows, had a Communist association, more marked in Mosul than in Baghdad, where all arms were turned in after duty; these militia men were as tightly controlled as the more bourgeois French revolutionary National Guard, but were less widely used. They wore something approaching the uniform then already associated with guerrilla freedom-fighters and searched passers-by (chiefly motorists) for arms, more frequently than efficiently. The middle class did not like them but only the self-important found fault.[23]

In the mass of Communist source material to which Batatu has had access there is a great deal which is ambiguous. He gives examples of accounts of mass rallies greatly exaggerated by the Communist press, especially in *Ittihad al-Sha'b* ('People's Union').[24] This is normal, and it is more interesting that he hedges about his claims for Communist influence: it is only '*part* of the credit for the rise of the workers' (in respect of pay increases) that he claims for the party, and later he says just that 'wide masses were *still hospitable* to its ideas'.[25] Very moderately he asserts: 'The July Revolution had aroused to political life thousands of people from the classes working with their hands, and *many* of these had turned towards the Communists.'[26] All this relates to the period following the Revolution and hardly at all to 14 July, and these are very moderate claims; in fact it seems that the Communist Party realized that the masses were not crucial. Conducting a review of their post-revolutionary policy, the Party admitted a strategy preoccupied with seizing power in the army, so that 'the "masses" would play only "a supporting role"';[27] but I think that Batatu is absolutely right when he says that the manual workers were becoming politically conscious (whether it was under Communist influence or otherwise). He is identifying something important that developed rapidly after 14 July, and that grew largely out of the successful experience of that day.

## Opinion with Experience

Qasim's claim to have 'exploded the volcanoes of revolution' was a very good metaphor. Batatu describes how on 14 July Communist Party members issued forth from 'homes and hideaways' onto the streets, adding, less picturesquely, that 'nationalists of all hues had also come out' (his nationalists are usually also-rans). He says of the crowds on the streets that their numbers 'must have had a greater weight in determining the historical outcome . . . than one might at first glance have been disposed to admit'. He is right, not so much in the hypothetical claim that they obstructed '*possible* hostile counter-action' (none existed), but when he speaks of the 'tremendous psychological effect'.[28]

Anyone who was present can have seen only a small part of the action taking place over a densely populated city. I can cite only my own experiences. I think that by mid-morning there were still men coming onto the streets, perhaps arriving from neighbouring villages; in any case a continuous stream of cheering and shouting men, mostly in small groups, seemed to be hurrying somewhere, but as if to a fair, not to storm the Bastille. Possibly they ended up at the Ministry of Defence, where crowds did converge in a dense mass and were difficult for the army to control. No one who was on the streets that morning will doubt the cheerful air of spontaneity with which this celebration of sudden freedom began; the prevailing mood was a sense of release and liberation, and perhaps of almost personal escape from the many burdens of which only a few had in fact been lifted. The crowds were shouting triumphantly against Abdulillah and the imperialists, and in praise of the army, and this without the planning and inevitably stereotyped slogans of a later date, when the Communists could call out a 'rally' from what had by then become their home districts. There was no sign that these crowds had been organized. They did not all seem to come from the same direction, and they were not a single crowd, but more closely resembled holiday parties calling out to each other. I do not remember that there was a single placard – placards take more preparation – there was just that infectious carnival atmosphere of 'bliss was it in that dawn to be alive'.

The United States Ambassador, Waldemar J. Gallman was misinformed about 'hoodlums recruited by agitators'.[29] Crowds are called out just as often by natural curiosity (an urge to celebrate, to see what is happening, or just to join in the fun) as they are by 'agitators', or in the alternative terminology, 'activists'. Some such no doubt joined in, but there is no evidence that they initiated anything. It takes time and preparation in favourable conditions to organize a crowd. The officers themselves, whose thoughts had been concentrated on occupying selected targets and areas, first bothered to address the people directly when they called them out by radio – and later sent them home again under curfew, because they had by then become over-excited. Perhaps the hoodlums had turned up.

It may seem macabre to put it in this way, but the carnival period culminated in 'killing and dragging'. There was some confusion about the bodies. I was told that one burning in a side-street was that of Fadil Jamali, who was found alive in a village a little later and shown on television. This violence earned the Iraqis an unenviable reputation, not only in the West, but also in other Arab countries. (This was before the Lebanese fighting and the military suppression of the Palestinian uprising. There are in any case historical precedents in Europe.) Any crowd contains all sorts, kindly people and killers, the latter often people who are unaware of their latent capacity. The fact of the killings (mostly mistaken identities, apart from Nuri and the royals), the re-imposition of visible controls, the return of habitual anxieties, and an increase in uncertainty, may have helped to dampen feelings down in the next few days and to encourage xenophobia fed by the usual fears and rumours. Carelessness is easily and angrily attributed to sabotage. My driver offered us refuge in his house; it was both a generous gesture, because he did not have to make it at all, and an unnecessary one, because there was no real danger, but the bare fact that he thought of it implies that some slight hint of menace had come into being. The realities that enforce a revolution returned only too soon. At different levels of sophistication a 'wait and see' attitude, even without spoiling the fun, may have been there from the outset. There is no evidence of any difference between popular uncertainties and those of intellectuals.

Batatu recognizes that in the period immediately after the Revolution an awareness of class interest arose in addition to older forms of allegiance: events had 'sharpened the divisions between the various sects and ethnic groups. At the same, the labourers and the poor, regardless of race and religion, feeling their strength, were voicing openly their desires and expectations.' This smacks a little of revolutionary romanticism, but it means that new ideas did not supersede old ones. It is of course true that the 'sectarian' category is also economic, and of course Shi'ism has long been 'the ideology of the underdogs'.[30] A sectarian correlation remains, but certainly not an exclusive one. Batatu notes the number of Iraqis in politics, from ministers to Communist politbureau members, who were of mixed parentage, among them of course Qasim. This may be the characteristic Iraqi pattern of the remoter future. Meanwhile, it is likely enough that the Shi'a associated Britain with the Sunni domination of which the royal family was the type. Shia and Sunnis had somewhat different reasons for rejecting the old regime. It was always the Sunnis who would deny quite sincerely that there was discrimination, as those always do whom discrimination favours. This factor militated against Shi'i awareness of one world-wide Arab nation, and soon enough it helped to sober the delirium of 14 July. It in no way mitigated the welcome the Shi'a gave the Revolution, and I doubt if they were worrying about the pan-Arab menace on the day, but its unanimity could not long survive the 'hybrid character' of the new regime, with such various pre-existing centrifugal forces 'making for uncertainty'.[31]

The crowds were fairly comfortable with Qasim: 'the populace was still attached to him' in 1963 'and the old shouts for him were already reechoing',[32] but initially the people were simply anti-colonialist. The popular hero then was *al jaysh*, 'the Army'. It seems doubtful if even those in the know among the dissident officers were aware of Qasim's political principles[33] (if he had any except pragmatism); certainly no one prepared photographs of Qasim in advance (nor for that matter did they prepare any of Arifa for immediate distribution. Probably no one was sure who would come out on top. What did appear immediately on Baghdad streets were pictures of Gamal Abdel Nasser, and it was a day or two before these could be replaced by those of Abdel Karim. A widespread opinion is that the Baath were responsible; in any case it is likely that the United Arab Republic's embassy was one channel. At the time Nasser seemed to be everywhere, though I am not sure about the districts which were later predominantly Communist in sympathy. The chief indicators were small general shops, often the kind just set into the wall of a building, as well as kiosks and street vendors' stalls, and many of these apparently already had Nasser's picture positioned somewhere unobtrusive; now that the police would raise no objection it was everywhere to be seen. I realize that these small entrepreneurs and shopkeepers do not count as 'workers and peasants', but no better evidence of popular feeling at that moment exists. An Arab orientation prevailed, all the stronger because it directly opposed the British Baghdad Pact policy. Nasser was the symbol of resistance to a colonial regime; the Qasim alternative soon became clear, but it was not there at the beginning. Some months later montages of Nasser were on sale in the streets, with his head superimposed on the body of a fat, old woman, but this was in support of Qasim's policy of Iraqi isolationism. For the moment, most citizens felt a little lost and were looking for a lead.

Batatu discusses the leadership of the various parties and groups. Because of his full access to Communist Party records, he weaves the story of the Revolution about the Party. We are shown events through the Party's eyes and I have cited some of this material. He has found less of particular interest about the Baath at that stage, when it had not yet emerged dominant among the nationalists who were originally united, not by party membership, but by anti-colonialist sentiment.

In his full discussion of the sources available for the Free Officers' movement, Batatu gives us the expected analysis of their social origins: 'middle or lower middle-income families', presaging the 'men of middle condition' who would rule in the years to follow.[34] It is clear that Communist connections with the movement were pretty thin. It is evident from most of the tables in the book that many political activists of all persuasions came from roughly the same social origin. One point should be noted: the oath taken by the Free Officers 'shows an . . . attachment to *at least the forms* of Islam' which 'requires no explanation.'[35] This is true, but it would be tendentious to imply that this was no more than a matter of forms, and Batatu rightly indicates the deep religious commitment, as well as an 'ideological heritage' from the 1941 revolt led by Rashid Ali al-Gailani. He cites generously from two distinguished and sympathetic officers, Rif'at al-Hajj Sirri and Nadhim at-Tabaqchali, on the eve of their execution in 1959; their love of country was grounded in religion: 'Arabism is truth, and the Quran is truth, and Islam is truth.'[36] Even before the Islamic revival, all classes followed the religious norms, and I would need evidence that this was not true equally of the masses in the districts that supported the Communists. Among the officers, Batatu confesses that many of them made poor Communists: 'much of the party's recently won support' in 1959 'was of the wishy washy kind'.[37] This was at a time when many were tipping the party to win, thus creating a bandwagon effect. It is not clear whom the British Ambassador, Sir John Troutbeck, was thinking of when he referred to 'the lessening influence of Islam';[38] if he thought this true of the Arab world generally, later events have shown that it was a monumental error, but I believe that it was a misjudgment even for Iraq alone. We may reasonably take as typical of the army in 1958 Arif's first broadcast announcement on behalf of the officers: 'Trusting in God . . . we have undertaken to liberate the beloved homeland from the corrupt crew that imperialism installed.'[39]

Barely mentioned by Batatu, the People's Court, under its president, Fadil Abbas al-Mahdawi, played a major role in the break with the idea of Arab unity, at least on the propaganda side. This was double-headed. The court was strictly concerned only with the trials of the old imperial 'lackeys', and in this sense it was Mahdawi who finally saw the British off; but it was also he who had most to say in public about other Arab regimes, and he enjoyed an exchange of abuse with Nasser, and also with Aboud in the Sudan. It was almost as though he was endorsing the recent British build-up of Iraq to counterbalance Egypt and Syria, then linked in the United Arab Republic experiment, but of course without the unrealistic pretence of the Baghdad Pact alliances.

Mahdawi was a man of no Western education, and self-taught in Arabic literature, but he was an omnivorous reader with a real curiosity about the world, a grown-up street urchin, yelling abuse at some stranger, but also quick to learn from him and to educate himself. He was a bully in court, but he would argue endlessly with witnesses and even the accused, usually far more knowledgeable than he was, about points in Arabic literature, and he would also deride some points of Western culture about which he knew nothing. For example, an old-regime radio announcer was put on trial, perhaps to relieve political tension, and a broadcast quiz programme was cited: 'Do you know why Schubert's symphony was unfinished?' Mahdawi ridiculed the evidence about this trivial question, and all Western music with it. Two days later he found occasion to provide a lecture on Beethoven. He gave the impression of working the encyclopaedia hard at home.

Yet the court allowed the public, including women who seemed like the legendary *tricoteuses*, an astonishing degree of 'audience participation'; a chorus was encouraged, it is not certain by whom, to intimidate the accused and to threaten them with nooses during long periods of shouted abuse. This created sympathy for the often courageous and apparently unmoved victims; I saw this reaction

myself from a random group of young officers.[40] Qasim allowed
Mahdawi a free hand to act out his play on his own stage. The
People's Court in 1958–9 stands up well to comparison with the
indiscriminate selection that preceded the 'defence' of the French
nation in the September Massacres, and it was not an instrument of
governent such as the Committee of Public Safety made of the Paris
Revolutionary Tribunal. There was a good deal of 'off with his head'
in Baghdad, but Qasim executed very few of those whom Mahdawi
condemned; the sound and fury hardly signified at all. Condemned
prisoners were kept for a long time in suspense, then sent for by
Qasim, kept waiting till the small hours, lectured by him interminably,
and released.[41] This court helped audibly and visibly to clear the old
regime away. It gave an impressive sense of purge to all who had
access to a television screen, if only in a café or public place, or to
radios, which were even then everywhere. It sealed the total success
of the Revolution in breaking with the past.

The international background to events in Iraq was changing, and
the old colonial concerns about government had naturally disappeared.
The British were adjusting, not only to the new situation in Iraq, but
also to the new range of international preoccupations. With Nuri
gone, they easily disengaged from their other 'friends'; they had
always wanted to find better (and the Americans had always wanted
their own).

Had the men of the old regime hoped for British intervention? If
they had expected a repetition of 1941, they had forgotten that that
was only an item in a world war, which in turn had never seemed
very important in Iraq. The British always knew that any decision
must be left until the moment came, and when it did, the Foreign
Office was realistic and gave priority to wider international
considerations. In due time gleeful stories circulated about an old-
style politician who claimed his fair reward from Whitehall and was
turned away 'like a dog'.[42] If the British and the regime had
misunderstood each other, it is not surprising that they misled the
Iraqi nation. Diplomacy was now the top priority it should always
have been. There was no more than a normal delay in recognizing
the new regime; Ambassador Michael Wright's recommendations
followed the rules of his profession.

The world kaleidoscope began to fall into the pattern now long
since familiar. Britain now began more rapidly to adjust from the
Middle East strategy of protecting communication with India, a
shibboleth that died hard in the Suez aggression, to the later one of

cold war. The two strains of thought are interwoven in the British documents just antecedent to the Revolution and in the State Department material which demonstrates how America stood – some hesitation notwithstanding – behind the British.[43] Unlike the Iraqis, the Americans had long been aware of British weakness. They did not know it, but they were then about to step into the shoes of the British as most-hated nation, although they did not yet fully enjoy the notoriety they would achieve throughout the Arab world by their attachment to Israel. At that time they could still reasonably hope to succeed Britain as patron of the Arabs, but, as Iraqis saw it, they were not offering a real alternative: one American ambassador had seen a future for Fadil Jamali in replacing the 'old gang', but to Iraqis he was only a new recruit to it, largely perhaps because of his crusading views on Communism. Fadil rather bravely preached these views on trial before Mahdawi (Iraqis of all persuasions consistently showed outstanding bravery), so that the broadcast was echoed all over public places, but the new regime could safely allow it; many Iraqis, like other Arabs at the time, tended to dislike Communists, but as a purely local problem and without sharing the Western 'world conspiracy' attitude. Even during the rivalry for power under Qasim, one can almost say that Moscow was seen as the pawn of the local Communists, rather than vice versa.

The Iraqis were at least as bad at 'reading' the British as vice versa. They never understood the reasoning behind the West's fear of Communism, because their own perspective was so different. As the British tended to oversimplify the Iraqis, so the Iraqis in turn regarded the British as monolithic. It puzzled them for example, how the paper then called *The Daily Worker* should appear for sale in Baghdad beside other foreign papers, possibly because they supposed the Communist Party to be banned in Great Britain, but more probably because the idea of class warfare, or of an exploited class, in a colonialist country simply never occurred to them. It was not stupidity on their part, but they were slow to recognize new trends, or to open themselves mentally to the world into which they were just entering.

The British were increasingly beginning to see their advantage as lying in competitive free trade in an open market, rather than in markets artificially restricted by paternalist British official administrators. In Britain this was the epoch that soon gave birth to the slogan 'You've never had it so good'. If the Iraqi perception was outmoded, that was surely because the British actions they perceived were behind the times, behind at any rate the early signs of a future development that was not yet unambiguously clear. In civil service circles the old order was not changing obviously, but it was on the point of a landslide. The generations overlapped. Some diplomats were insensitive to local opinion and over-sensitive to superiors at home who belonged essentially to the old order. There were brakes on change. Senior British policy-makers clung to nineteenth-century traditions, and America was in the grip of an anti-Communist obsession; both remained dependent for far too long on client politicians in satellite countries and neither had finally adjusted to the post-colonial world. It has continued to be a short-sighted policy to depend on allied regimes lacking a sufficiently broadly-based local support.

Much the same faults as had vitiated the political and economic activities of the great nations had corrupted their cultural and educational functions. Both derived from the same, now moribund, assumptions. In early days, the British (and not the British alone) began 'cultural relations' in amateur fashion by offering that side of their 'culture' that appealed to them, and, therefore, by extension, should appeal to everyone else. So clear was the donors' idea of what they should offer that it did not occur to them to try seriously to find out what the recipients actually wanted, still less what they needed, because how could they want anything but what they were given? It was difficult to recognize that the horse taken to the water could not be made to drink. That may sound absurd, but, without exaggeration, it is how people once thought, and, to some extent, how many still do.

Behind the perceptions of different cultures and countries there lie almost infinite gradations of misunderstanding. Most major countries send cultural missions, or at least give cultural responsibilities to their diplomats, all over the world, the Arab countries included. This work ought to be free of the constantly changing exigencies of political diplomacy; it ought in fact to set the example of how good relations between countries of unequal strength can be. Most missions now try to realize this aim, or at least to minimize the fluctuations of political and economic relations in that one respect. In the 1950s the lines between cultural (or educational) work and information work were less clear-cut.

'Information' is one-sided, a country's perception of itself in the form in which it hopes to project it. It is boastful and openly political, and makes no pretence to any element of exchange.

Cultural affairs are in theory distinct, are usually handled separately, and admit the principle of reciprocity. It is disastrous if the 'informational' concept infects the cultural field; books, language teaching, scholarships to study abroad, artistic manifestations, lectures, for example, may or may not be of interest to the receiving country. When they are not of spontaneous interest to the recipient, they are only a disguise for 'information'. Nowadays, social studies, science and technology (barely distinguishable from 'aid') are often of common interest, but these did not figure seriously or fruitfully in the 1950s. Even now there is rarely an exact equivalence in exchange. Only countries not dominated by the entrepreneurial market familiar in the West have always been able to offer opportunities for artists to exhibit or musicians to perform. When the British authorities, for example, sent a book about Scottish lochs to Iraq, they were prisoners of the 'informational' belief that readers would absorb whatever was put in front of them. It was possible to mitigate the unresponsiveness of Western culture through local exhibitions and concerts to which both sides contributed, but even this was confined to the Western styles which many Iraqis had acquired.

The absurd attempt to tell people what to want was integral to the colonial situation, and it was a sign of how people felt before the Revolution that after it took place cultural relations immediately became a matter of closer negotiation in more restricted areas than before, but this at least secured the real object, which was to identify the intersection between what one side has to offer and what the other side wants. This experience brought out unambiguously how pervasive suspicion of British influence had been, even when its intention was least intrusive.[44]

The coming changes in the country were not at all clear in July 1958, but there were unmistakable glimmerings. Let us take the case of a Briton whom chance had placed at that time, in that place, in an official but totally unpolitical position, and who could hardly fail to have a good idea of what was going on. What was the honest thing to do:

This is what the pseudonymous author, 'Caractacus', said:

The traditional answer is 'resign', but a family man waits until he is sure that he should. My own work, what I was actually doing, was honest in itself, even good and constructive, and I felt no personal guilt about it, but there is also the question of the guilt of a community. If Britain was responsible, even only in part, for the regime, if Britain was just *believed* responsible, individual Britons had a responsibility too. I need not resign, but I did not think I could do nothing either. So I did something. I wrote a book. In it I said that the true British interest was to take local opinion into full account, and not to stage-manage an inefficient and unpopular regime. It was to withdraw, and leave Iraqis to run Iraq; and not just a few whom we had chosen ourselves, and weren't wanted by other Iraqis. Whether they ran it well was not our business now, if it ever had been, any more than our affairs were theirs. At the lowest, it was not in our national interest to commit ourselves to what could only in the end be the losing side. If in Iraq, if thoughout the Arab world, we could deal with men representative of their people, and not with our own shadows, we could have a future of practical co-operation.

So did I lack the courage of my convictions when I adopted a pseudonym? Was this disloyal to the employers, whose bread it was, after all, that I ate? I would have told the truth if they had asked me outright, but I soon found that an unspoken agreement seemed to be operating: if I did not provoke them by breaking silence, they would not confront or penalize me. It seemed likely that, if it came to the push, I should at any rate be transferred out of the Arab world, where I had begun to know the people and to study the culture; I should have to start again from the beginning. With cultures as with people, you can only fall in love for the first time once. The one thing necessary in intercultural, as distinct from political, work is just the thing that is too often neglected, and also too difficult, once it has begun to make progress, to repeat – that is, really to get to know and like the other man's culture.

There is no evidence at all that 'Caractacus's' book, *Revolution in Iraq*, affected British opinion, still less policy, in the slightest. It may be, as I said of the intellectuals of Iraq, and in general, that it did express a growing feeling among the British people. Yet in the summer of 1958 the British landed troops in Jordan and the Americans in Lebanon. Why should Iraq have been immune? Would it have been so, in fact, if there had been any chance of success, any support in the country for intervention, or if the Revolution had not been such a success from the word 'go'? Frederick Axelgard's research has confirmed that an Anglo–American contingency plan was hurriedly devised, and aborted.[45]

Whatever it meant for Iraq, the Iraqi Revolution was a decisive moment in the history of imperialism, but it is not likely that the Free Officers were thinking about the world historical perspective. Perhaps they would not have cared greatly about it. They knew the importance of the Revolution for the history of Iraq, though they did not know all that it would imply for the future, and they thought they knew its importance for the rest of the Arab world. It is too soon to write the later history of opinion in Iraq, or to make a final assessment of the consequences of what happened in 1958. I suggest that this is a question without an answer.

## Perspective

If 'history is a pattern of timeless moments', a perspective of various revolutions through the many ways we perceive them may help us to recognize a pattern, and so to clarify our perception of the Revolution in Iraq. The basic question that gets asked in any comparison of revolutions is, what makes any of them a revolution at all? What happened in Iraq in 1958? Was it perhaps after all 'only a coup'?[46] I suggest that it is a mistake to think that these are two incompatible categories. A coup may or may not be followed and completed by a revolution; it is only one means to power and in itself quite neutral. It is a myth that a revolution must begin with an act of 'the people'. In that sense, 'the people' are themselves an ancient and benign myth; it is to 'the people' that revolutionaries, who by definition have usually not been elected, like to appeal, only to find that they have to educate their supporters into supporting them. Whether power is seized by an army coup or by a militant party group makes very little difference; either may later prove fissiparous, but both are trained to act together and can dominate the masses. We cannot disqualify coups from being revolutionary only because some coups have been reactionary, nor even because the prestigious French Revolution began with an experimental scramble for power which did nothing to make it more effective, and about which successive schools of historians dispute. In Baghdad the initial coup was endorsed, on the spot and later, by days of popular excitement reminiscent of the Paris *journées*, but it is not popular endorsement that makes a revolution; it is not even the extent of the changes that result (many not immediately visible, and most bound to be endlessly arguable), but such indisputable changes as are seen to occur and are recognized as revolutionary at the moment they occur. A revolution is when everyone thinks it is.

A broad perspective of revolutions brings out their common character, and the particular case in Iraq becomes clearer each time we examine a number of them together in some single light. Hanna

Batatu has told us that his interest in the English Civil War and the French Revolution influenced his choice of subject.[47] The Iraqi case lends itself to comparison. Only when I heard the 'Marseillaise' played on the radio on the day of revolution did I remember the date. I am not at all sure that it was played because it was appropriate, but it was no less so if it was just part of a rousing medley of Western music. In the coming months, to watch the parties jostling each other for Abdel Karim Qasim's inconstant support called to mind the uncertainties of 1792–94. The essentially experimental character of the French Revolution, as different leaders argued and manoeuvred, with shifting support from Paris and the provinces, was constantly paralleled in Iraq. The difference was the presence of the 'sole leader', and there the closer parallel is with the English Civil War, with Qasim well cast as Cromwell. The striking resemblance between all three events is the process of trial and error which circumstances forced on all the actors. There was no orderly procession of events following a revolutionary plan.

It was peculiar to the USSR and China that an organized party established the revolution in accordance with a preconceived theory which could only be discussed within the fixed limits of the party leadership; for them, too, there was trial and error, but Lenin and Mao both knew how to slot practical politics into political theory – and vice versa. Leninist Marxism, however, was too concerned about a correct method of seizing power, and this incidentally bogged down the Iraqi Communist Party. In Iraq the rise of the parties, when they were allowed into the light of day, came after a revolution which individuals of very different tendencies and political preferences had brought off. After the first uprising, insurrectionary days seem to have been organized by one or other of the parties in Baghdad, again, of course, as in Paris, but not, as there, discussed and planned in public by parties with constantly and visibly fluctuating membership and policies.

Also, it may be that in Baghdad there were more spontaneous occasions of which one party or another was able to take advantage than we think. As Batatu has pointed out, no study has been made of the crowds in Iraq, as has been done for Paris. In Cairo, Gamal Abdel Nasser was a pragmatic reformer who could take up a doctrine and drop it without problem, as seemed wise to him – to that extent he resembled Qasim, but he had the finer instinct for political survival and much better luck. There was less social stability and still less homogeneity in Iraq than in Egypt, but again both revolutions were experimental, and dogmatic only in that at various times various participants held conflicting dogmas. The USSR and the Chinese People's Republic have never been exempt from experimentation, and it seems safe to say that Iraq falls into a general pattern which includes most, if not all of the great revolutions of history.

There are some other similarities which may be more fortuitous. The English Civil War and the French Revolution have in common the fact that in each a king was killed as a traitor to his people. The Iraqis do not seem to have set out to kill their king, but Batatu quotes evidence that the officers meant to exile him (perhaps on the Faruq model) and put Abdulillah, the ministers and other beneficiaries of the regime on trial for their lives,[48] thus conforming to the pattern of the People's Court. In England and Iraq professional soldiers made the revolution. In England the army was specially recruited from articulate dissidents, among whom the conflict of incompatible beliefs was never satisfactorily resolved, but it reflected differences within the nation itself; it is clear that in France conscription brought the *armées révolutionnaires* (and the National Guard) closer to the nation. Yet I think that, at the beginning, the harmony of the 'people' of Iraq, or of the people with the army, was greater than in the two other regicide examples.[49] The corollary of this was that, when the Revolution began to devour its children, there was a high rate of mortality among the officers. The Indian 'mutiny' (or 'war of independence') was also a cultural conflict that extended well beyond the army in which it began, and to that extent it resembles the Iraqi case. In China the Long March of the People's Liberation Army was decisive, but perhaps resembles the English example more than it does the Iraqi. The way in which the Chinese (and the Cubans too) made much of the friendship and identity of interest of the army and the civilian population recalls at least the very early days of 1958 in Iraq.

A revolutionary conception that the Iraqis and the Americans had in common was that it was essential to expel a foreign presence and, curiously enough, the same foreign presence. The French had had their own reasons for xenophobia, and so in our time had the Chinese. The English and the American revolutions were both initially concerned with taxation without representation, which, put like that, is no longer an issue, but revolutions are always *inter alia* about who shall govern (which carries with it the power to tax) and often about whose consent shall matter. It is most unlikely that Iraq's

final constitutional position will prove to be the same as England's –
the English monarchy was not an alien one – but final constitutional
settlements are rare. The French have had more formal constitutions
than anyone, but change and development continue there, as
everywhere. The distribution of the powers of government, almost a
daily issue in the United States, is part of our perception of any
revolution, which experiments to find stability until, with the passage
of time, the moment comes for another instalment. The constitutional
problems of a revolution are only one aspect of the social reform and
nation-bulding to which it gives an impetus, and which any newly
privileged class is likely to favour. Revolution turned the American
colonies into a nation, and quickened the social development of
France. In Iraq, too, revolution brought out, from the disparate 'old
social classes' of an Ottoman province, a national identity which
under the old regime was only just beginning to appear.

A special aspect of the expulsion of foreigners is the opening up of
new opportunities to more and different people, not only, as in the
USSR and the Chinese People's Republic, where there was a serious
attempt to raise up an underclass and simultaneously to create a new
privileged class, but also in Egypt and Iraq, where the 'new' class was
already in existence. Conforming to Tocqueville's analysis, an
innovative and already active class, identifiable less in terms of
property than of privilege, saw the need to clear away old garbage to
make room to experiment and develop. The poor of Iraq felt some
uncertain and insecure advantage in the revolutionary situation, not
because they held effective power in any form, but rather as
beneficiaries of paternalism.[50]

It is less important to expel foreigners than to exclude *foreignness*.
Not less than the Iraqis in their revolution, the Americans in theirs
were anxious to rid themselves of foreign rulers, whose culture,
however, they shared, took for granted and did not want to change.
In over two hundred years they have given a jointly developing
culture only a relatively slight twist of their own. It is quite a
different matter wherever there is a real cultural divide. Any failure
to control technology causes all cultures to deteriorate in proportion
as they fail to absorb it. This is so much the more serious for nations
that have not originated the technology, and are in the process of
absorbing it from foreign sources, that it seems to become imperative
for them to control the foreign impact on their cultures. The
'colonialists' have wielded the technological power which every
weaker country believes it must assimilate in order to be free. The

problem is, how? Most recent revolutions of this century have been anti-colonialist, but they have come in different shades. China tried without success to destroy its own history in order to construct its distinctive variant of a Western political formula. Islamic culture is traditionally more aggressive, and its humiliation has been all the greater. The Iranians have taken the offensive at the head of that Islamic extremism which is a third attempt to shake off the baneful influence of the West, as so many Muslims, not all fanatics, see it. In turn 'lackey' national sovereignty (like Abdulillah's and Nuri's) and defiant nationalism (like Nasser's) failed to get rid of the problem of Western superiority. When I use the term 'failed' I mean 'failed to the general satisfaction', and when I use the term 'superiority', of course I do not assert that the West is superior, or that it is inferior. I mean only to say that Muslims have tried to show, first, that the West need not, then that it must not, and now finally that it cannot, dominate Islam; that Islam, whether as a culture or as a religion, is not inferior.

In the 1950s the typical Western 'imperialist', harking back over a long age of European domination, was shocked by the bitterness of the Egyptian and Iraqi nationalists, felt outraged at what he considered their impudence, and affected to jeer at their education (often better than his own). An Iraqi officer captured by the British invasion force in 1941 claimed his rights under the Geneva Convention. The reaction he got was: 'What do you know about the Geneva Convention?'[51] Yet the West was perfectly familiar with and even shared the national aspirations of patriots, that is, if they were Europeans. At least there was no incompatibility of principle. Communism was another matter, but it, too, arose in the West and was (as we have seen) primarily a Western preoccupation. Sir John Troutbeck's reasons for the attraction of Communism in the 1950s (even his claim of the 'lessening influence of Islam') apply equally to the rise of Islamic extremism. Modern liberals are more profoundly shocked than the old colonialist was, when in Islamic extremism they meet the total rejection of contemporary Western values and what looks to them like a list of human rights that has been stood on its head. If one world is to be isolated from infection by the other, there will be a reversal of the priorities of each and total loss of mutual understanding. It was not so in the 1950s. The Geneva Convention story is a case in point, for Muslim moderates had long ago accepted additions to traditional Islamic law – for example international law and diplomatic practice.

What has happened since? In Egypt, Gamal Abdel Nasser tried to side-step religion, Anwar Sadat expected to manage it, while Husni Mubarak wisely drags his heels. Today we can see how creeping Islamization has so far been largely political, and seems likely at most to influence rather than to replace the juridical establishment. This offers a model of how the nationalism of the 1950s may be reinforced by the tendencies of the 1980s. It is not the pattern in Iraq, where the religious question is complicated at home by differing forms of Islam, and where abroad it is the filling in a Syrian–Iranian sandwich. When we look back to the events of 1958, we are struck by how little the religious question arose and how secure and normal the religious background then seemed to be. Nationalism has gone on to take more secularist forms, but sooner or later Iraq will have to come to terms with a general religious tendency of the Arab world. Nothing that happened in 1958 will make that difficult, but the country's religious divisions may save it from fanaticism.

We should also consider the opposite of rejection. The debt of any revolution to the influence of others is bound to be largely a question of guess-work, and yet in many cases some debt is undeniable and is occasionally identifiable. The interdependence of French and American thinkers is an obvious case in point. The French Revolution may have been a remote model for the Iraqis, because European history is often taught in the Arab countries from the arrival of Bonaparte's armies in Egypt, and the extension of French revolutionary principles to so much of conquered Europe has given it a kind of cumulative universal prestige. It is obvious that in Iraq the Egyptian Revolution was an influence, as the fount of pan-Arab feeling and as a model of successful defiance of theWest, but it may be more nearly correct to speak of 'convergent development' in closely similar situations. There have been so many revolutions in the twentieth century that the era of anti-colonialism is a mesh of mutual influences.

It is not mutual dependence that is most important in revolutions, but almost the reverse. The greatest need in every case I can think of has been for self-reliance, though not all revolutions exemplify this in quite the same way. If a revolution does not spring from and lead to self-reliance, it will not be a revolution at all. Chairman Mao's insistence on self-help has often been anticipated. This is a quasi-rule that applies universally and aside and apart from our sympathies. A remark by Robert E. Lee is apt: 'The cry is for too much help', he said, speaking of possible British support for the Confederacy. 'I am mortified to hear it. We want no aid.'[52] No revolt that depends on outsiders will achieve independence. The documents cited by Roger

Louis demonstrate how important it was that Britain should get out of Iraq – important for Iraq, because the revolution that freed it from at least the paternalist incubus was seen to be self-generated, and important for Britain, which was freed from the inherited habit of colonial thinking, and important, in retrospect, as proving the accuracy of the general Iraqi perception at the time.[53]

I have tried in a tentative way to place this revolution in a wide historical context in order to shed a little light on its perception, both in the present and in the past. The few points I have touched on in summary are only a beginning, but I hope that it is useful to hint at the possibilities, if only because, however slight, they already bring out so many revolutionary similarities. One that I have not mentioned is the escalation of violence between conflicting sides after the initial revolution, either the suppression of further change as counter-revolutionary, or the revenges of a 'White Terror'. This, too, seems a nearly invariable rule, probably inherent in the security of all revolutions which by definition have destabilized an establishment.

Naturally revolutions come at times of major change of all kinds in the world at large. Exactly the same things may not be happening everywhere simultaneously, but it seems that, for whatever reason, similar outbreaks do come in different places at about the same time, partly perhaps from contagion, but more because the same pressures are finding much the same relief. Historians have discussed this curious fact like epidemiologists discussing the spread of bubonic plague. Revolutions are not clones, but the most cursory examination shows that every one of them has a great deal in common with many of the others. I have been concerned with appearances and with how they relate to facts, because you cannot talk about the one without reference to the other. Perceptions by different people at the time seem to have corresponded not only with the facts but also therefore with each other. Western Embassy officials, especially the British, and the men of the streets and market-place thought in different terms as well as in different languages, but we now know that they all saw the same thing, whatever they thought about it, and however reluctant they would have been at the time to admit the fact.

All this is to say nothing about the consequences of the Revolution. What the Iraqis wanted was the foreigner out, and that they got. Any new wounds now are self-inflicted. If so much has happened since that it somewhat dims the Iraqis' perception of their first successful revolution, we may still think that their vision at the time was right and unspoiled. There was little limit then to what

might be attempted; for the moment the future seemed open. It is in
their subsequent history that revolutions differ most. It may be that
in the long run the history of opinion does not matter, in the sense
that concerns and indignation die away as if they were just plants
making room for new growth. It is with surprising speed that a
political belief, for which only a little earlier men and women were
glad to die, is replaced by some new and equally sincere concern; but
opinion matters in the sense that, unless we understand it, we cannot
understand the events that some strong motivation has shaped, still
less the people who helped to shape them.


## Notes

1. Hanna Batatu, *The Old Social Classes and the Revolutionary Movements of Iraq*
(Princeton, 1978), p. 36.

2. Ibid., p. 5.

3. This is based on my recollection of Sir Michael Wright's comments. Roger Louis
has now provided evidence (see the following chapter, 'The British and the Origins of
the Iraqi Revolution').

4. See Gilles Kepel, *Le prophète et pharaon* (Paris, 1984), pp. 207–8.

5. The contempt of the Communist leader, Fahd, for 'petty bourgeois intellectuals'
is interesting; his hopes for 'the people's intelligentsia' are naive. See *Old Social
Classes*, p. 508.

6. Alexis de Tocqueville, *L'ancien régime et la révolution* (Garden City, New
Jersey, 1955). See also his *Oeuvres complètes*, vol. 8, *Mélanges* (Paris, 1865), chap. 2,
p. 66.

7. *Old Social Classes*, p. 679.

8. See Louis, 'The British and the Origins' p. 31 below; 'the British were identified
indelibly with the Hashemite dynasty and with Nuri.'

9. For the execution of Fahd, see *Old Social Classes*, pp. 568–69.

10. Ibid., Book One, Part II, ch. 5, esp. pp. 55–57, 64, 73–132.

11. Personal recollection, notably of the Naqib family of Basra.

12. *Old Social Classes*, Book 1, Part II, ch. 9, esp. pp. 236–44.

13. Ibid., p. 805: 'Royalists possessed at bottom little more than the appearance of
power.'

14. English eighteenth-century parallels came naturally to Englishmen: see Louis,
'The British and the Origins', pp. 33, and 35–6 below. For Troutbeck on the danger
threatening the 'Royal House', see ibid., p. 35.

15. Book Two, 'The Communists . . . to the Fifties', is a party history; more
relevant here is the scheme of Book Three, 'The Communists, the Ba'thists, and the
Free Officers from the Fifties to the Present', which goes up to 1975. Access to much
Communist material makes that party the pivot of the story, and gives an 'insider's'
impression of events. Of course this does not affect the author's historical judgement.

16. On the revolutionary situation, Louis, 'The British and the Origins', p. 58,
discloses an astonishing statement by Wright: 'His language is unequivocal: "For it is

quite certain that, today, a revolutionary situation does not exist."' See Batatu, *Old Social Classes*, p. 806, for comparison of 'coup' and 'revolution'.

17. Batatu speaks of Qasim's 'passionate concern for the wide masses of the labouring poor', *Old Social Classes*, p. 839.

18. Ibid., p. 843.

19. Ibid., p. 905.

20. Ibid., p. 901 cf. Batatu's own phrase, 'capriciousness or erraticism', p. 835.

21. Ibid., p. 959.

22. Ibid., pp. 897–99. For fair-weather Communism on the fringes of the party see also pp. 922–23, 1000.

23. Ibid.; personal recollection.

24. Ibid., p. 859 (for February 1959), p. 900 (*Ittihad al-Sha'b* of 4 May 1959: concerning May Day rally). It is frequently cited for news of public demonstrations and public Communist activities and interests. I am not at all sure that Batatu, for all his historian's caution, does not overestimate the significance of mass rallies called out by the party; see p. 828.

25. Ibid., pp. 841, 923 (my emphasis).

26. Ibid., p. 849. This is said with reference to using recently released political prisoners to indoctrinate new party members.

27. Ibid., p. 934.

28. Ibid., pp. 804–5.

29. Walldemar J. Gallman, *Iraq under General Nuri: My Recollections of Nuri al-Said, 1954–1958* (Baltimore, 1964, quoted by Batatu, *Old Social Classes*, p. 806.

30. *Old Social Classes*, pp. 869, 983–85.

31. Ibid., p. 814.

32. Ibid., p. 977.

33. Ibid., pp. 789 ff; for Free Officers' movement see esp. pp. 767–89; also p. 763.

34. Ibid., p. 1125.

35. Ibid., p. 777.

36. Ibid., p. 772.

37. Ibid., p. 902.

38. For Sir John Troutbeck's analysis of Communism in Iraq in the 1950s see Louis, 'The British and the Origins', pp. 40–41 below.

39. Batatu, *Old Social Classes*, p. 802.

40. Personal recollection. I attended the court once, but watched it frequently on television in the presence of a variable grouping of young officers (as far as I was concerned an entirely haphazard one).

41. Personal information from released prisoners; common knowledge at the time.

42. Personal recollection of stories circulating in Baghdad at the time.

43. See chapters by Louis and Axelgard in this volume. For the formative period of imperial dissolution in the Middle East, see Wm. Roger Louis, *The British Empire in the Middle East, 1945–1951: Arab Nationalism, The United States and Postwar Imperialism* (Oxford, 1984), Introduction.

44. Personal experience.

45. Disclosed at Austin in discussion, but not recorded so far as I have seen. See Frederick Axelgard's chapter in this volume.

46. See Batatu, *Old Social Classes*, p. 806.

47. See Hanna Batatu's chapter, p. 211 below, and n. 2, above.

48. See Batatu, *Old Social Classes*, p. 795.

49. That the army should not be considered a social class apart was also the opinion, reported by Batatu, ibid., p. 851, of the plenum of the Central Committee of the Communist Party in September 1958, when they warned against 'ideas which regard the army as a mass separate from the class make-up of society'. Their doctrine is not invalidated by the good solid tactical reason they had for holding it.

50. For urban and rural social change under Qasim, see Batatu, *Old Social Classes*, pp. 836–42, 806–7.

51. The writer was told this by Col. Salim al-Fakhri (see ibid., index).

52. Letter of 29 December 1861, cited by Bruce Catton, *Terrible Swift Sword* (New York, 1963), p. 110.

53. Louis, 'The British and the Origins'. It will be clear that my views are generally in agreement with those of Roger Louis, and I am gratified to find that much of his documentation vindicates earlier views of mine.

# 2

# The British and the Origins of the Iraqi Revolution

## Wm. ROGER LOUIS

The subject of British imperialism in Iraq, indirectly at least, is basic to Hanna Batatu's overall interpretation. He draws at least three conclusions that are significant. The first is that the British themselves were uneasily aware as early as the period of the Second World War that, in their own self-interest, too much depended on their principal collaborator, Nuri Said. 'The weakness of our long-term position in Iraq', Batatu quotes from a Foreign Office document of 1943, 'undoubtedly consists in the extent to which our eggs are concentrated in Nuri's somewhat unstable basket.'[1] From the British vantage-point, the long-range future appeared to be unsatisfactory. What could be done about it? Could revolution be averted? The second conclusion is that the British miscalculated, like Nuri, on the pace and way in which the resources should be developed and the revenues invested. 'At bottom', Batatu writes, 'the question is one of elaborating the institutions and building the skills that could employ the huge oil revenues in a socially effectual way.'[2] The third point, certainly the most fundamental, is that the British helped to create the set of shifting alliances among the propertied classes, the shaikhs, and the political and military leaders of the country. One of his principal arguments, as I read it, is that during the 1920s and 1930s the British represented part of the triangular basis of power in Iraq. They rivalled the monarchy and the socially-dominant landed classes. The institutional policies initiated by the British continued to work in favour of the existing social order.[3]

My comments will develop those points, among others, by concentrating on the period antecedent to the Revolution and by analysing British thought on the nature of Iraqi society. At the same time I shall try to relate discussion on internal matters to external issues that Batatu deals with less extensively. Those include the Baghdad Pact and the question of Palestine. I shall use as examples the ideas of two British officials who commented substantially on the affairs of Iraq, Sir John Troutbeck, Ambassador in Baghdad 1951–54, and Sir Michael Wright, the Ambassador from 1954 until the Revolution in 1958. Troutbeck and Wright were representative latter-day British proconsuls. The former was contemplative, ironic, and learned, the latter more interventionist and much more inclined to give credence to the dangers of Communism and the cold war. Both of them considered the prospect of revolution in Iraq, though Wright minimized the possibility. What type of revolution did they fear?

In Batatu's book the British are shadowy figures. 'The English', in his term, are an abstraction. In *The Old Social Classes* one has to read almost between the lines to establish firmly in one's own mind that until 1958 Britain remained the dominant foreign power in Iraq propping up the monarchy, that British troops were stationed at air force bases in Habbaniyah and Shaiba, that British officials held key posts as 'experts' in the Iraqi government, and that the Iraq Development Board was largely a British invention. It would do Batatu an injustice to conclude from his book that British imperialism was a negligible force in the Iraqi state of the 1950s, but how is one to distinguish between the institutional legacy of the British mandate and the active influence of British soldiers and poitical advisers?[4] For the historical record, what was the British view on those matters? Did British influence still count in the 1950s? If so, in which ways did it manifest itself? Could the British still intervene decisively, either directly or indirectly? Did the Iraqis still believe that they could? One is reminded of the feigned perplexity of Harold Beeley, who wrote as a member of the Foreign Office in1951: 'I was often puzzled after my conversations in Iraq to know whether the complaint against us was that we interfered and ought not to interfere or that we ought to interfere and failed to do so.'[5]

Batatu certainly cannot be accused of approaching his subject from an Anglocentric point of view. But among the British themselves the comparisons between England and Iraq sometimes seemed compelling. Stewart Perowne, the Oriental Counsellor in the British Embassy in Baghdad in 1947 described the Regent, Abdulillah, as a statesman with 'a great admiration and liking for Britain and for British methods and persons. His cars, his aircraft, his clothes, his hunters, his fox-hounds, even his swans, are British, and so are many of his closest friends.'[6] As Perowne analysed Iraqi politics, he found echoes of the thoughts of Queen Anne and the Duke of Marlborough, parallels of corruption in eighteenth-century England and in twentieth-century Iraq, and a march of nineteenth-century progress that had finally reached Baghdad. He once compared Nuri with Disraeli. Perowne of course is an eccentric example. But there were others who followed him in the belief that Nuri was a hero worthy of the times. Sir Michael Wright had less historical flair than Perowne, but the interpretation was similar. For example Wright once reflected on Nuri's momentous innings in Iraqi politics: 'Nuri had been called back in August, 1954, to become Prime Minister for the twelfth time. The old champion had rolled up his sleeves and walked down the pavilion steps to bat on a rapidly crumbling wicket.'[7] As will be seen, Wright was aware of Nuri's shortcomings, but throughout the critical period 1954–58 there was a tendency on Wright's part to dwell, in his own words, on 'The Achievements of Nuri Said'.[8] It is virtually certain that all British contemporaries would have treated Nuri as a much greater figure in Iraqi statecraft than Batatu does in his book.

What were the assumptions which the British made about Iraq? It is useful here to explore the ideas of Sir John Troutbeck, who had a long record of service in the Middle East. From 1947 to 1950 he had been head of the Middle East Office in Cairo, where he had co-ordinated regional policy. He was thus familiar with general problems such as that of Arab unity as championed by the Arab League. He took it for granted that British influence in Iraq was beneficent, and indeed that the Iraqis owed their very independence to Britain. 'When all was said and done', he wrote in 1952, 'we had delivered Iraq from Turkish rule and given her her independence, provided a long succession of honest and able administrators for the country, built the railway system and handed it over practically free of charge, and created the oil industry upon which the financing of further development depended.'[9]

Though he may not have agreed with all of the implications, Troutbeck was expressing the rudiments of what has become known as the 'colonial state'.[10] Batatu leaves this generic idea rather implicit in his analysis, but the following synopsis of the British era in Iraq would seem to me to complement parts of his argument. During and after the First World War, Britain imposed a territorial unity on the three former Ottoman provinces of Basra, Baghdad and Mosul. The boundaries of the new territory were accompanied by an army to police the frontiers. Iraq under the administration of the British was a nascent modern state. It gradually possessed not only boundaries but also a system of administration and justice, a constitution and a bicameral legislature. The British developed an infrastructure of road, railways and telegraphs. They created a central bureaucracy with all of the trappings of Western government, including offices with files, typewriters and telephones. Internal security was provided by the Iraqi Police Force with its own Criminal Investigation Department. All of these measures in one way or another served British self-interest, yet at the same time British administrators could emphatically claim that they served the Iraqi government in the best tradition of the British civil service.

One function of the colonial state is to provide a basis of revenue, which the British did through the 1929 law on the national tax system, which benefited their collaborators, the large landowners. Another function is to regulate land tenure, which the British did by inheriting the Ottoman land law of 1858 and overseeing the enactment of the land law of 1933.[11] Still another function of the colonial state is economic development. In 1925 a British, French and American consortium called the Iraq Petroleum Company secured a concession over Iraqi oil. In 1950 the Iraq Development Board was created to invest a large part of the profits of the Iraqi government into such projects as irrigation and flood control, agricultural development and land reclamation. Yet another fundamental function of the colonial state is to provide internal security. In 1941 the British responded to an uprising led by Rashid Ali by reoccupying the country and restoring the monarchy. Thus there was no doubt that Iraq was a puppet state.[12] Though the mandate had ended in 1932 and Iraq had become 'independent', it was clear that the Iraqi government was dependent on Britain. Troutbeck would have used a slightly different phrase – a 'friendly' rather than 'dependent' government, perhaps – but he would have recognized the functions of the Iraqi state as created or directed by the British. It would be unfair to Troutbeck, however, not to point out that he would probably have regarded the entire concept of the 'colonial state' as a convenient scapegoat by which Iraqis could blame British imperialism for their own shortcomings.

Though Troutbeck was a man of equable temperament, it irritated him that Iraqis remained resentful and suspicious of the British presence. He was once provoked into reducing them to a racial stereotype:

> The Iraqi, it seems to me, or at any rate the townsman, will never forget a grievance. Being one of the laziest of mortals and having no family life, he will sit in his cafe for hours on end surrounded by his cronies, brooding over his grievances and talking interminable politics. By a mixture of tact and firmness one may keep him sane and good-humoured for a time, and a joke may turn his thoughts at a difficult moment. But there is a side to his nature which is embittered, frustrated and fanatical.
>
> Seeing little but squalor and stagnation all round him, he will not admit even to himself the obvious answer, that he belongs to a peculiarly irresponsible and feckless race.[13]

The Iraqis did not seem capable, even in their own eyes, of keeping pace with events in the Middle East. 'Bagdadi lawyers and coffee-house politicians', Troutbeck observed after the Egyptian revolution of 1952, 'seem to regard it as almost a matter of honour to have a *coup d'état*. It has happened in Egypt and Syria, and even in the despised Lebanon. The Bagdadis are hanging their heads in shame; they have not yet even murdered a Prime Minister.'[14]

Troutbeck was representative of his era. He held what a contemporary writer described as 'the theory of the two standards', by which the British, so it was believed, had progressed to an advanced stage of civilization while the Iraqis had developed only to an eighteenth-century equivalent.[15] Troutbeck had no doubt whatever that the Iraqis had been granted independence prematurely in 1932. 'There is not the smallest doubt that Iraq achieved her independence too soon.'[16] In holding that view, he was a quintessential British official. But he also espoused more sophisticated and less paternalistic ideas that set him apart from most of his contemporaries. Troutbeck believed that the British should force the pace of reform and modernization in their own self-interest as well as for the sake of Iraq. 'If nothing is done', he wrote in April 1953:

> the position of the Royal House itself may be in danger. We are always being accused here of interfering in Iraqi affairs in the wrong direction; I think that the moment has come when we must make a real effort to move things in the right direction both in our own interests and in those of Iraq.[17]

The issues that preoccupied him as he tried to exert a positive influence were the ethnic and religious composition of the Iraqi state, 'radical' nationalism as espoused by unemployed Iraqis with some degree of education – the 'effendis' – and certain matters that needed to be addressed urgently such as tax reform.

Above all Troutbeck was aware of what he called the 'artificiality of the Iraqi state. British rule had imposed a fragile unity over the six and a half million diverse peoples who espoused disparate religious beliefs. Since agriculture provided the livelihood of the majority of the Iraqis, it was not surprising that Troutbeck called attention to the 'agrarian misery' of the rural areas. Traditionally the British had upheld the authority of the tribal shaikhs, who were, in his phrase, 'horrified' at the idea of land reform. Quite another set of problems, he identified with the Kurds of the northern part of the country. They formed about one-fifth of the total population. 'In time of trouble', he observed, 'their loyalty could not be wholly guaranteed.'[18] The principal political element were the Sunni Arabs, who constituted only about one-quarter of the population but exercised a traditional dominance of the Shia Arabs, who formed about one-half the population. Troutbeck once gave a curious explanation of how British policy had enhanced Sunni supremacy: 'a similar problem had arisen in the old days in India when the Hindus were much further advanced than the Muslims and were therefore being given all the appointments.'[19] Whenever he summarized the ethnic and religious reasons for unrest, Troutbeck recognized the part played by 'the politically conscious, truculent and unemployed effendi . . . [undermining] the stability of the country'.[20]

Troutbeck's method of analysis of the tension within Iraqi society differs of course from Batatu's. But the British interpretation was consistent and coherent. It may have been Anglocentric, and it may have used, for example, Indian analogies that today seem absurd. Nevertheless, Troutbeck's explanation took the same thrust as Batatu's on a basic point. Iraq was not a nationalistically cohesive state. To use Batatu's words, 'the national or patriotic idea was in 1958 still very weak'.[21]

Troutbeck believed that since 1932 the quality of administration in Iraq had steadily declined.

So today we have a country with all the material means for progress at its disposal but with an administration so rotten and chaotic that it is more than doubtful whether it can take advantage of them . . . The British administration disappeared before new roots had time to establish themselves.[22]

In the face of administrative incompetence and corruption, how could fundamental problems be resolved? The question filled Troutbeck with despair as he reiterated in his own mind some of the larger issues: 'tax reform, the useful employment of the young effendis, the low standard of efficiency and honesty in the administration and the moulding of the different races and religious sects into a united whole'. Troutbeck had begun his career in Turkey. He had witnessed the transformation of Turkish society under the leadership of Kemal Ataturk. In surveying the problems of Iraq, he reflected pessimistically that there was no leader of the same stature. 'No Ataturk has yet emerged in Iraq. Nuri Pasha, on the other hand, still has plenty of kick in him.'[23]

Part of the revolutionary indictment against Nuri was that he had irrevocably aligned himself with the forces of 'feudalism'. Troutbeck quite clearly regarded the issue of land as the basic problem of the country. Nuri supported the wealthy landowners and opposed agrarian reform that might have reduced the size of landholdings. Troutbeck estimated that the large 'landlords' held close to 70% of the cultivable land while small landholders or 'peasants' owned less than 15%. The landowners were predominantly Sunni. The unequal relationship between Sunni and Shia Arabs pervaded all aspects of society and government. In Troutbeck's words, 'it is the Sunni minority that still holds most of the big jobs whether in Government, administration or army.'[24] This was his recurrent theme: 'the old guard of Sunnis . . . are neither greatly interested in internal reforms nor willing to share the sweets of office with the Shias.'[25] As if he were forecasting the eventual revolution, Troutbeck commented in 1953: 'The kind of things that were worrying me as likely in due course to lead to an explosive situation were the facts that the rich paid practically no taxes, that there were still innumerable peasants without land of their own, that the cost of living remained very high and that the split between the Sunnis and Shias seemed to be getting wider rather than otherwise.'[26]

Nuri dominated the shifting coalitions of the landed aristocracy and political or military leaders, many of whom, like Nuri himself, had served as young officers in the Ottoman Army.[27] The Iraqi elite in the professions, as well as in the civil service and the army, drew inspiration from an earlier age. Collectively this miscellany of the 'old gang', Troutbeck's phrase, exerted a fragile control over Iraqi society; but it was by no means comparable to the 'old guard' that existed, for example, in Egypt.[28] The interlocking but variable elite of Iraq, in the British judgement, probably consisted of no more than four hundred men of whom only about fifty were influential in national affairs. Again, they were mainly Sunnis. In 1953 almost all officers of the Iraqi Army of brigadier rank and above were Sunnis.[29] The problem for the British was that they themselves were so closely associated with Nuri and the monarchy that in turn they were inextricably linked with the coalition of interests that had grown up around the Hashemite regime. According to Troutbeck: 'one of our major embarrassments here was that everyone tended to identify us with the elder statesmen.' In Troutbeck's view, Nuri himself frustrated all efforts to prove that the British were sincere in wishing for improvement in the standard of administration and the quality of life in Iraq:

There is no sign that Nuri believes in reform. He believes rather in paternal government, the strong hand distributing gifts of welfare, which can be paid for not by taxing the rich but rather by extracting further revenues from the oil companies.[30]

Nuri believed that a firm hand controlling and distributing the benefits of the oil riches would eventually lead to general prosperity and political stability. Here Troutbeck was convinced that Nuri's attitude would be challenged by the younger generation of Iraqi nationalists. 'I find it hard to share his [Nuri's] confidence', Troutbeck concluded, 'that they [the Iraqis] will accept forever a position in which the wealthy landowners have so great privilege and so little burden of responsibility. It is certainly the view of the younger modern-educated Iraqi that this position cannot last.'[31]

Whatever the complexion of the actual government, Nuri and the 'old guard' continued to control the economy, the parliament and much of the political press. For example, from September 1953 to April 1954 Fadil Jamali presided over two governments as prime minister. The British followed the developments under his leadership with considerable interest because he represented a younger generation determined to introduce social and economic reform. Jamali was a Western-educated Shi'i. He held a Ph.D. from Columbia University. He did not have an anti-British reputation. Nevertheless the British had ambivalent feelings about him, in part because of the nature of the Shia regime. Troutbeck commented:

The old Ottoman-trained Iraqis were for the first time discarded and . . .
Dr Jamali's Government . . . marks something of an epoch in Iraq's history
. . . The younger men are keener, work harder and . . . are less corrupt and
more genuinely interested in reform than their seniors.

On the other hand they are more parochial in outlook, more chauvinistic
and somehow smaller men. The Shias . . . bear all the marks of the
underdog. The greater their power becomes, the more difficult will Iraq be to
deal with.[32]

Jamali, moreover, proved to be ineffective as a reformer because of
the political basis of Nuri's strength. A Foreign Office minute
summed up the British perception of the static nature of the old
social classes: 'Whatever the colour of the Prime Minister, Iraq is at
present governed by the old guard of landowners whose leader is
Nuri Pasha es Said.'[33]

Troutbeck's despatches reveal that Jamali may have been an
ineffective social reformer but that he was much more closely
associated with the origins of the Baghdad Pact than is commonly
known. Troutbeck wrote in December 1953 that Jamali was 'very
anxious' to strengthen Turco–Iraqi ties: 'Communism was a danger
to them both and they ought to combine to resist it.' Troutbeck was
initially sceptical: 'Dr Jamali is a man who scintillates brain-waves
and this idea of his of wishing to strengthen Turco–Iraqi relations
may prove nothing more than a flash in the pan.'[34] The Foreign
Office response, however, gives a clue to more positive calculations
that were not ephemeral and led indeed to the creation of the
Baghdad Pact:

Iraq lies on the exposed south-eastern flank of N.A.T.O. and even out of
the context of American plans to line up Turkey, Iraq, Persia and Pakistan,
we should welcome any improvement in Turco–Iraqi relations . . .

The Egyptians and the other members of the Arab League will be annoyed
but this should not worry us unduly: on the contrary it would be to our
advantage to prevent the Iraqis from co-ordinating their policy on Middle
East Defence with the Egyptians.[35]

Troutbeck had mixed sentiments about the wisdom of accentuating
differences in the Arab world over the issue of defence, but there was
no doubt in his mind, or anybody else's, that Nuri was the driving
force behind Iraq's eventual strategic alignment.

The main problem as Troutbeck saw it at the end of his tour of duty as Ambassador in late 1954 was that Nuri could not endure as a permanent fixture. Though he regretted Nuri's reluctance to pursue social and economic reform, he believed that Iraq needed to be ruled by a strong hand and that Nuri, though no Ataturk, provided an indispensable stabilizing element. In one of his last despatches Troutbeck discussed the issue of stability in relation to Communism:

Of course his [Nuri's] methods are not such as would appeal to nineteenth century liberals, and no doubt the cry will soon go up that Iraq has become a Fascist state. Nevertheless I am quite convinced that strong Government is essential in Iraq . . .

The most alarming feature in Iraq today seems to me that stability still depends on one man – Nuri Said. He cannot last for ever, but no one of his calibre has appeared on the scene during my term of office and there seems no one else capable even of maintaining order. The Communists and their friends are quiet for the moment but, if Nuri were to disappear, there is no doubt that they would quickly raise their heads again.[36]

The Communist movement in Iraq, in Troutbeck's judgement, might eventually bring about a revolution unless it could be effectively combatted. Earlier in the year he had commented on the 'striking increase in left-wing and Communist sentiment'.[37]

Since Batatu's book devotes so much attention to the question of Communism, it is useful to present Troutbeck as a contemporary witness on the subject. He devoted several passages to it in his swan song of 9 December 1954. He emphasized the spread of Communism not only among the urban population but also in religious circles and in rural areas:

It [Communism] is fed from many sources – the traditional resistance to Western imperialism, chronic indignation at the corruption and selfishness of the ruling classes, the hard living conditions of the poor, the lack of opportunity for the young men who pour out of the colleges year by year, and lastly the ideological gap left by the lessening influence of Islam.

As a result, though there are few Communists in the strict sense of the word, the mass of the intelligentsia at least give a ready ear to Communist propaganda.

Nuri . . . believes that strong government is the answer. So it may be so long as the government remains strong. But when he is not Prime Minister, the government is weak. The most disturbing feature of my period of service here has been the steady growth of Communist sentiment from the time that Nuri relinquished the premiership in the summer of 1952 till he resumed power a couple of years later.[38]

In the eyes of the Communists, and indeed for Iraqis generally, the British were identified indelibly with the Hashemite dynasty and with Nuri.

In comparing the analysis of Troutbeck and Batatu, where they differ above all is on the part played by the individual in the political process. Batatu holds that neither Nuri nor the Regent 'was as free as he seemed to be'.[39] Troutbeck on the other hand believed that individuals and political groups – Nuri, the Communists, the British – could make a difference in the eventual outcome if they demonstrated political will power and tenacity of purpose. There is another important point, however, where there is less of a divergence between Troutbeck and Batatu. Troutbeck often warned that Nuri was regarded as a traitor to the cause of Arab nationalism because of his association with the British. The three emotions of 'Arabism, Islam and anti-imperialism', Troutbeck wrote, 'meet in concentrated fanaticism on the question of Israel.'[40] Troutbeck would not have disagreed with Batatu's statement that the Palestine tragedy accelerated the pace of change in the Middle East; but he would probably have seen a much closer connection than Batatu between external events and the drift towards revolution in Iraq.[41]

*   *   *   *   *

Sir Michael Wright, like his predecessor, was a man of rigorous intellect, but Wright had less intellectual curiosity about Iraqi society. He was an 'old Middle East hand' by experience rather than by temperament. During the early part of the war he had served in Cairo. Apparently the formality of the British Embassy under Lord Killearn left an inspirational mark on Wright. At least the way he ran the embassy in Baghdad bore a resemblance to Killearn's rigid style of pomp and imperial circumstance. Wright himself was a man of courtly dignity. Even his wife referred to him as 'His Excellency', or less formally as 'H. E.' While Troutbeck was 'one of the best-loved members of the Diplomatic Service', Wright did not inspire personal warmth.[42]

Wright saw the affairs of Iraq in the context of the cold war. He once described the Baghdad Pact as 'an agreement which committed Iraq to side with the Free World against possible Soviet aggression'.[43] No British official at the time would have taken exception to that obvious statement, but there was a world of difference in outlook between Wright and Troutbeck. The latter believed that the

Communist movement in Iraq and elsewhere in the Middle East was essentially nationalistic. Troutbeck once quoted from an Iraqi newspaper to sum up the Iraqi attitude towards the cold war:

> The call of the West finds no echo in our hearts. We do not understand them because we do not feel ourselves to be part of the so-called "free world" which they say they are defending. We are part of the oppressed world which is struggling against them to achieve its freedom and throw off their yoke.[44]

That attitude, Troutbeck continued, should not be confused with Communism and did not imply identification with Moscow. The danger of a Soviet or Communist take-over did not appear to most Iraqis to be an immediate threat. Wright, on the other hand, believed that most intelligent Iraqis recognized that 'Communism represented the greatest of the dangers to Iraq and to her development.' More specifically, he held that the events in Iran in 1953, when the Shah had been temporarily forced to flee the country, had awakened those in responsible positions in Iraq to the danger of 'a Communist or near-Communist Iran on her frontier'.[45]

Wright made certain assumptions about the nature of Iraqi society that influenced his views about the other Arab countries and the Baghdad Pact. He believed that Iraq's 'natural orbit' caused the country to gravitate towards Iran and Turkey rather than towards the Middle East proper and 'the old and sterile policies of the Arab League'. By creating a new regional group that would include Pakistan and Iran, then other countries, notably Egypt, might eventually see the light and be persuaded to throw in their lot on the 'right side'. Wright elaborated on the Shia–Sunni part of the equation:

> I do not feel sure that the natural orbit of Iraq is purely an Arab one. I am becoming increasingly impressed by the degree to which Iraqi eyes are turned on Persia, to which the Shias look as the leading Shia power, and to some extent on Turkey, particularly in the case of the Sunnis.
> It was events in Persia which really awoke Iraq to the Communist danger ... Turkish traditions are far from negligible; and links of sympathy with Britain are stronger than is often supposed. On these and other grounds ... I question whether the Arab League, if that is more or less what we mean by the Arab fold, is, in fact, the right framework for Iraqi policy.[46]

That line of thought led Wright to the conclusion that it would be best to support Iraq as a pillar of the 'Free World', regardless of the reaction of the other Arab states. He was convinced of the urgency of the situation: 'Is it not better for us to have an Iraq prepared to take a staunch attitude, even if it is an independent one, on Communism and regional defence, rather than an Iraq more or less bound to accept policies of the Arab League . . . ?'[47]

Batatu is surely closer to the truth than Wright on the general issue of the Baghdad Pact. Iraqis did not see their national destiny as coinciding with the fate of Iran and Turkey, and the pact itself isolated Iraq from most of the Arab World.[48] There is another issue, however, on which I believe that Wright had a better sense of proportion of contemporary affairs than Batatu. This is the impact of the Suez crisis of 1956 on Iraq.

'Disbelief and consternation' were the words Wright used to describe the Iraqi reaction to the invasion of Egypt by Britain, France and Israel in November 1956. The problem was not that the British used force against Nasser but that they consorted with France and Israel, 'the one regarded as the arch-colonizer and the other the arch-enemy of the Arabs'. As if expressing his own disapproval, Wright added: 'It was, as our friends said, un-British.' Part of the trouble, Wright explained, originated with the students, who had 'nothing to lose but their studies'.[49] In much more serious vein Wright described how the Suez invasion placed Nuri together with the young King Faisal II and the Crown Prince Abdulillah in mortal jeopardy:

The action of her Majesty's Government [at Suez], because it was linked with action by Israel, placed him [Nuri] personally, as well as the King and Crown Prince and all those in Iraq who had so actively pursued a policy of friendship with Her Majesty's Government, not only in the gravest political difficulty but in danger of their lives, and imperilled the continued existence of the régime and the monarchy.[50]

By all British accounts, Nuri took a stout-hearted attitude and precariously retrieved the situation. According to Wright: 'Nuri, growling like a wounded bear, took the line: "I will save the Iraqis from themselves and the British from themselves."' Wright specifically described how Nuri managed to hold the government and the monarchy intact:

He put heart into his colleagues, into the Army, and into senior officials . . . .

He devoted his main criticism to internal security and refused to yield an inch to demonstrations or criticism, the first time in the history of Iraq that a

Prime Minister had maintained this attitude at a moment of critical tension.[51]

During this period of sustained crisis Nuri held the position 'with a courage and steadfastness beyond praise'. But it was a close call. After the crisis had passed Wright reported that Nuri was still in power, 'but with the ground heaving under his feet'.[52]

The following excerpts from the diaries and letters of Michael Ionides reveal the Iraqi political consequences of the Suez crisis, again from a British perspective but one that differed from Wright's. Ionides was the British member of the Iraq Development Board. He had been trained as an engineer and had Middle Eastern experience since the 1920s. He was sensitive to the criticism of younger Iraqis who felt aggrieved at Nuri's out-and-out support of the British. He wrote in December 1956:

> There are bitter complaints from the younger men, up to 30 or 40, that Nuri has never brought the next generation along, has kept everything to himself, never built up the structure of Government and Parliament, never even tried to make elections work as other emergent countries have done.
>
> He has given no outlet for discussion, they say, no means for the younger people to take any part, keeping them in suspense and in complete ignorance as to what is going on, laying Iraq open to charges of doing nothing for Egypt and everything for the British, charges they cannot find evidence to refute, however much they might wish to.

Commenting on the social structure of Iraq, Ionides continued: 'At the top of the pyramid there is the minority of diehard no-goods, fearing chiefly for their wealth and security, going with the wind as long as it is fair.' On another occasion he assessed Nuri's position after Suez:

> The gap between Nuri and the people of Iraq has been growing fast and when he goes, it will not be just Nuri going out of power; it will be the end, or the near end of a phase when British influence, formerly dominant but steadily declining, clung on the last solid pro-British rock, Nuri Pasha, while the tide of affairs went on, beyond his control and beyond British control.[53]

Ionides was thus an acute observer of Middle Eastern affairs. He emphasized the immediate political origins of the Iraqi Revolution, though as an economic expert he would have been the last to have denied the underlying economic and social causes.

In reading contemporary evidence such as that of Wright and Ionides, one cannot but be struck by the deliberate political interpretation that stands in contrast to Batatu's overarching emphasis on 'structural changes and dislocations'.[54] This is more than a difference between officials or men of affairs, on the one hand, and a scholar on the other. This is a clash among those trying to understand the causes of revolution. Where does the balance lie between the immediate and the long-term, between the emphasis on certain individuals such as Nuri and the more impersonal economic and sociological forces? It does no discredit to Batatu to reassess the less scholarly but none the less substantive point of view that the Revolution was as much, if not more, political as it was economic, at least in immediate origins.

At one level there is no conflict. Contemporary British observers would certainly have agreed with Batatu that the issue of the exploitation of the oil wealth played a central part in the developing crisis before July 1958. Wright wrote in the aftermath of Suez that Nuri had been lucky because 'the country was prosperous and that there was no economic discontent which others could exploit'.[55] Oil revenues had risen from £40.8 million in 1952 to £86.4 million in 1958.[56] Nuri's gamble was that this huge wealth would create prosperity and bring about a lasting political stability without unduly disturbing the basis of the land system. Through the eyes of British witnesses of the time, what in fact happened?

It was an article of faith held by most contemporary British observers of the 1956–58 period that a race was taking place between development and revolution. Wright wrote in 1957 concerning the progress in recent years:

> The benefits of the oil revenues were beginning to be felt in the lives of the ordinary people and whether in housing, education, health, flood control or irrigation, there was a sense of progress and expanding horizons, and of considerable pride in the manner in which the formidable tasks were being tackled.

At the same time he was aware that the 'younger intellectuals', for example, 'considered that progress was too slow, and in particular that the somewhat feudal influence of the tribes, with their own law and their grip on land, must be made to give way more rapidly to more modern ideas'.[57] Nuri consistently gave the same answer to the charge that progress was too slow. Iraq needed the framework of 'internal stability' within which reforms could gradually be introduced. Wright summarized Nuri's outlook: 'to be over-hasty in undermining tribal structure and traditions before there was something adequate to put in their place would only lead to chaos'.[58] With the benefit of hindsight, it should be stated that Wright too easily aquiesced in Nuri's point of view. Thus he, and with him the British government, forfeited the opportunity to use what influence it still possessed to intervene, as Troutbeck would have put it, on the 'right side' of history.

Michael Ionides had insight into Nuri's temperament and limitations:

Despite his energy, he never found time enough to promote reforms which were getting more and more pressing. I do not mean only such things as land reform, springing from ideas of social advance, but also the kind of practical measures which were needed to bring all the new projects we [the Development Board] were building under efficient administrative control. I doubt if Nuri fully understood the need for these reforms.

The complexity of affairs induced by this sudden economic expansion [in the 1950s] demanded a range of experience which he did not possess, and a concentration of thought and effort which he had no time to give.[59]

To do Nuri justice from a British point of view, Wright probably best summed it up when he wrote that 'he is a sincere patriot working according to his own lights for the betterment of all Iraqis.' He added that Nuri's plans definitely did not include 'the breaking up and sharing out' of the great landed estates.[60] Wright thus detected one of the underlying causes of the impending revolution. He was uneasily aware that the British, by continuing to align themselves with Nuri, had irrevocably identified themselves with 'the class and way of life which he represents'.[61]

\*    \*    \*    \*    \*

Quite apart from the importance of certain individuals such as Nuri, what of the general spirit of the times? Can one understand the Iraqi Revolution without taking fully into account the ideas about Arab nationalism that were prevalent in early 1958? On 14 February King Faisal announced on radio and television the 'union' of Iraq and Jordan. The two 'sister countries', he proclaimed, thus offered proof that 'the Arab nation has awakened and is alert and determined to restore its glory'. The two branches of the Hashemite family would work together to provide common economic policies, customs laws, educational curricula, perhaps even a unified military command. Sir Michael Wright summed up the essence of the scheme as 'a confederation plus economic and financial unification'.[62] 'The dream of Arab unity is as strong in Iraq as in the other Arab countries', he reported, but on the other hand there could be little doubt that the Iraq–Jordan union was 'almost wholly' a response to the Egyptian and Syrian decision two weeks earlier to form the United Arab Republic.[63] People of Baghdad generally believed that the Iraqi–Jordan union was 'imposed by the [two] Monarchies' or was 'Western inspired'. Nuri's ambition might be eventually to include Kuwait, Saudi Arabia and other Arab countries in the union, but to the average Iraqi the United Arab Republic represented the genuine path to Arab unity. According to Wright, 'there will be the problem of selling the confederation to the Iraqi man in the street, who is likely to be somewhat unimpressed by its advantages as compared with those of joining the United Arab Republic'.[64]

The creation of the Egyptian–Syrian union was a turning-point in Middle Eastern affairs. Wright believed that it would influence the course of events in Iraq: 'The decision of Egypt and Syria to form a United Arab Republic changed the whole atmosphere.'[65] He had no doubt that Nasser was the catalyst of Arab nationalist thought, not merely on the question of unity but on such issues as Algeria. The years 1957–58 were of course critical ones in the Algerian Revolution as well as in the impending Iraqi Revolution. By all British accounts, the subject of Algeria was one of the principal topics of discussion among Iraqi intellectuals. Sam Falle, the Oriental Counsellor in the Baghdad Embassy, summed up the theme of conversation in the coffee houses of the city with the words 'The Baghdad Pact, Palestine and Algeria'.[66] In all of those issues the British detected the malevolent hand of Nasser. In Iraq there was no question of his immense popularity. 'Colonel Nasser is still the hero of the broad masses of the population', Wright reported in February 1958.[67] Nasser appeared to be riding a wave of popular sentiment that would not be stopped by such artificial counter currents as the Iraq–Jordan union. Wright related the underlying sentiments of Iraqi politicians, businessmen and tribal leaders, as if there were almost an inevitability as well as a resolve behind Nasser's plans: 'the Egyptian revolution is not intended to be for domestic consumption only but to be followed by a similar form of revolution in Iraq, Jordan,

Lebanon and ultimately Saudi Arabia'.[68] In any event, it appeared clear to the British in Baghdad that 'events outside Iraq' would play a large part in the domestic issues of the country.[69]

Wright attributed the creation of Nuri's last government in March 1958 to the external danger of Nasser and the United Arab Republic. 'The formation of this new Government [in Iraq] was a direct answer to President Nasser's challenge', he wrote.[70] In comparison with previous regimes, Nuri's combination of ministers represented a strong alliance that included politicians with progressive social and economic programmes. Two prominent figures were Fadil Jamali, the Foreign Minister, and Abdel Karim al-Uzri, the Minister of Finance. 'Dr Jamali's words tend to be intemperate', Wright observed, but nevertheless Jamali was 'a firm believer in the dangers of Communist penetration in the area through Soviet co-operation with Nasser.' Wright regarded him as distinctly above the average cut of Iraqi politicians: 'he brings to the Government two most valuable qualities, courage in standing up for his convictions, however unpopular, a rare quality among Arab politicians, and a sincere belief in social reform'. Wright was beginning to attach increasing importance to the issue of economic inequity in Iraqi society. One of the reasons could be seen in Baghdad itself. 'Ordinary people' migrating fromn the countryside were creating 'slums of mud huts' at a perturbing rate. Thus Wright welcomed the presence of the new Finance Minister as an indication that Nuri was at last beginning to take in earnest the question of social reform. Wright wrote of Abdel Karim al-Uzri:

> He is a somewhat doctrinaire economist and land owner with progressive views and many ideas . . . for carrying out social and economic reforms and for spreading the benefits of the oil revenues among all classes of the population.
>
> As Minister of Finance he is likely to press for reform of the tax structure and the introduction of land taxation, coupled with limitations on the size of estates, which will be popular with the ordinary people but may be strongly opposed by the tribal Shaikhs and large landed proprietors who will see their interests threatened.[71]

Wright therefore held out hope for social reform, but he did not want to be too optimistic: 'the Palace and Nuri will not wish to deliver too strong a frontal attack on one of the main groups to which the Government will look for support.'[72]

Wright's conscious effort to assess the influence of the United Arab

Republic on Iraqi politics led him to paradox. The British in their own self-interest did not wish to sharpen inter-Arab rivalries, despite the allegations of critics of British imperialism. Wright was fully aware of the charge that the British, by dividing the Arab world, sought to prolong the longevity of the British Empire. He regarded this hoary suspicion as nonsense. He thought that endemic tension was dangerous and might well jeopardize whatever influence the British still possessed. He believed Nasser to be a real danger to the British position in Iraq and by no means an imaginary threat. Nasser's propaganda struck a sympathetic chord among the intellectuals, the younger generation of officials, and above all the poorer people who believed that they were being excluded from the benefits of the oil wealth and the development projects. The paradox was that Nasser's challenge might at last galvanize Iraq's political elite into moving at a more rapid pace in economic reform. Wright's expression of the 'paradox' is tortuous, but it repays study. It catches the delicate balance between the external and internal affairs of Iraq as perceived by the British in March 1958:

We are confronted with the paradox that although we cannot wish for the continued sharpening of inter-Arab relations which President Nasser's present policy appears to involve, and although we may fear that in the long run the Iraqi régime will have the greatest difficulty in maintaining itself against the danger to it which President *Nasser*, working on a discontented population largely favourable to his aims, represents, yet in bringing together into one Government these disparate elements *he has perhaps produced the one combination which, given time, could carry through some of the internal reforms which are needed to give Iraq stability.*[73]

Again, Wright did not wish to be too optimistic. Nuri's past indifference to social reform hardly inspired confidence that there would be a dramatic change. But clearly the British believed that the game was still in play.

If Wright found it paradoxical that Iraq's salvation might come from the challenge of the United Arab Republic, he found it ironic, and depressing, that the two regimes of Nuri and the Shah bore similarity. Both were authoritarian. The British might do their best to press for reform in Iraq, but would they be any more successful than they had been in the pre-Musaddiq era in Iran? Perhaps it can be inferred from Wright's sentiments that he might have agreed, at least in his moments of despondency, with Batatu's premise that the tensions in the structure of the post-colonial state would determine the course of events more than world policies or actions of the political elite. In any event it makes one pause to reflect why the Iraqi Revolution took place in 1958 and the Iranian Revolution some two decades later. According to Wright, the mounting opposition in both countries had comparable middle-class strengths. Iraqis and Iranians alike held exaggerated notions about the extent of British influence: 'There are striking similarities between the situation in Iraq and Iran, such as the potentially explosive element of political frustration under an authoritarian régime, especially among the growing middle class, as well as the belief in Britain's dominant and, to some, sinister role.'[74]

Wright's reflections on the opposition to Nuri's regime led him to conclude that Iraq was not in a revolutionary situation. He was confident in his assessment, both in reports to London and in conversation in Baghdad. It would not be fair to blame him for failing to predict the Revolution. Men of equal and greater intellectual acumen did not foresee the civil war in Lebanon or the Revolution in Iran, or much earlier for that matter, the American and French Revolutions. Nevertheless, it is legitimate to inquire where Wright went astray in his judgement. Much of his analysis on the eve of the Revolution was shrewd, imaginative, and balanced, but in retrospect it is clear that he erred on the problem of the army and on the question of development.

Wright wrote his last full-blown report on the Iraqi political system in April 1958. It is worth examination because it reveals the strength and weakness of British political analysis on the eve of the Revolution. Like Stewart Perowne before him, Wright believed that the political balance of power in Iraq resembled Britain's at the time of the accession of George III. Such an extraordinary comparison makes one wonder about the influence of historical scholarship. Had Wright read Namier's famous work on eighteenth-century politics?[75] In any event he believed that political power resided in the 'Palace' (by which he meant Faisal II and Abdulillah). The key to the political balance lay in the skill with which the palace worked through the politicians who were not organized in political parties but rather revolved around a small political elite whose outstanding leader was Nuri. Here lay the significance of Wright's comparison of Iraq with eighteenth-century England:

The King appoints and dismisses Prime Ministers and need not pay much attention to the two Houses of Parliament, for the Senators are appointed by him and the Deputies, although elected by a wider suffrage than was the unreformed House of Commons in Britain, are selected as candidates by a process in which the influence of the régime plays such a large part that in the countryside few elections are contested and in the towns the opponents of the régime stand very little chance of election.[76]

The only underlying principle from one regime to the next, Wright thought, was probably 'the safety of the régime itself'.

In recent years a succession of governments had been drawn from the professional politicians 'who belong largely to the landed upper class' but also included 'a certain number of self-made men', including Kurds. Whatever the change of government, all Iraqi politicians embraced what Wright called 'a fundamental concept': only after the successful exploitation of the oil wealth could a 'modern' political structure replace the existing system. Here Wright offered a basic definition that may be taken as the sophisticated British view on the rudiments of Iraqi society in 1958: 'a feudal order based largely on tribes, the army and a strong monarchy'.[77] Wright thus explicitly identified the army as part of the triangular structure of power.

The eighteenth-century analogy helped explain the rapid turnover of Iraqi governments. Like Perowne, Wright saw that the Iraqi political groups did not represent political parties in the British sense but rather shifting alliances more similar to the Italian *combinazione* (in Perowne's words, 'a transient association of a few interested individuals for a transient material end').[78] The palace sought to preserve its own influence, like George III, through prerogative and favour. The principle at stake was nothing more and nothing less than self-interest and survival:

The Crown Prince has not believed in keeping any one man longer in office than a particular situation requires. The political objective of the Palace is in fact to preserve the position and influence of the Hashemite dynasty and to ensure that Governments depend on its favour rather than on parliament or on political parties; changes are therefore made with regularity so as to ensure that no group has a monopoly of power and can build up a position in which it can challenge the prerogatives of the Palace itself.[79]

The politicians who co-operated with the palace shared political power from time to time; those who did not formed the opposition.

The principal flaw in Wright's judgement lay in the assessment of the forces opposing the regime. He characterized the 'Opposition' as consisting of a few prominent but ineffective public figures including Muhammad Mahdi Kubba, the leader of the right-wing nationalist movement, and Kamil al-Chaderchi, a Communist lawyer and journalist, whom Nuri had jailed on the pretext of anti-Suez sentiments.[80] For the most part the politicians who protested against Nuri's regime belonged 'to the urban middle-class and are largely lawyers, businessmen, professors and teachers'. 'These men and their associates do not make up a "ragged band"', he wrote, 'for their material prosperity is marked.' Nor did he attach much importance to the political clichés they voiced on Arab nationalism, which, in his opinion, were identical with the propaganda of Nasser's 'Radio Cairo'. He held in short that the 'Opposition' in Iraq merely effervesced the froth of Arab nationalism: 'passion for unity, strong opposition to Israel, revolutionary ardour against conservative régimes and xenophobia'. Nuri's opponents believed in liberalism and reform at home, and neutralism abroad. Many of them thought that Iraq should have a British form of democracy. They did not necessarily oppose the monarchy. Most wished to introduce reform gradually. They all shared the aim of a more equitable distribution of the oil profits, but so also did Nuri. With such critics, who needed a revolution? Only slightly did Wright veil his contempt for what he regarded as the main opponents to Nuri. It is therefore not surprising that he came to an emphatic conclusion that revolution was improbable. His language is unequivocal: 'For it quite certain that, today, a revolutionary situation does not exist.'[81]

Not everyone shared Wright's optimism. On the Foreign Office copy of his despatch, one official, probably R. H. Hadow, inscribed next to Wright's non-revolutionary sentence a large exclamation mark – ![82] Hadow was a member of the Levant Department. He held strong views on the need for internal reform and was sceptical whether Wright had identified the true nature of Nuri's opposition. What of institutional loyalty? Here Wright made another comment that caused dissenting astonishment. He remarked that 'the Army, although it has in the past erupted into politics, is at present showing no signs of doing so . . . it is likely to go on supporting the régime.' Thereupon Hadow drew another large exclamation mark – ! What were Wright's reasons for arriving at conclusions that aroused such provocative comment in the Foreign Office? What led him to take such a favourable outlook on the army, which in turn coloured his assessment that Iraq was not in a revolutionary situation?

To some extent Wright relied on the judgement of his military attaché, Brigadier N. F. B. Shaw. He was not a man of outstanding ability. He competently managed the military side of his mission, but he was at sea in larger political issues such as the loyalty of the officer corps.[83] His predecessor, Brigadier A. Boyce, had kept a sharp eye on possible subversive units or officers in the army.[84] By contrast, Shaw concentrated his attention on parades and ball-bearings. It is an interesting question whether Wright, given better advice, might have modified the official assessment of the embassy. It is true that on the subject of the army he had strong opinions of his own that in turn fortified his ideas about Nuri's successor. With a scornful view of the politicians, Wright saw the army as the possible salvation of Iraq. As for the collective military establishment, Wright wrote that both the army and air force 'have shown an example of loyalty and steadiness which has not been rivalled by the forces of any other Arab state.'[85]

No one could predict how long Nuri might last, but it was certain that it would be difficult to find a civilian counterpart. The problem with the army, Wright conceded, was that it might produce 'an Iraqi Nasser'. But a strong leader might be the best that the British could anticipate. If, like Nuri, he remained loyal to the monarchy, the situation would not be unsatisfactory. Loyalty to the Hashemites was of course a large assumption, but Wright seems to have made it without too much mental agitation:

When the time comes for Nuri to leave the political scene, there may be no alternative to a more authoritarian régime based on the Army with a soldier as the strong man behind a civilian figurehead. This is not an attractive prospect in view of the danger of instability through the emergence of an Iraqi Nasser or through competition among Army officers for power.

It would, of course, provide an easy target for the attacks of the Opposition and of Nasser, and it would be distasteful to those who remember the 1936–41 period which was dominated by the Army. But it may be the best we can hope for. Provided it was based on the Hashemite monarchy it would probably retain the Western connection and it might hold the fort for a time.[86]

Such was Wright's conclusion about the future of the Army and Nuri's successor. If it seems in retrospect too optimistic in its premise that the army would remain loyal to the monarchy, it was no more so than his other major conclusion about development. Wright appears to have concurred entirely in Nuri's judgement that things would remain quiet in Iraq because of the benefits of development. Poverty itself would not be a cause of revolution. 'I do not believe', Wright concluded, 'that poverty or lack of economic opportunities by themselves will, so long as the oil flows, produce an explosive situation.'[87]

It is easy to ridicule someone whose assessments proved to be wrong. It is less easy to recapture the spirit of the contemporary debate and to bear in mind that it seemed plausible to uphold the point of view of Wright and Nuri. Wright's outlook at the time commanded intellectual respect in part because of the conspicuous progress in building cotton factories, drainage pumping stations, bridges and river transport. Speaking to Wright's staff in March 1957, the Minister of Development took pride in describing such projects as the new electricity power house in Baghdad. 'This is nothing', he said, 'wait till you see 1960.' Wright's attitude was equally robust. 'The long-awaited results of planning and spending are now becoming visible', he wrote, 'and Iraqis are taking interest and pride in their country's development.'[88]

Unfortunately for Wright, the field reports by Sam Falle demonstrated that the evidence of material progress could be interpreted in another way. Falle assessed the unevenness of development in different parts of the country and the way economic progress affected, or did not affect, different parts of Iraqi society. His approach has stood the test of time better than has Wright's. Falle was one of the ablest of the younger British officials. He was linguistically gifted, energetic and gregarious. He had an enquiring intellect. In late 1957 he had reported on a trip he made some 250 miles by Land Rover to the south of Baghdad to Kut and Amara. In the area around Kut he observed 'unemployment, widespread poverty and actual hunger'. There were no significant development projects under way, though test borings were being carried out for a new bridge. In Kut itself there were a few new buildings that included a school and a hospital. But he described the roads in the town as 'unspeakable'. In Amara about half the population of 54,000 lived in 'conditions of hideous squalor and poverty'. The only obvious development project was a new bridge. Falle took care not to present only one side of the picture; he spoke to some 'peasant smallholders' who were doing 'tolerably well', but the general standard of living he could describe only as being 'shamefully low'.[89]

Wright would have been well advised to read Falle's report quite carefully. Instead he penned a perfunctory despatch to the Foreign

Office commenting merely that he would do what he could to 'encourage' the Iraqi government to 'tackle' the issues raised by Falle.[90] These were problems, however, that usually proved to be intractable at the government level in Baghdad. Falle raised questions that were basic to Iraqi society, not least the influence of the shaikhs and the issue of land tenure. Wright accepted Nuri's view that 'the tribal system', though not yet dead, was 'dying'.[91] The transition to the new social and economic order in Iraq would be facilitated by reclamation of waste lands that would open up opportunities for small landowners. Thus the old system of land tenure would be left to reform itself. 'New lands' became the shibboleth of the Nuri regime. They would be the supreme test of the development programme. In Amara, which was supposed to be the home of the pilot scheme, there were plans for draining and filling a large swamp where 'the lower middle class' could build about 4,000 houses. Falle was exceedingly sceptical whether this plan was feasible. For the scheme to be workable, the local shaikh would have to provide free houses which, according to Falle, he had no intention of doing.[92]

'The main cause of the trouble', Falle reported, 'is the large feudal landowners.' In the Amara scheme, the reclaimed land owned by the government would be distributed in equal measure to 'existing tribal leaders' and to 'fellaheen' or peasants.[93] The problem was that the local shaikhs received the better part of the 'new land' and their relatives most of the rest of it. Even among the three hundred 'peasant smallholders' to whom reclaimed land had been allocated, the shaikhs retained control over both the water pumps and the water itself. Falle wrote: 'This system which puts the new smallholders at the mercy of the shaikhs, who have the pumping machinery, is clearly most unsatisfactory.' The conclusion he drew about the 'predatory landlords' carried him in the opposite direction from Wright's belief that Iraq was not in a revolutionary situation. 'The peasants are oppressed and hardly able to scrape a living', he wrote. Falle's report dealt only with a district, but it is clear that he believed comparable conditions to exist throughout the country. These were circumstances that could well lead to 'Communism and anarchic nationalism', if not revolution.[94] This was a clear warning. It was not heeded.

Straight to the end, Nuri and Wright were preoccupied with such external questions as whether Kuwait would join the Iraq–Jordan union rather than more mundane issues of land distribution and water pumps. Nuri was in London two weeks before the July

Revolution. In conversation with Selwyn Lloyd, the Foreign Secretary, he ranged over topics such as the prospect that Lebanon might join the Iraq–Jordan union and the possibility of Iraqi intervention in Syria to break the link with Nasser.[95] For his part, Wright did not question fundamental assumptions. He continued to believe, like Nuri, in a firm paternalistic internal policy as the best way to guide Iraq through a dangerous period. He thought that the union with Jordan fulfilled the Iraqi 'emotional demand for unity'.[96] He judged that the monarchy was 'the cementing factor' in Iraq's national life without recognizing the extent to which Iraqis themselves regarded it as an alien institution. The new union with Jordan fortified the old belief that behind the Hashemite dynasty stood the British. But Wright himself remained confident that Iraq was not in a revolutionary situation.

*　*　*　*　*

On 14 July 1958 at 7:10 a.m. Wright sent one of his last telegrams from the British Embassy in Baghdad. He stated simply that since 6:00 a.m. a revolutionary government had seized power. He reported fighting throughout the city. He did not know of the fate of the King, the Crown Prince or Nuri.[97] The Station Commander at the Royal Air Force Base in Habbaniyah, in a superb example of British understatement, reported later in the day that the situation was 'confused and interesting ... we are minding our own business'.[98] The military community fared better than the British civilian population in Baghdad, though as revolutions go it could have been worse. Only one member of Wright's staff of about twenty-four was killed, not deliberately but by a stray bullet. The embassy was looted and burned. Wright himself rose to the occasion. He acted honourably and courageously. By late afternoon he had evacuated his staff to the New Baghdad Hotel. The first news to reach London was through the American Ambassador in Baghdad who reported that Sir Michael and Lady Wright were both 'remarkably calm and cheerful'.[99]

Two days later, having set up emergency headquarters in the New Baghdad Hotel, Wright reported that Nuri had been killed on the afternoon of 15 July. 'I understand he was discovered in woman's dress. He either shot himself or was killed by the mob.' It took a few more days to confirm the details, but on the 20th he telegraphed with certainty that the King and Crown Prince had been shot and that the 'bodies of the Crown Prince and Nuri were dragged naked round the town'.[100] As if to confirm his own views on foreign influences on Iraqi policies, he noted that 'the town is full of photographs and emblems of Nasser especially on military vehicles.'[101] From Wright's point of view, it would have missed the spirit of the Revolution not to have associated it with Nasser and the sense of Arab nationalism with which Iraqis identified themselves.

Wright's initial assessments portrayed the events of 14 July more as a *coup d'état* than as a revolution. 'Certain Army Units', he reported, conducted the operation under the command of a 'very small' directorate or 'controlling group'.[102] It was clear from the outset that the leader was Brigadier Abdel Karim Qasim, who became the new Prime Minister. In an appreciation of the new leadership written a month after the takeover by the new regime, Wright commented in balanced vein:

The Prime Minister, Brigadier Abdul Karim Qassim is soft-spoken and friendly to meet. He is said to be a devout Muslim and dedicated to the service of his country. He is unmarried and lives very simply. Apart from a few remarks in some of his speeches his conduct so far has been essentially moderate and restrained . . . He has a good reputation as a competent army officer and as far as it is possible to judge enjoys confidence in the army.[103]

Within a few weeks, Wright used the phrases '*coup d'état*' and 'revolution' interchangeably. The analogy that sprang to his mind was the Egyptian Revolution of 1952. Qasim and his fellow officers, like the Free Officers rebelling against Farouk, were sincere, upright idealists who believed that they were acting in the best interests of their country. The new regime, Wright reported, 'is essentially an Administration of liberal reformers.'[104]

The Foreign Office came to a similar conclusion about the origins of the Revolution and the aims of the Iraqi military officers:

A revolutionary situation very similar to that existing in Egypt prior to the Neguib–Nasser *coup* of 1952 has been building up in Iraq for years. Wealth and power have remained concentrated in the hands of a few rich landowners and tribal sheikhs centred round the Court, while a growing middle class of politically conscious Arab 'intelligentsia', supporting the ideals of Arab Nationalism . . . have been denied an effective voice in the affairs of their country . . . .

As in Egypt, the *coup d'état* in Iraq seems to have been actually organised by a small number of army officers acting with great efficiency and secrecy.[105]

Revolutions in the Middle East often represent a shift of power from one generation to the next. In this sense Wright actually anticipated the new order, though he did not foresee the revolutionary events. 'The group of politicians of the generation of Nuri and with their roots in the 1920s', he had written in April 1958, were 'fading away'.[106]

Some of them, including Nuri, came to a much more brutal end than Wright or any of the other British observers of Iraq ever believed to be possible. One of the most striking descriptions of the Revolution came from the pen of a British official in Jordan, C. H. Johnston. He related a detail about Nuri's death that conveyed the atmosphere of mob violence. After Nuri's body was dragged through the streets 'a car was driven backwards and forwards over it until it was flattened into the ground'.[107] So ended Britain's principal collaborator in Iraq. 'I had the impression', Johnston wrote, 'that if the Russian revolution had been put into execution by the Mau Mau the effect would not have been very much different.'[108]

### Notes

1. Hanna Batatu, *The Old Social Classes and the Revolutionary Movements of Iraq* (Princeton, 1978), p. 347.

2. Ibid., pp. 1133–34.

3. Ibid., pp. 11–12.

4. By contrast he is explicit about Britain's waning economic influence. See *Old Social Classes*, pp. 266–70. See also especially Joseph Sassoon, *Economic Policy in Iraq 1932–1950* (London, 1987).

5. Minute by Beeley, 30 March 1951, F[oreign] O[ffice] 624/199 (Embassy records). All references to British archival records are to documents at the Public Record Office, London.

6. Quoted in Wm. Roger Louis, *The British Empire in the Middle East 1945–1951: Arab Nationalism, The United States and Postwar Imperialism* (Oxford, 1984), p. 315.

7. Wright to Lloyd, 'Confidential', 11 January 1956, FO 371/121640.

8. Wright to Lloyd, 'Confidential', 4 July 1957, FO 371/128041.

9. Troutbeck to Eden, 'Confidential', 31 October 1952, FO 371/98747.

10. For my own ideas on this useful concept in the African context, see Prosser Gifford and W. R. Louis (eds), *Decolonization and African Independence: The Transfers of Power, 1960–1980* (New Haven, 1988), introductory chapter.

11. The following works on land tenure in Iraq are particularly useful in

understanding British assessments which, in Troutbeck's case, invariably included the legacy of the Ottoman land law of 1858: T. Khalidi, ed., *Land Tenure and Social Transformation of the Middle East* (1984); Albertine Jwaideh, 'Midhat Pasha and the Land System of Lower Iraq', in Albert Hourani, ed., *St Antony's Papers 16: Middle Eastern Affairs*, 3 (London, 1963); and Doreen Warriner, *Land Reform and Development in the Middle East: A Study of Egypt, Syria and Iraq* (London, 1957); see also especially Peter Sluglett, *Britain in Iraq 1914–1932* (London, 1976), chap. 6.

12. See Mohammad A. Tarbush, *The Role of the Military in Politics: A Case Study of Iraq to 1941* (London, 1982).

13. Troutbeck to Eden, 'Confidential', 31 October 1952, FO 371/98747.

14. Troutbeck to Eden, 'Confidential', 31 October 1952, FO 371/98747.

15. 'Caractacus', *Revolution in Iraq* (London, 1959), p. 95.

16. Troutbeck to Eden, 'Confidential Guard', 9 December 1954, FO 371/110991.

17. Troutbeck to Sir James Bowker, 'Secret', 3 April 1953, FO 371/104678.

18. Troutbeck to Eden, 'Confidential', 9 December 1954, FO 371/110991.

19. Troutbeck to Bowker, 'Confidential', 29 May 1953, FO 371/104678.

20. Troutbeck to Bowker, 'Secret', 3 April 1953, FO 371/104678.

21. Batatu, *Old Social Classes*, p. 36.

22. Troutbeck to Eden, 'Confidential', 9 December 1954, FO 371/110991.

23. Troutbeck to Eden, 'Confidential', 28 November 1952, FO 371/98736.

24. Troutbeck to Eden, 'Confidential', 9 December 1954, FO 371/110991.

25. Troutbeck to Bowker, 'Secret', 3 April 1953, FO 371/104678.

26. Troutbeck to Bowker, 'Confidential', 29 May 1953, FO 371/104678.

27. See David Pool, 'From Élite to Class: The Transformation of Iraqi Political Leadership', in A. Kelidar, ed., *The Integration of Modern Iraq* (London, 1978).

28. On the theme of the fragility of the Iraqi ruling group, Batatu's interpretation should be compared with that of Elie Kedourie, 'The Kingdom of Iraq: A Retrospect', in his *The Chatham House Version* (London, 1970).

29. Troutbeck to Bowker, 'Confidential', 29 May 1953, FO 371/104678.

30. Troutbeck to Eden, 'Confidential', 9 December 1954, FO 371/110991.

31. Troutbeck to Eden, 'Confidential', 6 October 1954, FO 371/110991.

32. Troutbeck to Eden, 'Confidential', 11 January 1954, FO 371/110986.

33. Minute by K. J. Simpson, 24 February 1954, FO 371/111007.

34. Troutbeck to Roger Allen, 'Confidential', 23 December 1953, FO 371/110997.

35. Minute by P. L. V. Mallet, 6 January 1954, FO 371/110997.

36. Troutbeck to Eden, 'Confidential', 3 September 1954, FO 371/110991.

37. Troutbeck to Eden, 'Confidential', 11 January 1954, FO 371/110986.

38. Troutbeck to Eden, 'Confidential', 9 December 1954, FO 371/110991.

39. Batatu, *Old Social Classes*, p. 1115.

40. Troutbeck to Eden, 'Confidential', 9 December 1954, FO 371/110991.

41. For Batatu on Palestine, see *Old Social Classes*, p. 603.

42. The comment about Troutbeck was made by Lord Hankey in *The Times*, 9 October 1971.

43. Wright to Macmillan, 'Confidential', 17 May 1955, FO 371/115759.

44. Quoted in Louis, *British Empire in the Middle East*, p. 713.

45. Wright to Lloyd, 'Confidential', 8 February 1957, FO 371/128038.

46. Wright to Sir Evelyn Shuckburgh, 'Secret', 10 May 1955, FO 371/115511.

47. Ibid.

48. See Batatu, *Old Social Classes*, e.g. p. 766.

49. Wright to Lloyd, 'Confidential', 7 December 1956, FO 371/121662.

50. Wright to Lloyd, 'Confidential', 8 February 1957, FO 371/128038.

51. Wright to Lloyd, 'Confidential Guard', 11 July 1957, FO 371/128057.

52. Wright to Lloyd, 'Confidential', 8 February 1957, FO 371/128038.

53. Michael Ionides, *Divide and Lose: The Arab Revolt of 1955–1958* (London, 1960), pp. 188–89.

54. For example, *Old Social Classes*, p. 1113.

55. Wright to Lloyd, 'Confidential', 11 July 1957, FO 371/128057.

56. Edith and E. F. Penrose, *Iraq: International Relations and National Development* (London, 1978), p. 167.

57. Wright to Lloyd, 'Confidential', 8 February 1957, FO 371/128038.

58. Ibid.

59. Ionides, *Divide and Lose*, p. 125.

60. Wright to Lloyd, 'Confidential', 4 July 1957, FO 371/128041.

61. Wright to Macmillan, 'Confidential', 17 May 1955, FO 371/115759.

62. Wright to Lloyd, 'Confidential', 14 February 1958, FO 371/134023. Wright and others believed that the proposal originated in Jordan: 'this Union resulted from an initiative of King Hussain.' Wright to Lloyd, 'Confidential', 25 February 1958, FO 371/134025.

63. Wright to Lloyd, 'Confidential', 25 February 1958, FO 371/134025.

64. Wright to Lloyd, 'Confidential', 14 February 1958, FO 371/134023.

65. Wright to Lloyd, 'Confidential, 25 February 1958, FO 371/134025.

66. Falle to R. H. Hadow, 'Confidential', 1 February 1958, FO 371/134197. R. H. Hadow in the Foreign Office noted that Falle had hit upon 'the kernel of the matter'.

67. Wright to Lloyd, 'Confidential', 25 February 1958, FO 371/134025.

68. Wright to Lloyd, 'Confidential', 28 December 1957, FO 371/134197.

69. Wright to Lloyd, 'Confidential', 11 March 1958, FO 371/134198.

70. Ibid.

71. Ibid.

72. Ibid.

73. Ibid. Emphasis added.

74. Wright to Lloyd, 'Confidential', 22 April 1958, FO 371/134198.

75. L. B. Namier, *The Structure of Politics at the Accession of George III* (London, 1929).

76. Wright to Lloyd, 'Confidential', 22 April 1958, FO 371/134198.

77. Ibid.

78. Louis, *British Empire in the Middle East*, p. 320.

79. Wright to Lloyd, 'Confidential', 22 April 1958, FO 371/134198.

80. For Kubba and Chaderchi, see Batatu, *Old Social Classes*, esp. pp. 300, 303, 306–07, 812–13.

81. Wright to Lloyd, 'Confidential', 22 April 1958, FO 371/134198.

82. Wright to Lloyd, 'Confidential', 22 April 1958, FO 371/134198.

83. Shaw wrote in a military assessment dated 26 February 1957: 'The British attack upon Egypt had a certain effect upon junior Army officers who were distressed at the British policy, but due to careful handling ... there were no unpleasant incidents.' FO 371/128067.

84. As far as the possibility of a *coup d'état* is concerned', Boyce wrote in 1954, 'I

have still not noted any personality within the Army whose influence, bearing or actions lead me to believe that he might embark upon such an adventure.' Annual Report, 'Secret Guard', 12 February 1954, FO 371/111023.

85. Wright to Lloyd, 'Secret Guard', 16 March 1957, FO 371/128067.

86. Wright to Lloyd, 'Confidential', 22 April 1958, FO 371/134198.

87. Ibid.

88. Wright to Lloyd, 'Confidential', 12 April 1957, FO 371/128061.

89. 'Report on a Trip by Mr S. Falle, Oriental Counsellor, to Kut and Amara, December 17–20, 1957', FO 371/134197.

90. Wright to Lloyd, 'Confidential', 31 December 1958, FO 371/134197.

91. Wright to Lloyd, 'Confidential', 22 April 1958, FO 371/134198.

92. Report by Falle, 17–20 December 1957, FO 371/134197.

93. Ibid.

94. Ibid.

95. Lloyd to Wright, 'Secret', 4 July 1958, FO 371/134220.

96. Wright to Lloyd, 'Confidential', 22 April 1958, FO 371/134198.

97. Wright to Foreign Office, 14 July 1958, FO 371/134198.

98. Political Office with Middle East Forces to Foreign Office, 'Emergency Top Secret', 14 July 1958, FO 371/134198.

99. Viscount Hood (Washington) to Foreign Office, 'Emergency Secret', 14 July 1958, FO 371/134198.

100. Wright to Lloyd, 'Immediate Secret', 17 July 1958, FO 371/134199.

101. Wright to Lloyd, 'Immediate Secret', 20 July 1958, FO 371/134200.

102. Wright to Lloyd, 'Emergency Secret', 20 July 1958, FO 371/134200.

103. Wright to Lloyd, 'Confidential', 19 August 1958, FO 371/134202.

104. Wright to Lloyd, 'Immediate Secret', 23 July 1958, FO 371/134200.

105. FO memorandum, 'The Immediate Outlook in Iraq', 24 July 1958, FO 371/123201.

106. Wright to Lloyd, 'Confidential', 24 April 1958, FO 371/134195.

107. C. H. Johnston to E. M. Rose, 'Secret', 28 July 1958, FO 371/134201. Batatu adds that the remains of Nuri's body were 'after burial, disinterred by an angry crowd and, like that of the intensely hated crown prince, dragged through the streets, strung up, torn to pieces, and finally burnt'. *Old Social Classes*, p. 801.

108. C. H. Johnston to E. M. Rose, 'Secret', 28 July 1958, FO 371/134201.

# 3

# Reflections on US Foreign Policy towards Iraq in the 1950s

## NICHOLAS G. THACHER

In his comprehensive and thoughtful work, Batatu has identified appropriately those foreign influences which significantly affected the flow of events in Iraq. Given the main focus of the volume, it is not surprising that much more attention is given to description of the evolution of Soviet rather than of American or British policies in the region. Thus, Batatu does not explore in much detail how American policies originated, and why Iraq appeared a likely collaborator. A brief discussion of these elements may provide some perspective on the other, principal themes of Batatu's book.

The post-Second World War era found the United States challenged to exert world leadership amongst a vast array of puzzling and unfamiliar circumstances. Dealing with the threat of expanding Soviet ambitions proved in some ways a task more recognizable in terms of classical power politics than the problems of relations with the new states rising from the remains of the European empires. In many cases, traditional ideological impulses pressed the United States towards vigorous support of full independence for the former colonies resulting, in the case of India, for example, in policies satisfactory to both countries during the early post-war years.

In the Middle East, the United States found, after the war, states which seemed much further along the road towards independence than in most of the regions of Asia and Africa. Iraq, in particular, had had in place the paraphernalia of self-government plus full international recognition since 1932. Sentiments of the kind which led the United States to urge on Britain the justice of India's claims to freedom played little part in determining US attitudes towards Iraq.

On the contrary, the earliest US initiatives in relations with Iraq were determined by the war-time exigencies of Britain's hard-pressed position in the Middle East but with little respect for Iraq's yearnings for full independence. Even after the war, US policy decisions continued to be significantly affected by considerations of British interests and the British role in the Middle East. The three principal aspects comprising the British factor included firstly US belief that Britain's position was inevitably in decline and secondly, that the United States was going to have to be involved in measures to substitute US power for the 'vacuum' allegedly to be caused by British withdrawal. Recognizing this, the United States nevertheless wished Britain to continue making whatever contribution it could to the maintenance of regional security. Finally, the United States was constrained by the realization that lack of careful attention to British sensitivities could set up awkward strains at other points in our relations with an old and close ally. (Frederick Axelgard's chapter in this book provides a thoughtful assessment of the impact on US relations with Iraq of our persistent inclination to give heavy weight to British interests.[1])

Despite differences of viewpoint, occasional friction and suspicion between the two allies and some distinct disadvantages to the United States of our willingness to play for too long in Iraq a role secondary to that of the British, there was yet a very considerable degree of agreement and co-operation on objectives to be achieved and policies to be followed with regard to Iraq. There were elsewhere in the Middle East a few examples of sharp US–British disagreement. In the case of Iraq, it might have been advantageous for all parties had the United States brought more insistently to Iraq's affairs a different and fresher viewpoint.

In Iraq, as in many other parts of the world, the people and institutions of the United States enjoyed in the immediate post-war years a considerable measure of goodwill among educated and politically conscious groups. Among a narrow element of the population, some of this was perhaps engendered by appreciation for a handful of American institutions such as a Jesuit-run boys' high school in Baghdad and a small American hospital there. Of greater significance was the inevitable respect, if not liking, accruing to a new great power, especially when linked to the hope that its influence would be used to lead the world to better things.

US policies in Palestine soon eroded whatever early favourable attitudes may have existed. American civilians living in Iraq, depending on their outlook, often felt free to disavow their government's actions. Government representatives had not, of course, the luxury of such objectivity. Useful contacts with Iraqis tended to be thwarted by persistent recriminations concerning US policies toward the Palestine issue. Defences or attempts at justification of US policies were often offered by US officials with limited personal conviction as to their validity, and, in any case, brought only renewed expressions of deep Arab resentment. Reporting these Iraqi sentiments to Washington had little effect since headquarters had heard it all before. Representatives in the field had warned frequently of the adverse implications of creating a Jewish state in the Arab homeland. Such reiterated warnings contributed also to the image of a 'State Department Arabists' clique. These officials were often (and still are) identified by Israel's more vociferous friends as sinister behind-the-scenes conspirators bent on undermining US ties with the Jewish state. The nature of their intentions and their inflence have been considerably misrepresented.

Firm US opposition to the British–French–Israeli attack on Suez in the autumn of 1956 and the subsequent US insistence on the Israeli withdrawal from Sinai brought a short-lived but positive and congratulatory Iraqi response. The Arab–Israeli issue, however, soon evolved again to provide a persistent shadow over US–Iraqi contacts. Yet despite these factors, it should in all candour be noted, too, that American officials, determined to enlarge their circle of Iraqi acquaintances, freqently encountered warm hospitality and a willingness over time to give priority to other topics.

Not only personal responses but also broader public and press reaction toward the United States tended to be hostile because of American support for Israel. The monarchical government under Nuri Said adhered to the sharply critical posture of other Arab governments in United States and Arab League forums. In private contacts with American officials, Nuri exhibited a more flexible line. Ambassador Waldemar J. Gallman writes that Nuri told John Foster Dulles in 1953 that he accepted the UN resolution enacting the partition of Palestine as a basis for negotiations either directly between Israel and the Arab states or through a third party. In other discussions, Nuri expressed deep misgivings as to the ultimate aims of Zionism, but felt that Israel would endure if the rights of the Palestinians were recognized and compensation paid for their property losses. Ever sensitive to the threat of isolation from the other Arab states, Nuri never expressed such views in public. More typical was his reaction to the Suez incident of 1956 when, in a desperate effort to offset the adverse implications of Iraq's maintenance of its ties with Britain, he declared publicly for a policy forcing all recent European Jewish immigrants to Israel to return to their countries of origin. Neither on the record nor off did Nuri seek for himself or for his country a proponent's role in Arab–Israeli negotiations, nor did the United States exhort him to do so.

Some other aspects of US–Iraqi official relations should be briefly noted. Under the terms of a technical aid agreement of 1953, the United States was, by the time of the 1958 Revolution, providing Iraq with about 100 technicians assisting with a variety of economic development projects. In general, this programme seemed to operate reasonably smoothly and without many of the mutually irritating aspects affecting similar endeavours in other countries. Politically it was non-controversial with little impact, either positive or negative, on relations between the two countries. Correspondingly, the activities of the US technicians did little to give the Iraqi government's own broad development programme a higher and more favourable domestic profile. Most observers fault the monarchy's economic planning for its failure to devote a more significant portion of the country's petroleum income to urgent popular needs in housing, health facilities and education.

While, as indicated, US technical assistance was probably effective in terms of achieving the limited goals envisioned, it had almost certainly another effect and that was on US policy-makers themselves. We should recall the great significance attached in the 1950s to economic development as a means of strengthening US ties with other states, encouraging the growth of democracy and opposing the expansion of Communism. The Marshall Plan, devised to restore Europe's economic vitality, and President Truman's Point Four, aimed at the developing world, were important milestones in this type of thinking. Thus the US technical assistance programme for Iraq tended to provide reassurance for the United States that, whatever the visible deficiencies of the Hashemite government, whose collaboration we were seeking, we were undoubtedly playing a useful and productive part in directly assisting Iraq's economic development.

As early as 1949, Iraqi officials commenced efforts to persuade the United States of Iraq's need for economic and military aid. In the initial stages, US consideration of these requests was weighed in the light of Iraqi attitudes toward the Palestine issue. As discussions progressed over the next several years, increasingly the United States attached importance to the degree of Iraqi interest in development of a Middle East security system. Early hints from the US side eventually stimulated a lively interest on the part of Nuri Said and a variety of suggestions on his part for dealing with Middle East defence.

At first those who saw Iraq's participation as threatening to its internal stability and tending to isolate it in the Arab world dominated the discussion on the US side. But gradually the idea that Iraq should be a reliable partner in a Middle East defence system became an argument used both inside the US bureaucracy and in contacts with the Iraqis regarding an American arms programme for Iraq. This theme continued to be important in the tortuous evolution of the project which included recurrent reservations and reluctance. At last, in April 1954, an agreement with Iraq was signed providing the basis for a $10 million dollar grant aid programme. It was to have a contentious existence, stimulating criticism in other parts of the Arab world and within Iraq itself, and continuing to suffer periodic British resistance.

Gallman and Batatu have recorded similar verdicts on US military assistance for Iraq. Batatu notes that in the 1954 political campaign the Communists attacked the US–Iraqi military relationship as a 'tentacle of imperialism'.[2] Gallman reports Nuri Said's persistent impatience and barely concealed dissatisfaction with the rate of US deliveries up until the very end of the Hashemite regime, though Nuri found satisfaction in the character of some of the major equipment received. Batatu states that the size and nature of the US arms which Iraq was receiving compared most unfavourably in the eyes of Iraqi military officers with the generous amounts and lethal potential of the Czech and Soviet equipment being acquired by their counterparts in Egypt.[3]

If the impact of these two major features of US policy in pre-revolutionary Iraq must be assessed as ranging between neutral and negative, then a third aspect, the results for Iraq of its participation in the Baghdad Pact, must be seen as unquestionably disadvantageous. Many of the risks and potential drawbacks of Iraqi participation were identified and discussed by US policy-makers from the very outset of the pact's incubation. Yet, except for some occasional vacillations, US policy and actions in the years 1951–55 revealed a continuing interest in the inclusion of Iraq in a Middle East defence system, whatever form it took.

Working-level officers in the State Department expressed, at various stages, reservations regarding Iraq's participation in a defence framework grounded principally in the three 'northern tier', non-Arab countries and involving close collaboration with Britain and the United States. Iraq would be seen as moving directly contrary to the nationalist and pan-Arab ideals of its neighbours and against the strong views of politically-conscious elements within Iraq itself. The pact concept aroused concern, too, in the offices handling Greek, Indian and Israeli affairs.

Secretary of State John Foster Dulles himself entertained such doubts and continued occasionally to mention them. On return from his much-heralded Middle Eastern trip of April 1953, he noted that 'the political situation is such that Arab states will not at this time openly join defense arrangements with a combination of Western powers.' Dulles found, too, that the British and French positions in the area 'had probably deteriorated beyond the point of repair and that the Israeli factor plus the Arab tendency to link the United States with the colonial policies of the European states were millstones around our necks.'[4] Somewhat paradoxically, however, Dulles seemed to hope at the same time that Iraq might be a special case and therefore a candidate for participation in a pact organization. His misgivings, however, persisted.

Thus, Gallman reports that Dulles told him before his departure for Baghdad that he thought Iraq would eventually join with Pakistan, Turkey and Iran in regional defence arrangements. While the Secretary hoped this might have a beneficial effect on the other Arab states, he admitted, too, the alternative possibility that such action on the part of Iraq's government risked causing it problems with its own people and with the other Arab countries. Such doubts contributed to the United States' decision to abstain ultimately from full and formal adherence to the Baghdad Pact Treaty, although we had played an important role in its creation and continued actively to participate in all its subordinate functions.

Dulles's interest in Iraq's participation was stimulated by Nuri's enthusiasm. Nuri was convinced that weak developing countries like his own needed powerful and industrialized friends. He was concerned with the threat of aggression from the Soviet Union and the Communist apparatus inside Iraq. The proposed defence pact, promising inclusion of the United States, held the prospect of a productive relationship for Iraq with the great new superpower of the Western world and eventually a replacement for the increasingly burdensome tie with the British.

A fighter in the struggle against the Turks in the First World War, Nuri considered himself as loyal to nationalist ideals as any other Arab. Yet he was deeply concerned with the risks of antagonizing Nasser, the powerful and effective articulator of pan-Arab, anti-imperialist sentiment. Nuri went to Cairo to consult with the Egyptians and afterwards claims Nasser had understood Iraq's need to proceed on its own to conclude a security agreement with the northern tier countries. When the Turkish Prime Minister Adnan Menderes came to Baghdad in January 1955, Nuri was still wary and suggested Menderes talk first with Nasser. But the latter, under heavy political pressure at home, rejected a visit from the prime minister of one of Egypt's previous imperial masters.

After issuance on 12 January 1955 of the joint Turco–Iraqi communiqué announcing the intention to collaborate for defence, Menderes visited other Arab countries to seek their participation, but without result. Nasser saw a challenge to his leadership, to his espousal of neutrality, and to his championing of an Arabs-only defence alliance. Radio Cairo stepped up its bitter attacks on Nuri and his policies.

Hoping to duplicate Nasser's success in arranging the British evacuation from the Suez Canal zone, Nuri concluded an agreement which brought the British into the pact and ended their control of the military airfields at Habbaniyah and Shaiba. There were limited options for the British to continue making use of the airfields (provisions, it seemed to Nuri, similar to the ones governing a possible British return to Suez), but the continued existence of vestigial British rights served only to heighten criticism and hostility against the Hashemite regime.

Iraq's decision to participate in the Baghdad Pact brought it into the closest relationship with the United States that has existed before or since, but the benefits of the pact for Iraq were not readily identifiable. Most benefits accruing from its economic programme, such as roads, railways, and radio communications, did not materialize until after Iraq's withdrawal.[5] The significance of the pact in its greater objective – as a deterrent to Soviet aggression in the Middle East – is even less obvious.

Certainly, Soviet aggression of the kind envisioned by the pact's architects never seriously threatened the Arab Middle East in the Baghdad Pact era. The closest approximation to an event of that kind were perhaps the possibilities available to the Iraqi Communist Party to take over power from Qasim in May of 1959. Batatu finds several reasons for Communist restraint at this stage but ascribes the most important one to 'pressure that the Communist Party of the Soviet Union brought to bear upon the Iraqi Communist leadership'.[6] The Russians were apparently motivated by the prospect of a possible adverse impact on their own foreign policy objectives which might stem from a possible Communist take-over in Iraq: they desired neither to risk their ties with Nasser, nor to damage their new policy of 'peaceful co-existence', nor to wreck chances for a visit by Krushchev to Washington, nor, it was even said later, to create the possibility of American military intervention in the event of a Communist assumption of power in Iraq. Thus, the very existence of the Baghdad Pact (even though Iraq was by May 1959 no longer a member), and such other US actions as the Lebanon landings of July 1958, no doubt contributed to Russian fears as to possible American intentions.

In other respects, the pact failed to fulfil hopes of the Hashemite government. For the particular reasons described above, US military assistance to Iraq was a disappointment. Iraq suffered, thus, the same delays and limitations experienced by many 'secondary' US military aid recipients whose territory did not border directly on Communist-held states. In addition, military assistance for Iraq was regarded with concern and sometimes strenuous objection by Israel's friends in the US.

To many officials who dealt every day with pact affairs, it had a degree of unreality. No specific US forces were assigned to meet possible pact-bred contingencies. US membership in the Baghdad Pact's counter-subversion committee led to only modest collaboration by the CIA with pact organizations (although, in all probability, there was considerable bilateral Iraqi–US co-operation in intelligence matters).

The US endeavoured to give substance and conviction to its participation in the pact by fairly generous contributions to the economic programme, by seconding four or five officers to assist in staffing the pact secretariat, by participating in occasional combined naval manoeuvres in the Persian Gulf, and by sending a US Air Force general officer to Baghdad to lead deliberations of the Pact military committee. None of this fully satisfied Nuri, however, who continued to urge that the United States become a fully-fledged member of the pact, as did Ambassador Gallman. But Washington decided to continue its reserved position, wishing to avoid further accentuation of the liabilities which the pact had created. American officials believed that accession to the treaty would create insufficient additional strengthening of the US role beyond that which had resulted from US membership in the various pact committees. Among other drawbacks foreseen for full membership would have been the difficult task of securing Senate approval for accession to the treaty.

The elements within Iraq opposed to the Hashemite regime placed the pact near the top of their list of bitter grievances. Batatu notes that combatting the Baghdad Pact was an important objective in the list of goals of the Communist Party's organization within the Iraqi military, 'the Union of Soldiers and Officers'.[7] A general directive to party committees on the eve of the Revolution asserted that the party's first goals should include: withdrawal from the Baghdad Pact; abolition of the bilateral agreement with Britain; and resistance to the Eisenhower Doctrine. But beyond such formal attacks on the pact in statements by a powerful opposition group lay a broad popular recognition that it had isolated Iraq from the rest of the Arab states, a position running directly contrary to the strongly pan-Arab mood of the time, and counter to the nationalist sentiment which sought an Iraq totally free of significant political ties with the West. The disadvantages for Iraq seem further to have been accentuated by giving the name of Iraq's capital to the organization and placing its headquarters there. Thus, on the occasion of many publicized meetings of the pact's council and committees, the very name of the treaty served to remind Arabs everywhere of Iraq's close association with the Western imperialists.

Batatu draws convincingly the portrait of a revolution whose basic impulse sprang from a several-decade history of powerful but futile efforts by the Iraqi people to overthrow a much hated regime headed by unpopular leaders following outmoded policies. The Free Officers had no stated ideological goals (unlike some of the other opposition elements which joined them, such as the Communists). As Batatu relates, they were a small group within the military forces and, given the necessity of operating in a clandestine manner, they were of course, unable to develop any extensive organization within the populace at large. Several of the opposition parties (the National Democratic Party, the Independence (*Istighlal*) Party, and the Baathists) knew a few days in advance when the coup was to take place but only the Communists seem to have been ready to take tangible steps to galvanize their cadres to support the Revolution at a moment's notice.

Batatu gives no assessment and, in fact, makes only passing

mention of a force that some other observers believe played an important part in creating popular attitudes in support of the Revolution. Radio Cairo's message was transmitted by a powerful broadcasting station and was easily received in many parts of Iraq. In a society possessing only a 15% literacy rate (probably somewhat greater in urban areas), the advent of small, cheap radios established a new medium of communication more pervasive and convenient than anything most people had theretofore known. In villages, populations previously almost entirely cut off from all news or contact with the world outside their own huts and fields were gradually educated on the fine points of anti-imperialism in general and the specific iniquities of the Baghdad Pact.[8] In the cities, of course, Nasser's ceaseless and flamboyant rhetoric was available on a wider scale.

To provide general public access to Radio Cairo's output, as in a shop or a cafe, entailed some risk of suppression and penalty by the authorities, as did public display of Nasser's photograph. But certainly the Egyptian attacks must have served to heighten the sense of grievance of the Free Officers, as it did of the inhabitants of Baghdad's slums who so readily poured into the streets on 14 July. Irrefutable assertions cannot be made on this topic since systems for public polling did not, of course, exist in the Baghdad of the 1950s. There is, however, plenty of evidence of the grave concern which hostile Egyptian broadcasts in the Nasser era caused foreign governments, including those of Saudi Arabia, Jordan and the Hashemite regime in Iraq. Nuri's request for urgent US assistance in increasing Iraq's radio broadcast power met, despite embassy urgings, only with a bureaucratic and delayed response from Washington.

As Batatu states, particularly in his account of the 1952 *Intifadah*, Iraq's Communists made anti-American propaganda a significant part of their repertoire from the outset, resulting in the burnings of the US Information Services offices. Radio Cairo, targeting its hostility at US Middle East policy on the Baghdad Pact and the Eisenhower Doctrine, successfully delineated America as an enemy of pan-Arabism and a friend of imperialism. But on the day of the Revolution, when the British Embassy was burned, there were no corresponding attacks on any American installations. (This could be partly explained by their more remote location from the city centres as compared to the British compound.)

Iraqi troops were placed around the embassies. Fearing further outbreaks, Qasim declared a curfew and martial law. Three American civilians, along with three Jordanian officials, were set upon and killed by a mindless mob as they were being transported through a narrow street heading to the Ministry of Defence. Unfortunate as was this incident, it did not foreshadow any period of terrorist attacks on Americans. The Revolution did bring, however, a period of distinct coolness in US–Iraqi relations. On the American side, there were acute misgivings as to the prospects for stability in Iraq, and the State Department ordered evacuation of all US official dependents – a move to which the Iraqis at first objected but in which they soon acquiesced. Qasim hastened to assure Gallman of his desire for good relations with the United States. Later Qasim personally attended the first meeting of a joint US–Iraqi committee convened to consider Iraqi compensation for the families of the three US victims of mob action. (Eventually each was awarded about $200,000.) The Baghdad Pact headquarters, meanwhile, were closed and padlocked by the Iraqi government, although it did not formally withdraw from the pact until March 1959.

Although at the highest level the new government was correct and neutral in its attitudes towards the United States, less friendly attitudes prevailed at working levels of the administration and among the populace. Troops stationed ostensibly to protect the US Embassy turned to harassing and searching embassy staff entering and exiting the premises. Staff members were followed on foot and in their automobiles, graffiti were inscribed on their houses. For months, American technical assistance personnel remained at their desks in Iraqi offices, virtually unnoticed and without being given anything to do. Their withdrawal was eventually at the initiative not of the Iraqis but of Washington, reflecting again Qasim's desire to avoid any specifically anti-American gestures. Complaints made to high levels of the government concerning the indignities mentioned above were courteously received with promises of remedial action that were rarely implemented. Another more distressing form of harassment was the arrest and prolonged detention of several of the embassy's Iraqi employees on trumped-up charges.

The record of US policy direction and implementation briefly outlined above is not a fully satisfactory one. Attainment of a proper perspective perhaps requires recognition that, in some respects, the disappointing outcome in Iraq was hardly unique. In the mid-1950s, expectations directed toward the new superpower of the West by the post-imperial nations of the developing world were overwhelming.

Disappointment with the extent and delivery rate of US economic and military assistance could probably have been noticed from Morocco proceeding eastward through India. With Iraq, however, the indictment could perhaps be more severe since a case may clearly be made that the United States contributed to destructive forces which were quite beyond the capacity of Iraq's fragile political institutions to contain.

Historians (whether academic or not) have the privilege and duty of analysing and appraising the mistakes of the policy-makers of the past. Such criticism is perhaps most telling when the critic can speculate reasonably on alternative policies which might have been followed or considered at the time. Today, we can legitimately ask: might it have been possible to discover some alternative arrangement to the Baghdad Pact which could have achieved much of the objective sought while substantially mitigating the drawbacks of the course actually followed? As described above, the general disadvantages and dangers for Iraq of participation in a Western-sponsored defence system were recognized by Dulles, by Nuri, by working-level State Department officers and even by outside analysts well acquainted with Middle East policy problems.[9]

What role was played by Waldemar Gallman, US Ambassador in Baghdad? He was an experienced diplomat: precise, thorough, compliant and conscientious. He had been Deputy Chief of Mission in London during several of the war years, an experience which left him with a mild anti-British outlook. Before coming to Baghdad, he had been Ambassador to Poland and South Africa.

Gallman shared the viewpoint of Dulles, Nuri and Menderes that it was a good thing for Iraq to be committed to a Western-sponsored Middle East defence organization. He maintained his enthusiasm for the Baghdad Pact, consistently urging full US membership even after Washington had become more cautious. He was aware of the weaknesses of the Nuri government, but felt that if we were to treat Iraq as an 'ally' we should do so vigorously rather than half-heartedly. Gallman was not alone in his not overly critical stance towards an Arab government that was willing 'to stand up and be counted' on our side, as the phrase went in the late 1950s, at a time when our policies had brought us so much hostility elsewhere in the Arab world. We might have benefited in some respects from having in Baghdad an ambassador who was of a more critical turn of mind than Gallman, but it is doubtful that such a person would have been able to have had much signfiicant impact on policy or the trend of events.

In retrospect, it seems almost inevitable that the United States and Britain would establish some Middle East defence system in the wake of the Communist guerrilla war in Greece, the Russian territorial claims on Turkey, the subjugation of Eastern Europe, the Berlin airlift, Mao's triumph in China, and the attack on South Korea. Throughout the foreign policy establishment, in the bureaucracy, at the White House, in the Congress, there was a general conviction as to the need for measures to strengthen defences of the Middle East.

A policy was accordingly sought which would aim both to reassure the Middle Eastern states and to deter the Russians. Despite the recognized drawbacks for Iraq, the decision was for the establishment of a NATO-style defence organization.

We may usefully ponder the fact that three conservative monarchies in the Arab world – Saudi Arabia, Jordan and Morocco – have survived since 1955, despite being identified as maintaining a degree of dependence on the United States. Since the end of the Second World War decades, the United States regularly, but usually discreetly, has assured the Saudis of our firm commitment to their security. The United States had occasion to provide tangible fulfilment of this commitment, as in the early 1960s when it responded with a show of force to Saudi requests for assistance against Egyptian air attacks from North Yemen. Undoubtedly, Saudi Arabia paid a price in Arab League circles where it bore the stigma of the 'friend of the Americans'. Yet over the years, US assurances, reiterated in high-level private letters or in communiqués following official visits, have provided important reinforcement for Saudi security. The US concern for Saudi security was, of course, among the primary reasons for the massive US response to the Iraqi invasion of Kuwait.

Thus, may we not conceive of a system of quiet assurances which might have been issued, perhaps in tandem by the United States and Britain, to co-operating governments as being more effective in strengthening Middle East defences than all the elaborate and well-publicized mechanisms of the Baghdad Pact?

Saudi rejection of pact membership was the result not of US restraint and wisdom, but rather of Saudi wariness and misgivings as to the impact on Saudi Arabia's relations with its Arab brethren. Indeed, there is little evidence in the record of the pact's evolution of any parallel line of US thinking which would have supported the idea that a system of quiet assurances, reiterated also to the Russians, could have placed a far lighter burden on the fragile political structures of those Arab countries whom we sought to enlist and protect. 'Pacto-mania' had its roots not only in the NATO model but also in attitudes carried over from the old imperialist days. The 'Eastern question' mentality which motivated the European powers in their endless games of power-seeking in the Middle East continued to characterize a great deal of post-Second World War thinking about the area. Preoccupation with these traditional interests tended to prevent a more penetrating understanding of the significance of pan-Arabism, the new nationalism, economic factors, communal forces and the ambitions of the rising middle classes. Both Nuri and Menderes shared, in many respects, the old-fashioned thinking and the enthusiasms of their British and US collaborators.

The decades following the Second World War brought an era of turmoil and change in the Middle East severely testing the leadership and vulnerable institutions of Iraq's then existing Hashemite regime. Conflict stemmed from the painful yet reluctant British withdrawal from the Middle East, the bitterly contested establishment in Palestine of a state for the oppressed Jews, the emergence of new and more vigorous forms of Arab nationalism, revived Soviet interest in the region, and the relentless US determination to forge a Middle East defence organization. A mere recital of these difficult issues indicates the dilemmas of Arab, British and American policy-makers alike in finding a solution for any one problem that did not immediately create risks or drawbacks in dealing with one or all of the others.

## Notes

1. In addition, I am particularly grateful to Frederick Axelgard for making available to me a copy of his doctoral dissertation presented at the Fletcher School of Law and Diplomacy of Tufts University on 'U.S. Policy Toward Iraq, 1946–1958', which provides an analysis of the evolution of US policy in those years. My chapter obviously takes a different approach in its brief comments on US policy. However, the lapse of over thirty years since any continuous contact with Iraqi affairs left many gaps in my recollection of events. Mr Axelgard's dissertation provided me with most helpful reminders of principal developments in relations between the two countries.

2. Hanna Batatu, *The Old Social Classes and the Revolutionary Movements of Iraq* (Princeton, 1978), p. 686.

3. Waldemar J. Gallman, *Iraq Under General Nuri: My Recollections of Nuri al-Said, 1954–1958* (Baltimore, 1964), pp. 16, 188–90. Batatu, *Old Social Classes*, p. 766.

4. Townsend Hoopes, *The Devil and John Foster Dulles* (Boston, 1973), pp. 180–84.

5. See Guy Hadley, *Cento, The Forgotten Alliance* (Fulmer, Sussex, 1971).

6. *Old Social Classes*, p. 903.

7. Ibid., pp. 803–04.

8. 'Radio Cairo' reached new octaves of shrillness in the spring of 1958. See Foreign Broadcast Information Service reports for the Middle East, 22, 23, 24 April 1958. Nuri is accused of ruling 'by steel and by fire, because all the people hate you'. He is warned as to what 'the Iraqi people will do to you'.

9. John Campbell, who has long been Director of Studies at the Council on Foreign Relations, had also served a couple of tours of duty on the Policy Planning Staff of the State Department by the time he published his book, *Defense of the Middle East* (New York, 1958). He notes (pp. 49 and 61): 'Militarily the Baghdad Pact offered no prospect of effective defence . . . Except in Iraq the whole idea of alliance with the West (in the Arab world) against the Soviet threat has had little appeal and tends to raise the old specter of Western imperialism.'

# 4

# US Support for the British Position in Pre-Revolutionary Iraq

FREDERICK W. AXELGARD

US policy toward pre-revolutionary Iraq is not a central concern of Hanna Batatu's work, *The Old Social Classes and the Revolutionary Movements of Iraq*. This is appropriate, since the US role in Iraq was limited and the impact of its policies on the social and political forces that led to the 1958 Revolution was, by and large, limited and indirect.

Nevertheless, this impact was not inconsequential, a fact that has become clearer in light of information available in the years since Batatu completed his research. Declassified documents, now available in archives in London and Washington, DC, shed new light on the manner in which the United States viewed its own role and that of Britain in Iraq, and how well it detected the evolving tensions that eventually produced the Revolution. To what degree did the United States detect a revolutionary situation and adjust its policies accordingly?

Relying on these recently available sources, this chapter examines America's role in supporting, and thereby prolonging, the domination of British influence in Iraq. Batatu's treatment of the British role in Iraq is wide in scope and frequently quite detailed. Though he acknowledges some positive British contributions to Iraq's development, Batatu in the main is critical of Britain's approach to the country, as shown in his overview of the British relationship with Nuri Said.

The regime, that the 'Second British Occupation' ushered in in 1941, took more and more the characteristics of an unaccountable and coercive rule in which visible authority lay in an uneasy partnership of Nuri and the regent, drawing its strength from its subservience to British power and to native vested interests.[1]

Batatu sums up this regime by stressing that it imposed martial law in Baghdad for nearly eight of the last seventeen years of the monarchy, and that its estrangement from the Iraqi people stemmed in no small part from its subservience to British influence and interests.[2]

These points require little elaboration here. What is of interest, however, is that one can now document the steps which the United States took to sustain the British presence in Iraq and its influence on the conservative political elite led by Nuri Said. Batatu's concern with US–British interaction is limited to discussion of the formation of the Baghdad Pact. This alliance is noted as one source of the Iraqi people's outrage against its government, but relatively little emphasis is placed on the US role in the establishment of the pact and in its short but turbulent history.[3] Batatu casts a more sceptical eye over US policies in the context of the Suez war of late 1956, and 'parallel intrigues' against Syria in which Washington assisted, 'with the transparent aims of isolating Egypt and pulling Syria into the orbit of the Baghdad Pact'.[4]

Our purpose here is to focus on the way in which Washington supported the British role in Iraq, dealing mainly with the years between 1946 and 1958. The thesis is not complex. It is simply to suggest that Washington took a relatively active role in backing Britain at key junctures in the last years of the Iraqi monarchy, and thereby indirectly contributed to the inability or unwillingness of Britain and the Iraqi government to address the social and political pressures that gave rise to the Revolution.

There is, however, at least one somewhat intricate and provocative feature in the account which follows. The declassified documentation now available for review indicates clearly that a good many US officials believed that British influence in Iraq during these years was in sharp decline, and that its perpetuation was upsetting the social and political climate of the country. Yet these documents show that the United States avoided efforts either to supplant British influence in Iraq with American influence, or to diminish or redirect it in a manner that would alleviate the tensions that were building up to the revolutionary upheaval of July 1958.

## The US, Britain and the *Wathbah* ('Uprising')

Our study can profitably begin with the Rashid Ali revolt of 1941, a pivotal event in Iraq's political history, and also an important harbinger of future US–British interaction in Iraq. There was widespread concern during this early period of the Second World War because of Germany's advances and British defeats, and this was an important factor in the US decision to support Britain in suppressing Rashid Ali al-Gailani.

US support in this regard was manifest in a variety of ways. The US Minister Resident in Iraq, Paul Knabenshue, urged Rashid Ali, while he was still prime minister in late 1940, to adhere to Iraq's treaty obligations with Britain. Subsequently, Washington agreed to British requests to cut off Iraq's access to US dollar credits and to block exports of American weaponry to Iraq. Then, in a dramatic sequence of events in April 1941, Knabenshue secretly spirited the Iraqi Regent out of Baghdad in the back of his car to the British base at Habbaniyah, enabling him to evade pressure to reinstate Rashid Ali as prime minister. This manoeuvre forced Rashid Ali to resort to illegal means to establish a new government, thereby ensuring a coup or revolt.

During the thirty days of warfare between British and Iraqi forces that followed the Rashid Ali revolt, Knabenshue provided periodic intelligence to the British on Iraqi military moves and gave safe haven in the American Legation to British subjects. Significantly, when the fighting was over, Knabenshue joined the British ambassador in greeting the Regent outside of Baghdad and accompanying him in his triumphant return into the city.[5] Notwithstanding the special circumstances in which it took shape, US policy of this time lasted well beyond the end of the Second World War, and in fact established a pattern that continued until 1958: to reinforce the British presence in Iraq while neglecting the emerging political currents that challenged the British-dominated status quo.

Washington took a similar position during the next major episode in Iraqi political history, the *Wathbah* of January 1948. By the late 1940s, the setting for US interests in Iraq had changed following the elevation of its diplomatic legation in Iraq to embassy status in late 1946. This step in turn followed a prolonged discussion within the State Department about the importance of Iraq to US interests. A series of policy memoranda produced between late 1944 and early

1946 was punctuated by the observation that Iraq was a rising power in the Arab world and 'it will be increasingly necessary for us to maintain closer relations with Iraq, since our standing in the entire area will to a considerable degree be dependent on the attitude of Iraq toward the United States.'[6]

This view of Iraq's significance and the honeymoon in US–Iraq relations following the establishment of a fully accredited embassy in Baghdad proved to be short-lived. In 1947, the cold war intensified and Britain served notice that it could no longer provide the requisite military and economic aid to Greece and Turkey. The United States then introduced the Truman Doctrine, by which it took over the task of supporting these two countries. These developments sharpened the questions of the future of the British strategic presence in the Middle East, and of American support for this presence as a hedge against Soviet penetration of the region.

To discuss such questions, British and American officials met secretly in Washington in late 1947. Iraq was far from being the central topic of discussion at these 'Pentagon Talks', but when it did come up, there were substantial differences in British and American perspectives. US officials showed a relative lack of interest, as evidenced in their documents about the range of special treaty relationships which Britain had in the Middle East. While they bluntly criticized the 'obsolete' British arrangements with the shaikhdoms of the Persian Gulf, they made no such criticism of the Anglo–Iraqi Treaty – except to express concern that the Iraqi government be allowed to hire non-British subjects as foreign advisers.[7]

British officials, on the other hand, spared no pains to express the seriousness of their concern about Iraq. The need for continued British access to the Royal Air Force (RAF) bases in Iraq surfaced several times in the 'Pentagon Talks'. In its opening statement, the British side cited Iraq as the case in point for arguing that 'we must obtain or maintain the requisite strategic facilities . . . in the Middle East in peacetime, or withdraw strategically from the Middle East altogether.'[8] Indeed, strategic access made Iraq perhaps the most important country in the Middle East for the British at the time.

The US side acknowledged the importance which Britain placed on the Iraqi bases, but the Americans argued at the same time that Kuwait should be built up militarily 'in case developments should make it appear that effective use could not be made of the Iraqi bases'. The British representatives, on the other hand, were confident that a renegotiation of the Anglo–Iraqi Treaty (discussions were already well underway by this point) would result in perpetuating British access to the Iraqi bases. To this, the US side responded (prophetically) that domestic pressures in Iraq might prevent the Iraqi government 'at the last minute' from granting Britain such access, and again stressed the value of a base in Kuwait 'in case British treaty negotiations with Iraq could not be successfully concluded'.[9]

Any doubts Washington had about the Anglo–Iraqi Treaty negotiations soon disappeared from view. Just a month after the 'Pentagon Talks', as Anglo–Iraqi talks over a new treaty began to intensify, the Foreign Office asked for, and received, US backing in the negotiations. The State Department instructed its chargé d'affaires in Baghdad, Edmund Dorsz, to meet with British negotiators in the capital and join the quest for a successful outcome of the negotiations with Iraqi officials. Dorsz contacted officials of the British Embassy in Baghdad, who secretly kept him informed of progress in the negotiations, and he agreed to wait for their cue, in order to time the US input for maximum effect.[10]

The cue came early in January 1948, and Dorsz dutifully encouraged the Iraqi Regent to see the negotiations through to conclusion – a view which had been prepared in co-operation with the British Embassy and approved by the State Department. The Regent, in response, expressed appreciation for US support of the negotiations.[11] In the days that followed, while Iraqi Prime Minister Saleh Jabr was in London to finalize the new treaty, Dorsz tried to convince some of its major Iraqi opponents of its merits, thereby fulfilling his pledge to the British Embassy to use 'every opportunity' to express support for the new agreement.

Dorsz's actions disturbed the State Department, which was anxious to avoid the impression that the Americans were 'acting as British tools' on this issue.[12] But Washington's concern over appearing to be manipulated by Britain was overtaken by the *Wathbah* – the eruption of widespread, violent opposition to the new Anglo–Iraqi Treaty initialled at Portsmouth in mid-January 1948. The explosion occurred while British and American diplomats were exchanging premature congratulations and expressions of mutual appreciation for the combined effort that had gone into preparation of the new treaty.[13]

Thus, ironically, the new treaty was blocked in precisely the 'last minute' fashion that US officials had predicted just three months earlier. Their actions, however, did little credit to their prescience. At no point after the 'Pentagon Talks' did these officials try to restrain Britain's efforts in pursuing the new treaty. On the contrary, they encouraged them, with few reservations.

Hence, in much the same way as during the Rashid Ali revolt of 1941, the United States had quietly backed British strategic objectives in Iraq, while ignoring the dangers in the local political situation. In contrast with 1941, however, American officials in 1947 expressed concern over the political viability of British objectives and methods in Iraq. The historical record gives no clear explanation as to why, between October 1947 and January 1948, the State Department appeared to suspend its doubts about the new Anglo–Iraqi treaty. Apparently Washington hoped against its own best instinct that such an agreement would prove viable and help stabilize Britain's regional security role in what was otherwise a rapidly deteriorating strategic setting.

In summary, by 1948 Washington had helped London to back Iraq's conservative political elite in two very damaging political crises. It was an inauspicious pattern, one whose troubling aspects seemed to be unaffected by the fact that American policy-makers had begun to sense the tumult that lay ahead.

## US–British Interaction in Iraq, 1950–1954

Between 1950 and 1954, American diplomats expressed increasing doubt that the British role in Iraq was sustainable or politically useful. Yet the United States continued to say that Britain had primary responsibility for the defence of the Middle East. In Iraq, moreover, US policy consciously resisted the temptation to challenge the political and military pre-eminence enjoyed by Britain.

The years 1950 to 1954 were complex and difficult ones for US–British relations in the Middle East. It was during this time that the United States attempted to mediate British problems with the governments of Iran and Egypt, which laid the basis for a significantly greater American role in these countries within a few short years. With Iraq, there were no difficulties similar to the crisis over nationalization of the Anglo–Iranian Oil Company in Iran, or the dispute with Egypt over the military base at Suez. Nevertheless, among themselves, American officials spoke openly of the need for Britain to deal with Iraq more equitably or renounce its treaty outright.[14] Washington also knew that Britain's status in Iraq had been damaged by Mussadiq's challenge to British authority in neighbouring Iran, but it did nothing more than encourage the British-dominated Iraq Petroleum Company to raise its royalty payments to the Iraqi government.[15]

By the time that the Eisenhower administration took office in January 1953, American foreign policy-makers had made a quiet judgement that the United States might soon have to take over the British position in the Middle East, and that Britain seemed prepared to accept a larger US role in the area.[16] A symbolic affirmation of this thinking was Secretary of State John Foster Dulles's trip to the Middle East in May 1953, an unprecedented American intrusion into this traditional British preserve. With respect to Iraq, the foreign policy establishment had arrived at even more concrete conclusions. In a State Department intelligence report submitted during Dulles's trip, US analysts interpreted Britain's military and political position in Iraq to be seriously weakened and likely to deteriorate further. The report criticized Britain's dependence on the conservative political leadership dominated by Nuri Said, and predicted with certainty the end of the Anglo–Iraqi Treaty relationship upon the treaty's expiration in 1957. It also downplayed the significance of Britain's military resources in Iraq, including Britain's two strategic air bases, and pointed to the 'ill feeling which the US inherits in Iraq as the active or tacit upholder of British supremacy'. Finally, the report offered a blunt prediction of the future consequences of the British performance in Iraq:

When the aging Nuri passes, power is likely to fall to a generation whose whole political outlook has been conditioned by the anti-British struggle and whose political life has expressed itself only in negative terms of opposition without ever facing the necessities of forming positive and viable policy. It is probably already too late to avoid the consequences for British influence of this development. The very success the UK has had in staving off the shift in the base of power – and, incidentally, maintaining short-term internal stability – is serving to harden the attitude of those who will one day be the new ruling group and to make them more suspicious, illogical and intransigent.[17]

Other factors contributed to the attractiveness of a greater US interest in Iraq. For example, Iraq was one of the countries included in the 'northern tier' scheme for regional defence, which grew out of Secretary Dulles's trip to the Middle East. In addition, Dr Fadil

Jamali was installed as prime minister in Iraq in September 1953. Jamali was the only member of the political elite at the time not to have a strong predisposition toward Britain. Rather, his American education and contacts generated the belief that there was a serious opportunity for greater American involvement in Iraq.[18] Indeed, Washington did appear to take advantage of Jamali's tenure by negotiating and signing a military assistance agreement with Iraq. This understanding was signed in April 1954, just days before Jamali left office. It is widely known that this US–Iraq agreement was politically unpopular in Iraq, and its conclusion was partly responsible for Jamali's departure from the prime ministership. What is less well known, but is clearly revealed in the now-declassified archival sources, is the weakness of the US commitment to Iraq outlined in this military assistance understanding.

To begin with, the military and political significance of the US–Iraq understanding of April 1954 was diminished, if not neutralized, by a secret US–British memorandum signed eight weeks earlier. To put matters in perspective, the Iraqi government had formally requested military assistance from the United States in March 1953. Months went by with no response forthcoming from Washington. Then, in November 1953, the US ambassador to Iraq urged Washington to take advantage of the comfortable margin of political support enjoyed by the new Jamali government, and to hasten conclusion of a military assistance agreement.[19]

The British Foreign Office, however, was concerned that, with the new Jamali government in power, Britain's relative influence in military matters in Iraq was endangered. London asked Washington for discussions about the proposed US military aid programme to Iraq, and Washington agreed. Ultimately, the decision to co-ordinate with Britain delayed for several months the beginning of US negotiations with Iraq on the particulars of the military assistance agreement. This delay meant that a troublesome political issue was raised in far less propitious circumstances than would have been the case had the US ambassador's suggestion been taken up in late 1953. In addition, the secret Memorandum of Understanding (MOU) which grew out of the US–British discussions formally subordinated US military assistance to Iraq to existing British plans for development of Iraq's armed forces. Washington agreed that its aid to Baghdad would be complementary in nature and that Britain would remain the primary source of military support for Iraq. Washington also grudgingly agreed to state that it had no plans to provide any assistance to Iraq's air force, and that there would be little, if any, provision for Iraqis to obtain training at US military institutions.[20]

The declassified documents reveal additional reasons to question the depth of the US interest which lay behind the US–Iraq military assistance understanding of April 1954. After months of delay owing to co-ordination with the British, and after wading through weeks of difficult negotiation with Iraqi officials, Washington came perilously close in mid-April to abandoning altogether the prospect of a military assistance arrangement with Iraq. The reasons for this eleventh-hour manoeuvre were complex. On the surface, State Department officials appeared to be seriously upset with Iraq's unwillingness to declare publicly its upport for US regional security proposals. Close examination of the record also suggests that concern over Israeli opposition to US arms for Iraq was perhaps closer to the heart of American reasoning. In any event, the US Embassy in Baghdad was told to suspend negotiations with Iraqi officials pending a review of the situation by the National Security Council, which it was said, 'may take some time'.[21]

For our purposes here, it is perhaps less important to know that there was a last-minute hitch in US–Iraq negotiations than to know of the US ambassador's response to it. Ambassador Burton Y. Berry, who was soon to leave Iraq to retire from the Foreign Service, responded to his instructions by giving a devastatingly accurate, long-term assessment of the political situation in Iraq. The unsettling nature of his warning to the State Department is not significantly diminished by the fact that it was mistakenly premised on the assumption that the US–Iraq military assistance agreement would fail to materialize.

By the Department's action we set in motion in Iraq a whole series of events that seem to me to be inimicable to our objectives in Iraq and the ME [Middle East]. The news [of the US breaking off talks] can only increase the frustration and disillusionment of Prime Minister Jamali who has from the first welcomed and accepted the agreement, asking only for changes in language to increase his ability to sell it to the public. I fear, therefore, he may resign shortly and we will, thereby, have lost the most outspoken of all Arab leaders against Communism as well as the Iraqi official who is most convinced of the desirability of Arab cooperation with the west. *He will probably be followed as Prime Minister by one of the "old gang." This will provide the opportunity for those who wish to change the order of things in Iraq through unlawful processes.* The development of the pattern from there on is well known: The merging of the interests of the Nationalists and

Communists into a common front, the beginning of government by mob action, denunciation of the British treaty, nationalization, and fostering campaigns to rid the country of foreigners. I beg you to bend every effort in NSC [National Security Council] review to see that the decision is taken in Washington that will halt this deteriorating process in Iraq, with its chain reaction throughout the ME.[22]

The record does not reveal a direct State Department reaction to Berry's evaluation. Nevertheless, within three days and following discussions at the highest levels of the US government, Berry was authorized to resume negotiations with Iraqi officials and was given sufficient latitude to enable him to wrap them up literally overnight. The US–Iraq military assistance understanding was concluded on 21 April 1954.

Significantly this experience reveals a certain level of awareness among US officials of the true nature of political conditions in Iraq. On the one hand, there was a clear understanding of the declining and politically destabilizing influence of the British. There was also a strong belief that a return to power of the 'old gang' of politicians headed by Nuri Said was a recipe for political disaster. By the same token, it shows little practical adjustment in US policy to take account of this awareness. Despite knowing the weakness of the British position, US policy-makers were nevertheless willing formally to subjugate American initiative in Iraq to British preferences, and thereby prolong and prop up the British position. In addition, soon after Ambassador Berry left Baghdad, the US Embassy in the capital directly contradicted Berry's warnings against the reinstalment of the 'old gang'. It sharply criticized the results of the free elections of June 1954, which significantly eroded the political power base of the 'old guard', and later applauded the overturning of these elections and the return of Nuri Said to the premiership some two months later.[23]

## US–British Interaction in Iraq, 1955–1958

These growing contradictions and American preoccupation with a regional defence scheme to foil presumed Soviet designs in the Middle East set the context for the final period of US–British interaction with respect to pre-revolutionary Iraq. The future Baghdad Pact began to take shape in 1954 with the conclusion of a mutual defence accord between Pakistan and Turkey. American officials exerted consistent pressure on Iraq to join this accord, using the temptation of higher levels of military assistance if Baghdad agreed to do so. Yet the encroachment of this American strategy (designed to succeed where the British-proposed Middle East Defence Organization and Middle East Command had failed) did not sit well with British officials. Moreover, it appears that Nuri Said appealed to the Foreign Office for help in resisting American pressure to 'hustle' him into a regional alliance.[24]

Matters changed dramatically in the first weeks of 1955, however. From all available indications, the Foreign Office and State Department were caught completely off-guard when Nuri and Turkey's Adnan Menderes announced their own mutual defence agreement in January 1955. The British and American responses to this development began to diverge almost immediately. London quicky interpreted it as an opportunity to ease out of the treaty with Iraq, while retaining military access to the country by joining the burgeoning regional defence system.[25] Accordingly, it joined the Baghdad Pact in April. Washington, on the other hand, began to shy away from a formal association with the grouping. Dulles publicly welcomed the Turco–Iraqi announcement as a 'very constructive development', but decided not to publish the congratulatory messages sent to Iraq and Turkey on the occasion, and quietly sent instructions to US embassies in the Middle East not to focus attention on the Nuri–Menderes communiqué.[26]

US officials also began to issue a variety of rationales that argued against an early American accession to the pact. By the time of the first Baghdad Pact council meeting in November 1955, this attitude seemed to have hardened into a resolute refusal to be drawn into the pact. At this juncture, British Foreign Minister Harold Macmillan strongly urged Dulles to consider joining the pact, arguing that US adherence would 'make a certainty of success of what is now somewhat doubtful'.[27] The American Secretary of State demurred. He also rejected Macmillan's proposal to move quickly to get other Arab countries into the pact.[28] In this manner, the United States and Britain exchanged roles with respect to the Baghdad Pact, with London becoming the active advocate of its virtues and Washington (ignoring its paternal responsibility for the alliance) showing only reluctance and diffidence. Washington's attitude did much to cement Iraq's isolated position in the pact, tied to the unpopular colonial power and cut off from the company of all other Arab states.

Perhaps the greatest pressure for the United States to join the

Baghdad Pact came following the eruption of the Suez war in late 1956. The leaders of Iraq, Pakistan, Iran and Turkey claimed that the very survival of the pact was at stake and full US adherence was essential. US military officials gave identical arguments. Finally, the US Ambassador in Iraq, Waldemar J. Gallman, saw accession as absolutely vital in strengthening the American political position in Iraq, following the discrediting of Britain by the Suez crisis.[29] President Eisenhower disagreed, however, reasoning instead that to join the pact under the prevailing circumstances would make it appear to the Arab world that the United States had been manipulated by Britain.[30]

Washington's conscious cultivation of a secondary position behind the British also influenced its approach to providing military assistance to Iraq during this period. Following the US–Iraq military assistance understanding of April 1954, British officials were intensely suspicious of American intentions. They were convinced, for example, that US military advisers sent to Iraq to implement the military aid programme seriously transgressed the limits of US support established in the US–British Memorandum of Understanding (MOU) signed in February. The British ambassador in Baghdad fretted: 'The whole situation seems to be distinctly disturbing. Before we know where we are we shall find Iraq swarming with American military advisers while we are left in the air.'[31]

Then, as the structure of the Baghdad Pact unfolded, British military officials developed another worry. Since the MOU with Washington was formally premised on the rights Britain enjoyed under its treaty with Iraq, the negation of that treaty when Britain joined the Baghdad Pact would likewise destroy the legal basis of the MOU. Unless the terms of the MOU were revised, there would no longer be any pretext for Britain to suggest that Washington restrain its military assistance to Iraq.[32]

As matters turned out, these British worries were exaggerated. During US–British discussions in Washington in the summer of 1955, the State Department made a far-reaching decision. On the one hand, it acknowledged that British adherence to the Baghdad Pact technically voided the US–British MOU on military aid for Iraq. Yet the Department also told British officials that the Eisenhower administration would continue to abide by the spirit of the MOU.[33] The primary means of carrying out this policy was embodied in Washington's decision to use most of the US aid funds for Iraq to make 'off-shore purchases' of British equipment. This policy made its way into a major NSC (National Security Council) document on the Middle East in mid-1954, and was developed further in US–British talks at the end of the year.

British doubts about American intentions persisted, however. To set things straight, a proposal was made for a US-financed off-shore purchase of British-made Centurion tanks for Iraq. When the State Department stumbled on the question of whether its prior assurances to Israel would permit the supply of tanks to Iraq, the dialogue was elevated to the heads-of-state level. British sources report that Prime Minister Anthony Eden won agreement from President Eisenhower to purchase 70 Centurions, while Britain would buy 10. Later, however, Washington would agree to purchase only 10 tanks, in conjunction with a British gift of 2. The Americans' seeming emasculation of the deal enraged Eden, but he accepted it in the hope that it would be only a first instalment.[35] London was further upset when Washington's slow processing of the off-shore purchase delayed shipment of the tanks for months. To top matters off, Ambassador Gallman noted with obvious displeasure that when the long-awaited delivery to Iraq occurred, only the two British-bought tanks were displayed for publicity while the American-bought tanks languished for days in the hold of the British delivery ship.[36]

The eruption of the Suez crisis sharpened the frustration of US military officials with the constraints imposed by the US–British MOU. Concern had already been expressed that Iraq was receiving far less militarily for its adherence to the Baghdad Pact than Egypt and Syria (the major opponents of the pact) were from the East bloc,[37] but the Suez crisis catalysed matters dramatically. In view of the threat that the crisis posed to Nuri Said's political survival, it was proposed that US interceptor aircraft with Iraqi markings be dispatched as a show of support. The State Department, however, blocked this on the grounds that it would violate the US–British MOU.[38]

During the course of 1957, pressure built within the Pentagon to have the MOU terminated, and for Washington to assume primary responsibility for training and equipping Iraq's military.[39] There appears to be no documentary evidence to suggest that this course of action was ever formally adopted. Indeed, an NSC study dated January 1958 calls for 'open cooperation in military assistance' for Iraq between the United States and Britain.[40] Nevertheless, by May 1958, the Departments of State and of Defense had agreed to a plan which would have completely converted the air force of Iraq to American aircraft by the end of 1959.[41] Delivery of the first instalment of these aircraft was delayed, however. Ambassador Gallman recounts that Nuri Said came to him just five days before the Revolution, pleading for delivery of the jets, implying that it was anticipated as a major political and military breakthrough.[42]

The jets and an American training crew arrived almost immediately after the Revolution. The aircraft were seized by the government of Abdel Karim Qasim and the training crew left Baghdad. The diffident and self-defeating nature of the approach taken by Washington in its relationship with pre-revolutionary Iraq is vividly symbolized in the image of these jets, stranded at an airfield near Baghdad, with the Iraqi Revolution erupting in the background.

## Conclusions

The purpose of this chapter has been to demonstrate how the United States consciously cultivated a secondary position, politically and militarily, behind British influence in pre-revolutionary Iraq. The climax of this effort occurred in the years just prior to the Revolution. During this time the pace of Britain's decline in the Middle East and that of the American ascent were in sharp contrast. With specific regard to Iraq, long-standing concern over the staying power of Britain and the British-backed elite led by Nuri Said came to a head. Above all else, Britain's participation against Egypt in the Suez war brought into the open the potentially suicidal consequences of Baghdad's retention of a close association to London.

The documentary record reveals that in this period, as in earlier ones, American diplomats and policy-makers were aware of the political tensions in Iraq caused by the conservative elite's ties to Britain. It also reveals that, also as in earlier periods, Washington made little effort to address this problem in practical terms. Whether the United States could have done anything significant to alter the evolution of events is of course highly debatable. Its last ambassador to the Iraqi monarchy, Waldemar J. Gallman, was clearly prepared to believe that a higher American profile in Iraq between 1955 and 1958 would have had a salutary effect, perhaps to the point of staving off the Revolution. Yet, at the same time, he also dismissed the Iraqi Revolution as 'simply a seizure of power by a small, determined cadre of officers', and referred to the crowds in Baghdad's streets as 'not representative Iraqis but hoodlums recruited by agitators'.[43]

Yet Ambassador Gallman's arguments on behalf of a more assertive American role in Iraq, and what it could have accomplished, bear some consideration. Why? Because his words echo so closely what American officials had been saying for over ten years about the British role in Iraq, and its consequences for the American position there. Had Washington acted on its beliefs earlier, had the Truman and Eisenhower administrations taken concrete steps to distance themselves from the British in Iraq or otherwise weaken the ties between Britain and Iraq's ruling elite, it is not inconceivable that Iraqi history might have unfolded differently.

But 'going with the British' was only one manifestation of the US tendency to discount the nationalistic politics which contradicted its broader regional strategies. American differences with the Arabs over Palestine, and a preoccupation with a presumed Soviet threat to the Middle East, also worked against putting pressure on Britain to lower its profile in Iraq or withdraw altogther. Bound irreversibly to these cornerstones of its strategy, Washington had effectively tied its own hands. Hence, even if it was aware of the social and political stress in Iraq, Washington could do no more than watch knowingly as the soil crumbled beneath both Britain's and its own positions there.

## Notes

1. Hanna Batatu, *The Old Social Classes and the Revolutionary Movements of Iraq* (Princeton, 1978), p. 345.

2. Ibid., pp. 345–47.

3. Ibid., pp. 679–89.

4. Ibid., p. 751.

5. *Foreign Relations of the United States, 1940*, vol. III (Washington, DC, 1949), pp. 716–26 (hereafter abbreviated as *FRUS*); and *FRUS, 1941*, III, pp. 487–513.

6. Memorandum by the Office of Near Eastern and African Affairs, 29 August 1945 (Department of State Records, Diplomatic Branch, National Archives, Washington, DC, File No. 711.90G/8–2945) (hereafter abbreviated as DS 711.90G/8–2945).

7. 'The British and American Positions', (*FRUS, 1947*, V, p. 514); and 'Specific Current Questions' (ibid., pp. 535–36).

8. Draft Notes for Remarks by the United Kingdom at the Opening of the United States–United Kingdom Talks on the Middle East, October 16, 1747 (*FRUS, 1947*, V, p. 567). See also telegram from the U.S. Embassy in London to the Secretary of State, June 11, 1947 (*FRUS, 1947*, I, p. 753).

9. Statements by the United States and the United Kingdom Groups, 'Iraq as a Factor in the Maintenance of Stability in the Middle East' (undated) (*FRUS, 1947*, V,

pp. 594–96), and 'Political and Strategic Questions Relating to the Persian Gulf Sheikhdoms' (undated) (ibid., pp. 599–601).

10. Letter from Denis Allen to Loy Henderson, January 12, 1948 DS 741.90G/1–1248); Telegram from the Department of State to the U.S. Embassy in Baghdad, November 26, 1947 (DS 741.90G/11–2647); and Telegram from the U.S. Embassy in Baghdad to the Secretary of State, December 13, 1947 (DS 741.90G/12–1347).

11. Telegram from the U.S. Embassy in Baghdad to the Secretary of State, January 5, 1948 (FRUS, 1948, V, p. 203). Dorsz also apparently sought an opportunity to communicate the same message to Prime Minister Saleh Jabr in the week prior to Jabr's departure for London. The meeting could not be arranged because of pressing 'parliamentary affairs'. (Telegram from the U.S. Embassy in Baghdad to the Secretary of State, January 6, 1948 [DS 741.90G/1–648]).

12. Telegram from the U.S. Embassy in Baghdad to the Secretaryof State, January 14, 1948 (DS 741.90G/1–1448); and Telegram from the Department of State to the U.S. Embassy in Baghdad, January 16, 1948 (FRUS, 1948, V, p. 205).

13. Telegram from the Department of State to the U.S. Embassy in Baghdad, January 16, 1948 (FRUS, 1948, V, p. 205); Letter from Allen to Henderson, January 12, 1948, and Letter from Henderson to Allen, January 19, 1948 (DS 741.90G/1–1248).

14. Memorandum by Assistant Secretary of State George McGhee to the Secretary of State, December 27, 1950 (FRUS, 1951, V, p. 5); and Iraq Policy Statement, November 9, 1950 (FRUS, 1950, V, p. 654).

15. CIA Report No, 00–B–37167, 'Iraq: Attitudes towards Foreign Powers' (Declassified Documents Reference System [hereafter abbreviated as DDRS] 1975, CIA 3J) (quotation); Telegrams from U.S. Embassy in Baghdad to Secretary of State, March 17 and March 29, 1951 (FRUS, 1951, V, pp. 285–86, 292–93).

16. Department of State, Office of Intelligence Research Report No. 5890. 'The British Position in the Middle East', October 21, 1952. Similarly, the Department's Policy Planning Staff found Britain's position 'wholly inadequate' to defend the Middle East from Soviet aggression (Memorandum, May 21, 1952 [FRUS, 1952–1954, IX, Part 1, p. 233]).

17. Department of State, Office of Intelligence Research Report No. 5980.2, 'The British Position in Iraq', May 21, 1953.

18. Despatch from the U.K. Embassy in Baghdad to the Foreign Office, December 1, 1953 (Records of the British Foreign Office, Public Record Office, London, File No. 371/104677 EQ10345/3) (hereafter abbreviated as FO 371/104677 EQ10345/3); and author's interview with Hermann F. Eilts, 21 November 1986.

19. Burton Berry letter to Parker T. Hart, November 10, 1953 (DS 611.87/11–1053); and Telegram from the U.S. Embassy in Baghdad to the Secretary of State, November 23, 1953 (DS 787.5 MSP/11–2353).

20. Foreign Office Note by G. H. Baker, December 8, 1953, attached to Despatch from U.K. Embassy in Baghdad to the Foreign Office, December 1, 1953 (FO 371/104677 EQ10345/3); Memorandum from Henry Byroade to Robert Murphy, March 4, 1954 (FRUS, 1952–1954, IX, Part 2, pp. 2371–72, Note 1); and Memorandum of Understanding Concerning the Provision of Military Aid to Iraq by the Government of the United States (FO 371/110820 V1193/39 and FRUS, 1952–1954, IX, Part 2, pp. 2371–74).

21. Telegram from the Secretary of State to the U.S. Embassy in Baghdad, April 8, 1954 (DS 787.5 MSP/4–854); Telegram from the U.S. Embassy in Baghdad to the Secretary of State, April 11, 1954 (DS 787.5 MSP/4–1154); and Telegram from the

Secretary of State to the U.S. Embassy in Baghdad, April 15, 1954 (DS 787.5 MSP/4–1154).

22. Telegram from the U.S. Embassy in Baghdad to the Secretary of State, April 16, 1954 (DS 787.5 MSP/4–1654) (emphasis added).

23. Despatch from the U.S. Embassy in Baghdad to the Department of State, July 14, 1954 (DS 787.00/7–1454); and Despatch from the U.S. Embassy in Baghdad to the Department of State, September 17, 1954 (DS 787.00/9–1754).

24. (Foreign Office Minute, January 11, 1955 FO 371/115484 V1073/26); and Telegrams from the U.K. Embassy in Baghdad to the Foreign Office, January 10 and 12, 1955 (FO 371/115484 V1073/6 & 11.

25. Foreign Office Minute, January 14, 1955 (FO 371/115484 V1073/152); undated Foreign Office communication (FO 371/115488 V1073/152); Foreign Office Minute, February 1, 1955 (FO 371/115488 V1073/154A); and Telegram from the U.K. Embassy in Washington to the Foreign Office, February 9, 1955 (FO 371/115489 V1073/196).

26. Telegram from the U.K. Embassy in Ankara to the Foreign Office, January 18, 1955 (FO 371/115486 V1073/62); and Telegram from the U.K. Embassy in Washington to the Foreign Office, January 17, 1955 (FO 371/115484 V1073/32).

27. Telegram from the Foreign Office to the U.K. Embassy in Washington, November 25, 1955 (FO 371/115469 V1023/26).

28. Communication to Macmillan, via the U.S. Embassy in London, December 6, 1955 (FO 371/115469 V1023/28).

29. Waldemar J. Gallman, *Iraq under General Nuri: My Recollections of Nuri al-Said, 1954–1958* (Baltimore, 1964), pp. 74–79, 185–88; Memorandum for the Joint Chiefs of Staff from the Director of the Joint Staff, November 29, 1956 (CCS 381 EMMEA [11–19–47], Section 50 from Record Group 218, Military Archives Division, National Archives, Washington D.C.).

30. Memorandum of Conference with the President, November 21, 1956 (DDRS 1978, White House 451A).

31. Letter from the U.K. Embassy in Baghdad to the Foreign Office, October 6, 1954 (FO 371/110824 V1193/104).

32. Telegram from the U.K. Embassy in Baghdad to the Foreign Office, February 22, 1955 (FO 371/115583 V1193–30).

33. Despatch from the U.K. Embassy in Washington to the Foreign Office, 'Extract from Record of Meeting on Middle East Defense held at the State Department, August 11, 1955' (FO 371/115587 V1193/133G, and Telegram from the U.K. Embassy in Washington to the Foreign Office, August 13, 1955 (FO 371/115585 V1193/94/G).

34. NSC Policy Paper 5428, 'U.S. Objectives and Policies with regard to the Near East', July 23, 1954; and Foreign Office Minute, February 22, 1955 (FO 371/115583 V1193/33).

35. Minutes of a Foreign Office Meeting, August 9, 1955 (FO 371/115586 V1193/95); Telegram from the U.K. Embassy in Washington to the Foreign Office, August 16, 1955 (FO 371/115586 V1193/97G/A); and Prime Minister's Personal Minute, August 19, 1955 (FO 371/115586 V1193/97/G).

36. Gallman, *Iraq under General Nuri*, pp. 174–76.

37. Message from the Chief, U.S. MAAG (Military Assistance Advisory Group) Iraq, to the Joint Chiefs of Staff, April 3, 1956 (CJCS 091 [Iraq]).

38. See Joint Chiefs of Staff Decision on JCS 1887/365 (CCS 381 EMMEA [11–19–47], Section 60).

39. Memorandum from Air Force Chief of Staff Nathan Twining for the Secretary of Defense, May 15, 1957 (CCS 381 EMMEA [11–19–47], Section 58).

40. NSC 5801, 'Long-Range U.S. Policy toward the Middle East', January 10, 1958, p. 29.

41. Memorandum for the Secretary of Defense (JCS 1887/460), June 19, 1958 (CCS 381 EMMEA [11–19–47], Section 71).

42. Gallman, *Iraq under General Nuri*, pp. 190–91.

43. Gallman, *Iraq under General Nuri*, p. 205.

# 5

# The Soviet Union, the Great Powers and Iraq

## JOE STORK

### I

Today, more than thirty years after the event, the legacy of the Iraqi Revolution appears ambiguous. Iraq was the first and, except for Iran in 1978–79, the only major oil-producing state in the Middle East to undergo a far-reaching political revolution. Though the country thoroughly nationalized its oil industry and more, its economic structure shares many features with the other traditionally-minded oil-producing states in the region. The decrees of the Revolutionary Command Council in recent years have authorized the privatization of major economic sectors. And in its regional and international relations, the Iraq of the 1980s aligned itself with the conservative Arab states and the Western powers, an alliance, however, which was shattered by Iraq's invasion of Kuwait in August 1990.

Yet Iraq's experience in 1958 was unquestionably revolutionary. The revolutionary moment was the month of July, but the revolutionary process can be located in the two decades preceding and following – from the *Wathbah* ('uprising') of January 1948 to the second Baathist coup of July 1968. Throughout this period, though the essential revolutionary dynamic was a product of internal social combustion, the revolutionary process bore some imprint of outside intervention from the region and from the great powers.

Hanna Batatu's examination of Iraq's social classes and revolutionary movements was barely concerned, in its nearly 1,300 pages of text and data, with the role of outside powers. Egypt and Syria, of course, figure in parts of his account, for they comprised the regional dynamic of Iraq's revolutionary struggle in the 1950s. The great powers, however, remain very much part of the backdrop.

Batatu artfully renders the structure of the social classes of the old order, and the ways in which those classes were influenced by Iraq's absorption into the world market in the late nineteenth and twentieth centuries. Later, his narrative conscientiously depicts the mortal combat between Communist and nationalist forces in the first convulsive years of the Revolution, and in doing so sheds light on the rivalries in Mosul and Kirkuk as well as the competition for political allegiances in the sprawling squatter neighbourhoods of Baghdad.

For the most part the hand of Britain, which after all supported Iraq's pre-revolutionary ruling strata and played a controlling role in the country's economic development, is inferred and implicit, though at certain points – the clashes over the still-born 1948 Portsmouth Agreement revising Anglo–Iraqi obligations, for instance – this ingredient is concisely present.

This is as it should be, for Batatu set out to record the history of classes and movements. In Batatu's book, it is the experiences of Iraqis caught up in a maelstrom of social change that resonate in the reader's mind, rather than abstract constructs of political science. But when this reader returned to Batatu's book a decade later, he found a history of the interventionist role of foreign powers that is in many ways more satisfying than that offered by the scores of books and monographs devoted exclusively to this topic.

If there is not here a detailed account of American plotting to counter the revolutionary outbursts of the 1950s, for instance, we at least have a fully nuanced understanding of why the Eisenhower administration moved its military forces into an interventionist posture, and, to a greater extent, of why Washington concluded that there remained in Iraq in the days after the Revolution no political forces of counterrevolution that could make intervention viable. Indeed, from Washington's vantage-point the events of July 1958 in Iraq anticipated those of February 1979 in Iran: a thoroughgoing political revolution tearing apart a core regime (Baghdad Pact, Nixon Doctrine), casting serious doubt on the stability of all pro-Western states in the region and raising fears of the 'complete elimination of Western influence in the Middle East'. Both revolutions prompted US military intervention elsewhere in the region to counter the 'trend toward chaos'.[1]

## II

Batatu's most complete discussion of great power influence concerns the important relations between the Iraq Communist Party and the Soviet Union. The party's base among working people as well as the intelligentsia, and its attention to the causes of economic and social oppression, made it the single most powerful political force in Iraqi society in the years surrounding the 1958 Revolution. The Soviet Union's own revolutionary history and its rhetorical championing of the rights of oppressed peoples everywhere earned it considerable political credit among other active opposition forces as well.

At key junctures, by Batatu's reckoning, state interests of the Soviet Union led to party stances and decisions that facilitated the devastating blows inflicted on the Communists by the monarchy and later by the Baath. Three distinct instances stand out: the Soviet stand on the partition of Palestine in 1947–48; the cautionary advice Moscow evidently proffered to its Iraqi comrades during the flood tide following the Revolution; and the ensnarements of co-optation and repression of the 1960s and 1970s that followed the Soviet emphasis on close collaboration with regimes such as Iraq following a 'non-capitalist road'.

The Soviet decision to support the United Nations' partition plan for Palestine in November 1947, and subsequent recognition of the new state of Israel in May 1948, had devastating consequences for Communist parties throughout the Arab world. Batatu details the impact in Iraq. There seem to be good grounds for faulting, with Batatu, Moscow's 'overestimation of the strength and possibilities of the Jewish left' and, more to the point, its 'insufficient awareness of the widening chasm dividing [broad segments of the Arab people] from their traditional, Western-oriented rulers' (602–3).[2] But on a key point his critique seems lacking. The proof of Soviet error, Batatu writes, 'lies in its episodic character: it had to be abandoned within less than two years'(602). Here Batatu seems to equate Moscow's momentary pro-Israel orientation with Soviet support for partition and creation of the state of Israel. On this point the Soviets have remained remarkably consistent to this day, and it would seem that, whatever elements of tactics and opportunism may have contributed to the initial decision, there was also an aspect of principle, of support for self-determination against nationalist exclusivity, which Batatu does not address.

Concerning the consequences in Iraq, however, Batatu writes convincingly that it 'weakened [Communist] authority among Arab workmen, disoriented and demoralized their supporters, tangibly reduced their ranks, and created the psychological preconditions for the ruthless suppression by the police of their cadres and organizations' (603). This had a number of results which Batatu, in his thorough manner, spells out elsewhere: one was the rise of Kurds to the leadership of the party and a consequent lack of attention to 'Arab issues' throughout the mid-1950s.

Batatu notes that there was another factor operating here as well. The Soviets under Stalin had adopted a stance of unremitting hostility toward the 'national-bourgeois' parties leading independence struggles in the Third World; Batatu cites one E. Zhukov, a specialist on the East, condemning (in 1949) the 'reactionary national bourgeois ideology in its various forms, be it Kemalism or Ghandism, Zionism or pan-Arabism' (821). Only after the Kremlin 'thaw' following Stalin's death did Iraqi Communist Party engagement with the pan-Arab cause revive.

This Soviet shift coincided with important developments in the Arab world: leadership of the pan-Arab movement passed from conservative to revolutionary hands; nationalists and Communists were compelled to unite against the Baghdad Pact and its premise of imperialist intervention; Gamal Abdel Nasser in Egypt embodied a progressive agenda for Arab unity; and Egypt and Syria had turned to the Soviet Union for military and economic aid. Batatu, perhaps wisely, does not attempt to assign different weights to these factors in accounting for the new correspondence of Communist and Arab nationalist interests. Yet one detects here too a thread of Soviet state interest in this set of developments, which at this time does not occasion Batatu's critical comment, though it contained some seeds of disasters to come.

Iraq's political history after its revolution, in the 1960s and 1970s, suggests that Moscow's alignment with 'national bourgeois' regimes could be at least as deadly to local Communists as the fierce hostility of the 'left period' associated with Stalin. But that is to jump ahead of what seems to be the turning-point in Batatu's narrative: the moment extending from the Mosul revolt of March 1959 through the Communist Party demand of 28 April 1959 for a formal role in Qasim's government, to the decision of the Communists in the days of 20–22 May 1959 to call off the 'educational' campaign for seats in the cabinet.

Batatu evokes the significance of this moment with powerful word strokes. The alliance between Communists and Arab nationalists, not only in Iraq but in Syria and Egypt as well, had come apart with the success of Iraq's Revolution on 'Bastille Day' 1958. The mutual antagonism of Nasserists and Baathists was displaced chiefly by their shared aversion to Communist leadership. Qasim's determination to remain autonomous from the new United Arab Republic created a unique opportunity for Iraq's Communists, an opportunity interpreted as a threat by nationalist and conservative forces well beyond Iraq's borders. 'In view of the origins and the nature of the forces involved', Batatu writes, 'the struggle could not but exceed the confines of Iraq . . . Communists and nationalists were thrown sharply into adversary roles. The struggle also precipitated a crisis in relations between the UAR and the Soviet Union' (861).

Ultimately, in Egypt and elsewhere, Moscow would accept the verdict of Muhammad Haikal: '[In] our country the friends of the Soviet Union are greater than the number of Communists' (as quoted by Batatu: 863). It was in Iraq, however, that the decisive struggle between Arab Communists and Arab nationalists was fought: 'a central fact in contemporary Arab history, truly tragic and, in a high degree, decisive' (864). The physical battlegrounds were in Mosul and Kirkuk, for precise reasons that Batatu details. But the Communists were not defeated here, and Batatu poses the question explicitly: why did they not press their advantage when Qasim refused their demand to join the government?

His answer is not nearly so explicit. The Communists feared that much of their popular support was new and opportunistic, and might evaporate if the party were to instigate a head-to-head confrontation with the popular Qasim. At one point Batatu describes the core of the conflict in terms of concrete class interests: in March 1959, he writes:

the real initiative belonged to the Communists . . . the laborers and the poor, regardless of race or religion, feeling their strength, were voicing openly their desires and expectations, while property owners and conservative people looked with eyes of alarm at the unusual processes around them and, in their great number, pinned their hopes upon the nationalists . . . (860)

A few pages later, however, he takes refuge in abstractions, characterizing the conflict between Communists and Arab nationalists, and Baathists in particular, as 'immanent in the historical situation and unavoidable. It flowed from the very inner course of development of communism and of pan-Arabism . . . from the intolerance of any competition, whether in the sphere of ideas or of power' (865).

Ultimately, Batatu invokes in the most direct and immediate way in his entire book the international context, the contest between the two rival powers, the United States and the Soviet Union. In Washington, CIA chief Allen Dulles called the situation in Iraq 'the most dangerous in the world today' (899). 'Perhaps the factor that had the greatest weight in the decision to beat a retreat', Batatu writes, 'was the pressure that the Communist Party of the Soviet Union appears to have brought to bear upon the Iraqi Communist leadership' (903). Moscow was not willing to jeopardize its relations with Nasser any further, or the campaign for 'peaceful coexistence' with Washington and specifically Krushchev's upcoming visit to the US. It seemed a distinct possibility that a Communist campaign for a government role would provoke Western intervention, supported by conservative and nationalist Arab regimes alike. In such a setting there would be nothing Moscow could do to save the situation.

From the retreat of May 1959 followed the massacres of February 1963, but, in Batatu's judgement, 'that the retreat in 1959 was a mistake is not so obvious'. Again he suggests that the great power factor was determinant: 'the party does not appear to have had much of a choice, if only because of the world distribution of forces and its own international links' (993).

This is a curious and not quite satisfactory resolution, and one senses the author's tentativeness in advancing it at all. The evidence of Soviet pressure on the Iraqi leadership does not seem conclusive, though the characterization of the Soviet and by extension the Iraqi Communist dilemma seems accurate, and it certainly must have been a factor. But was it as decisive as this reading suggests?

The term 'tragedy' is much misused by contemporary American political analysts, ascribing to fate the all too wilful and self-serving decisions of powerful elites – I am thinking here of the unfortunate subtitle, and in a sense subtext, of James Bill's otherwise excellent recent study of US–Iranian relations.[3] Batatu refreshingly avoids the term, yet in his thoroughness he conveys a powerful sense that, indeed, 'political forces get entangled in complicated series of causes which they themselves did not set in motion, and which are largely beyond their power to master' (994). It almost seems that Batatu's completeness in threading together the social and political history of this place and time makes it impossible to confer any satisfactory ranking on the ingredients of the disaster of February 1963 and the months that followed. In the reflective sorting of elements and influences, the 'world distribution of forces' deserves a place, last perhaps for purposes of narrative, but it is nevertheless probably not the most decisive factor.

The rest of the story is anti-climactic. The extremity of the Baath's anti-Communist vengeance in 1963 thoroughly alienated that short-lived regime from the Soviet camp. The rule of the Nasserist Arif brothers, however, coincided with Soviet endorsement of Gamal Abdel Nasser, which redounded on Soviet–Iraqi relations. Moscow resumed arms sales to Iraq; the July 1964 nationalization by decree of Iraq's largest enterprises appeared to lend substance to the 'road of non-capitalist development' line emanating from Moscow, all of which inclined the Iraqi Communist Party to look towards the Arif regime for its political future. A conference of Communist parties in Prague in December 1964 noted the 'similarity and, on many principal issues, the identity of aims and programs' between 'the two greatest progressive forces in the Arab East, the supporters of Cairo's policy on the one hand and the Communists and progressives on the other' (1038). The plenum of the Central Committee meeting in Baghdad in August 1964 had anticipated this rhetoric in its manifesto: 'the Plenum views the question of Arab unity in the light of the new phenomena emerging on the Arab scene, the phenomena of non-capitalist development ... ' (1037). This 'August Line' implicitly renounced any drive to capture state power: 'If we should admit of the possibility of Iraq developing along non-capitalist lines, it would inevitably follow that we could not steer a course toward the conquest of power by our party' (1039).

The full implementation of this policy was delayed nearly a decade. The reality of political life under the Arifs hardly allowed the Communists to perceive progressive possibilities in the regime, and pressure from rank-and-file party members eventually forced the leadership to adopt a stance of opposition. There emerged a militant left faction of the Iraqi Communist Party which took the name Central Command. Batatu judges them 'unrealistic' but at the same time 'pointing a way out of the dead-end alley to which the movement had been driven by its connection with the Soviet Union' (1071). To some extent responding to this challenge, the main organization (Central Committee) convened a Third National Conference in December 1967, which called for 'radical changes in the composition, policies and ideology of the regimes in the liberated

Arab countries' (ibid.) – mentioning Egypt and Syria and implying Iraq as well. Despite the Central Committee's affirmation of solidarity with the Soviet Union, Moscow responded by shutting down the 'Voice of the Iraqi People' transmitters in Eastern Europe (1072).

## III

Batatu's account basically stops in 1968. His chapter on the new Baath regime that took power in that year provides a valuable description of the party command, noting the ways in which it had changed since 1963. 'It is clear', he concludes, that it 'reposes ultimately upon a narrow social foundation' (1093). Relations between the regime and the Communists, even the pro-Moscow Central Committee Communists, alternated between bad and gruesome, and Batatu's account remains one of the best we have in English. Only in 1972–73, in the context of renewed Iranian aid to the Kurdish insurgency, the nationalization of the Iraq Petroleum Company, and the Treaty of Friendship and Co-operation with the Soviet Union, did the party accede to the regime's blandishments to join the government – 'perhaps not uninfluenced by advice from Premier Alexei N. Kosygin' (1109). On the last page of his narrative, Batatu writes that the party 'finally garnered some fruits from its commitment to a legal and evolutionary political path' – including a government announcement that it would tear down Nihayah Palace, the infamous torture centre where so many Communists and other regime opponents had come to horrible ends.

Batatu ends with an important and prescient 'however'. The 1975 Algiers settlement between Baghdad and Tehran and the collapse of the Kurdish insurgency 'sensibly changed' the conditions underlying the Communist alliance with the Baath. Indeed, over the next several years the party again came under severe repression, and scores of Communists were executed in 1978, the year that Batatu's book appeared. In the National Assembly 'elections' of 1980, Communists were excluded on the grounds that they 'follow a foreign line'. Today the party is in opposition to the regime and, it seems, in its greater part in exile.

Iraq's alignment in the 1980s among the great powers was most remarkable, and limitations of space confine us here to some brief comments. In the course of an eight-year war, in the most prolific oil-producing part of the globe, less than a thousand miles from the borders of one of the superpowers, Iraq managed to manoeuvre itself into alliance, partly formal and partly tacit, with all the major world powers and most of those in the region as well.

At one level this owes mainly to Iraq's adversary, Iran. If Iraq's alignment with the Soviet Union in the 1960s through the mid-1970s was a consequence of its own revolution and the struggle for internal hegemony and consolidation that ensued, then the curious constellation of states aligned with Baghdad in the 1980s, including the Soviet Union, was a consequence of the second major revolution in the Gulf, that which swept the Shah from power in 1978–79. The Iranian Revolution broke up local Gulf power relationships and fuelled Saddam Hussein's pretensions to regional hegemony. It was not Saddam's strength but his weakness that most accounted for his wartime enmeshment with the great powers. Saddam had proposed that Iraq would be the instrument of counterrevolution in the Gulf in the 1980s and had to resign himself to the fact that it would be only the instrument of containment. In the summer of 1990, it was his own regime that became the object of containment.

Iraq's shifting international alignment has apparently less to do with internal upheaval and the struggle of domestic political forces for hegemony, and more to do with the conflict between competing nationalisms and nation-states.[4] In the 1980s, for the Soviet Union and the United States, Iraq was less likely than Iran to upset their separate, competing interests in the region. In Moscow's eyes, supporting the territorial integrity of Iraq was not the same as supporting Saddam's pretensions to be a regional power, and any likely alternative to continued rule by the Baath would be even more hostile to Soviet interests in the region.[5] For Washington, the equation was even simpler: in the words of Brookings analyst Thomas McNaugher, 'Iran's strength makes Iraq important.'[6] Today, following Iraq's aggression of August 1990, the great powers who helped to engender Iraqi military might are attempting to construct a regional alliance to offset this.

Yet it would be too easy to lose sight of the fact that it is a dialectic of internal and external forces, trends and developments that produce these calculations. In a recent offering by the Council on Foreign Relations, Paul Jabber provided a usefully concise and unvarnished statement of US interests in the region: 'it is in the vital military and economic interest of both the United States and the Western Alliance to maintain unfettered access to the world's largest oil reserves at reasonable, acceptable prices.' In case we miss the point, he reiterates a paragraph later that: 'What is at issue is the price.' In practice, this interest can best be secured 'through the preservation of a regional system in the Gulf that safeguards the ability of the various local countries to set their own policies freely' – that is, to set prices 'acceptable' to the West. 'The emergence of any hegemonic power in the Gulf – whether local or external to the region ... could be disastrous for the West.'[7] McNaugher, reflecting American strategic thinking in the midst of the Gulf war, writes that

Either state [Iran or Iraq], unchecked by the other, could pose perhaps the most serious threat that the GCC [Gulf Co-operation Council] states could face. A balance between these two states is crucial to GCC security and to the protection of Western interests.[8]

This solicitude for preserving a 'balance' between Iran and Iraq is largely, though not uniquely, a post-Khomeini phenomenon. In the early 1950s, Britain and the United States and their oil companies had used Iraq together with other Arab states to isolate and combat Iran's efforts under Muhammad Mossadiq to assert Iranian control over its oil resources. In the 1960s and 1970s, it was Iran's turn to be used against Iraqi oil nationalism, and then there was little concern for 'balance'. It was on the way home from the 'detente summit' in Moscow in May 1972 that Kissinger and Nixon stopped in Tehran and subscribed to the Shah's campaign to establish unrivalled Iranian hegemony in the Gulf and, incidentally, to revive the Kurdish insurgency against Baghdad.[9]

From the vantage-point of an observer in Washington, it is easy enough to see Iraq as a mere catspaw in the great power games in the Gulf. But Hanna Batatu's work demonstrates with impressive clarity the fact that, for all the manipulative influence of outside powers on political developments in states such as Iraq, the internal dynamics of reform, revolution and repression play a formative role in producing regional and international alignments. The fact that it is not possible to conduct the same sort of inquiry into the Iraq of the 1970s and 1980s should not make us lose sight of this fundamental point.

## Notes

1. A good presentation of US manoeuvrings in 1958 can be found in Alan Dowty, *Middle East Crisis: US Decision-Making in 1958, 1970 and 1973* (Berkeley and Los Angeles, 1984).

2. All page references are to Hanna Batatu, *The Old Social Classes and the Revolutionary Movements of Iraq* (Princeton, 1978).

3. James Bill, *The Eagle and the Lion: the Tragedy of American–Iranian Relations* (New Haven, 1988).

4. Fred Halliday makes this point in relation to the Middle East generally in 'Gorbachev and the "Arab Syndrome": Soviet Policy in the Middle East', *World Policy Journal* (Summer 1987), pp. 415–42.

5. Roderic Pitty, 'Soviet Perceptions of Iraq', *Middle East Report*, 151 (March–April 1988), pp. 23–27.

6. Thomas McNaugher, *Arms and Oil: US Military Strategy and the Persian Gulf* (Washington, 198?), p. 177.

7. Paul Jabber et al., *Great Power Interests in the Persian Gulf* (New York, 1989), p. 2.

8. McNaugher, *Arms and Oil*, p. 177.

9. Two excellent accounts of US–Soviet relations and detente's 'linkage' to questions of intervention in the Third World are Raymond Garthoff, *Detente and Confrontation: American–Soviet Relations from Nixon to Reagan* (Washington, 1985) and Fred Halliday, *The Making of the Second Cold War* (London, 1983).

# 6

# The Impact of the Iraqi Revolution on the Arab World

## RASHID KHALIDI

I

Much can be learned about the course of development of the Arab world in the modern era from an examination of a major rupture such as the Iraqi Revolution, coming at a crucial time and in a crucial place. Within its broader focus, Hanna Batatu's *The Old Social Classes and the Revolutionary Movements of Iraq*[1] offers at least two lessons relevant to the theme of this chapter. The first concerns similarities in the processes of social development in several Arab countries in the middle of this century. Particularly notable is the phenomenon of the emergence of parties and other political forces based in the military, the trade unions, the intelligentsia and other parts of society, which were firmly based in the middle and lower middle classes, and whose members often had rural roots. In a number of Arab countries in the 1950s, notably Egypt, Iraq, Syria, Jordan and Lebanon, these groupings launched a forceful challenge to the old social order, although they were ultimately successful in seizing power only in the first three.

Of course the idea that the old social classes (or the notables, to use Albert Hourani's term; or the feudal classes to use the popular parlance of the day) were losing power and being replaced by lower-class elements was a common one in the Arab world in the 1960s and early 1970s. At that time, when new revolutionary regimes were being established in the Sudan, Libya and South Yemen, this seemed like an inevitable process, and the durability of the remaining Arab monarchies was as yet unforeseen. *Infitah* (the 'opening up'), which in Hanna Batatu's word was 'in practice a kind of economic

Thermidor'[2] was then, of course, still in the future. What Batatu did in his book was to explain the social basis of this process and give it a firm theoretical and empirical underpinning. He also pointed out – against the prevailing wisdom – that there was nothing inevitable or transcendent about the process he was describing, but that it was rooted in the specificities of the countries in which it took place.

The second important lesson is related to the first: while it is necessary to approach phenomena in the Arab world such as classes, parties or ideologies, within the context of the new twentieth-century nation-states, at the same time one must take into account their trans-national nature. This helps to explain several common processes which transcend the boundaries between the Arab states, such as the rise to power through military *coups d'état* of several predominantly middle-class regimes. This was emphasized even more clearly a few years after the appearance of *The Old Social Classes* in Batatu's later work, *The Egyptian, Syrian and Iraqi Revolutions*.[3]

These linkages become apparent only after studying, from a comparative perspective, the impact of the post-1952 revolutionary regime in Egypt on several other Arab countries, including Syria, Lebanon and Iraq (especially in the period 1955–58), and the impact on Iraq of the teachings of the Syrian Baath Party, as well as the example of the Egyptian Free Officers. Such linkages are not, of course, unprecedented, either in the Middle East or elsewhere. What is extraordinary, however, is the extent to which, rather than being a single unit, the Arab world seems to be a clearly defined sub-system of the international system, with its own boundaries, its own rules, and its own internal channels of influence. Certain events or ideas thus have a specific impact within these boundaries but not necessarily beyond them; likewise, certain behaviours are acceptable within them but not beyond, and vice versa. Largely as a function of the powerful impact of a single written language, and of the existence of a limited number of influential cultural and intellectual centres such as Cairo and Beirut, there is common discourse within this system which helps to define it as a separate sub-system, one which does not extend to other Islamic or developing countries, despite many parallels and similarities with them.

At the same time, in spite of its relative coherence, in the modern era this sub-system has shown itself highly permeable to external influences. The impact of etatist, nationalist and liberal ideologies in the first half of this century, the ideological impact of Communism from the 1940s until the 1960s, and the economic pressures of the capitalist world market are among the most salient of recent examples. To complete the paradox of cohesion yet separateness, all of the sub-units of this Arab system – its component states – are, for many purposes, completely unique and distinct.

## II

The above analysis naturally is relevant to any attempt to assess the impact of the Iraqi Revolution on other Arab countries. This impact was not a simple one. In actuality, the specificities of Iraq and its troubled experiences from 1958 until 1963 guaranteed that there would be no simple replication or imitation of the example of its revolution. For similar reasons it was also impossible to replicate the experience of Egypt, but that was not yet known or understood at the time. The Egyptian model was indeed for a time widely imitated, and many attempts were made to 'export' or 'import' one or other of its features. Thus, at least four Arab coups after 1952 (Iraq, North Yemen, Libya and the Sudan) were carried out by groups of 'Free Officers'.

None the less, the July 1958 Revolution in Iraq reverberated for a long time, and in many different ways, in the Arab world. There were many reasons for this. One of them was that it seemed to many Arabs at the time to constitute part of a trend, an irreversible tide of Arab nationalist revolutions led by military officers, sweeping away corrupt oligarchies linked to imperialism. Another was that it had taken place in Iraq, one of the largest, wealthiest and most powerful of Arab countries, a bastion of British imperial power in the region for over four decades, and a state which, with its oil revenues and powerful army, had long been a pillar of the status quo in the region. Moreover, coming in the wake of the unification of Egypt and Syria in the United Arab Republic only months earlier, the Iraqi Revolution, carried out like that of Egypt by a group of 'Free Officers', seemed to herald further steps towards Arab unity along a Nasserist path.

In consequence of these expectations regarding the Iraqi Revolution, for a short time afterwards there were no limits to the jubilation among some in the Arab world, or to the trepidation among others. Outside the region, Western governments seemed exceedingly fearful of a regional domino effect. Implicitly at least, some of their leaders believed the inflated rhetoric of Arab nationalism, and apparently equated it with the much-feared bogey of Communism.

Acting on these concerns, Britain moved immediately to shore up its remaining Hashemite client in the region, by despatching troops to the aid of King Hussein of Jordan. The Iraqi Revolution was a crushing blow to Britain's standing in the Middle East, particularly after the humiliation of the Suez fiasco. Britain was determined to prevent any further erosion of its position. The United States, too, reacted, landing marines and soldiers in Lebanon in response to a request made by President Chamoun in May and politely ignored until the events in Baghdad. Simultaneously, the destruction of the Hashemite regime in Iraq, the former rival of the Saudi government, drove the latter even closer to the United States. This confirmed its shift from a pro-Egyptian orientation, which had begun early in 1957 when King Saud, during a visit to Washington, embraced the Eisenhower Doctrine in return for American agreement to sell the kingdom weapons for the first time.

The extraordinary moves made by Britain and the United States in July 1958 are evidence that the Iraqi Revolution led many at the time to believe that, unless drastic action were taken, there might be no stopping the overthrow of Arab monarchies and the classes with which they were linked, and no stopping the shattering of ties with Western powers on which they depended. However, today, after an interval of more than three decades, 1958 in Iraq can be seen as the last of a series of thoroughgoing revolutionary upheavals in the *mashriq* (Arab East), indeed in the Arab world as a whole, and in many ways the most revolutionary of them all. In a sense, it marked the apogee of the Arab radical trend. Afterwards, the 1958 interventions of Britain and the United States and the crucial earlier shift in Saudi Arabia's regional alignment helped to create a barrier against the revolutionary tide in Jordan, Lebanon and parts of the Arabian Peninsula which, unlikely though it may have seemed at the time, was never to be breached. The bitter domestic sequels of the Iraqi Revolution in turn had an impact on this trend.

Revolutions were still to come in Algeria, North and South Yemen, Libya and the Sudan. But while all of them proclaimed their debt to the revolutions of Egypt, Syria and Iraq, most particularly the former, the upheavals in these three core countries of the Arab world had an impact, and certain elements in common, which were not shared by the later ones in the outlying Arab lands. Whether it was because of the distorting influence of a prolonged and brutal struggle with colonialism (as in Algeria, Libya and South Yemen), the abortive nature of the revolution itself (as in North Yemen), the successful interventions of conservative powers, the specificities of the societies involved, or the fact that they took place on the peripheries of the Arab system, these later ruptures with the existing pattern in the outlying countries differed in a number of significant ways from those in Egypt, Syria and Iraq.

Moreover, those places where revolutions were either aborted or did not take place took on a crucial importance, whether in the case of Jordan, Lebanon and Saudi Arabia, or Oman and the Gulf principalities. They marked not only the scenes of the first defeats for the Arab 'revolutionary tide', but also over time came to constitute the *points d'appui* for the successful conservative strategy developed by King Faisal and the Western powers in the 1960s and 1970s. This strategy has seemingly been vindicated by an *infitah*, fuelled by oil revenues and spreading from Egypt to other formerly radical nationalist regimes, which has produced a type of convergence between them and their conservative former rivals.[4]

It is important to look at the impact of the Iraqi Revolution on the Arab world in light of this post-1958 ebbtide, because in some ways this revolution can now be seen as marking the end of the age of innocence – and of the succession of easy victories – for Arab revolutionary nationalism in its initial emotional, undifferentiated form. Things would never again be as simple as they seemed in the immediate aftermath of the fall of the monarchy in Baghdad in July 1958. To understand why, it is necessary to examine some of the specific effects of this event in the Arab world.

## III

The major inter-Arab effects of the Iraqi Revolution of 1958 can be examined under three interrelated headings:

(1) Problems of nation-state nationalism (which Batatu calls either 'Iraqism' or 'particularism' in the Iraqi context)[5] versus pan-Arabism.
(2) Conflicts between Arab Communist parties and their Arabist rivals, notably the Baath and Nasserists.
(3) Problems for Arab states with links to the Soviet Union resulting from the UAR–Iraq conflict.

Although these issues are clearly closely connected with one another, for analytical purposes they will be dealt with separately, in spite of the inevitable resulting overlap and repetition. It is important to stress that the following treatment will necessarily be synoptic rather than exhaustive, and intended simply to suggest directions for possible future attention.

(1) The aftermath of the Iraqi Revolution marked one of the first moments in the short history of pan-Arabism when it came into open conflict with nation-state nationalism or particularism on a regional scale. Such conflicts had of course arisen previously within the context of the domestic politics of a single Arab state, notably in Iraqi politics in the 1936–37 period, but 1958 marked the first time such a clash had taken on regional dimensions, with the possible exception of the brief interlude of Arab independence in Syria from 1918 until 1920. At that time, a major element of the Damascene elite – and with them at times King Faisal – had often advocated the advancement and protection of the interests of the Syrian state, in opposition to many Palestinians and Iraqis involved in the Arab government in Damascus, who demanded a less narrowly based, more pan-Arab policy.[6]

Circumstances after the Iraqi Revolution were naturally quite different from in Damascus forty years earlier, although in some sense what was at stake was the same disagreement over the limits of the polity: particularist or pan-Arab. While this conflict worked itself out after 1958 strictly within the context of Iraqi politics, in the deadly struggle between Qasim and the Communists on one side, and Arif, the Baath and the Nasserists on the other, it had regional implications, and soon came to involve many regional actors. The regional clash which resulted was unavoidable, in large measure because of the fragmented nature of Iraqi society and politics, and the fragile nature of the Iraqi polity, highly penetrated as it was by external forces. Moreover, given the logic of the pan-Arabism which motivated the creation of the United Arab Republic, it was inevitably geared to inclusion of other Arab states, and involvement in their affairs. As Batatu remarks of this new entity: 'by the very principle of its being, it had an inherent tendency to reach out beyond its frontiers.'[7]

Even accepting the powerful impetus of such logic, it is important to note that it was often not as a consequence of the initiative of Abdel Nasser that the UAR became involved in Iraqi internal affairs, or indeed those of other Arab states such as Lebanon, Jordan, Yemen and Saudi Arabia, but rather as a result of the ideological zeal of his local partisans. In many cases this was a result of their desire to compensate for their internal weakness in a given country with the external support of their powerful Egyptian patron. This applied both to the Syrian Baath Party during the original union beween Egypt and Syria in early 1958, and to the Baath in Iraq immediately after the 1958 Revolution, when the party precipitated a controversy by its advocacy of Iraqi amalgamation with the UAR. Whereas in Syria the Communist Party had refrained from opposing the Baath over this issue in 1957, in spite of Khalid Bakdash's well-founded misgivings, this was not the case in Iraq. There, the Communists were far stronger, and had the examples of the fate of both Egyptian and Syrian Communists to warn them. As a result, they immediately opposed the Baath and the idea of union. In doing so, they were 'steering an out-and-out particularist course', as Batatu puts it.[8]

Thus, while Syria's union with Egypt did not raise the issue of particularism versus pan-Arabism, at least not at first, the Iraqi Revolution did so almost from the very beginning. In the aftermath of the defeat of Arif and his allies in internal power struggles during the first months of the new regime, it was natural that the pan-Arab forces in Iraq should gravitate to their powerful external patron, and natural in turn that Abdel Nasser should respond to their appeals. At the same time, it was equally natural that, in their opposition to the unionist and pan-Arabist trend, the Iraqi Communists should find themselves challenging not only local Arab nationalists, but also their patron in Egypt.

The slogan with which the Communists supported Qasim – 'the Sole Leader' – was not just a repudiation of Arif and the other Iraqi Free Officers; simultaneously, and in a much more important sense, it was a repudiation of the regional leadership of Abdel Nasser, and a quasi-declaration of Iraqi independence from him. The very title which the Communists conferred on Qasim served as as red rag to a bull for his opponents, both within the country and without. It was perceived to be, and was meant as, a challenge to Nasser in his newly-won dignity as leader of the Arabs after Suez and the union with Syria. Nasser's supporters would not have allowed him to leave it unanswered, even had he desired to do so. For if he was not the pre-eminent Arab leader, then where did that leave his followers in other Arab countries? The stage was set for a particularly violent confrontation, which erupted first in Mosul, and continued to break out periodically in different forms in Iraqi politics for many years thereafter.

In consequence, Iraq became for a time the primary arena for inter-Arab and other regional conflicts, just as Syria had been until the 1958 union, as is described by Patrick Seale in *The Struggle for Syria*,[9] and just as Lebanon was to become from 1975 until the present. In the same way that the nature of pan-Arabism in the early and mid-1950s was profoundly affected by the specific circumstances of Syria where this arena was located, so was the struggle between pan-Arabism and particularism in the Arab world shaped by the specificities of Iraq, notably its ethnic divisions and the presence of a powerful, deeply-rooted Communist party. Although the post-1958 period was the first time since 1920 that pan-Arabism had clashed so intensely and on a regional scale with nation-state particularism, this conflict between what one scholar has called *raison d'état* and *raison de la nation*[10] was to become a regular feature of Arab politics from this point on. As Batatu points out, it was the misfortune of the Iraqi Communist Party to be standing in the way when this first collision came.[11]

(2) Arab Communist parties had clashed with pan-Arab forces and with Nasser before July 1958. But whether in Egypt after the 1952 Revolution, or in Syria after the union with Egypt, these conflicts were essentially restricted to the confines of the politics of one Arab state. Evidence for this assertion can be found in the failure of the Syrian Communist Party to take sufficient heed of the earlier fate of their Egyptian comrades under Nasser in the lead-up to the union. Although Khalid Bakdash was clearly troubled by this precedent, as he showed by his departure from Syria just as the union took place, neither he nor the party actively opposed unity at this stage, and indeed in some ways they precipitated it by their tactical miscalculations, and their *muzayada* ('outbidding') of the Syrian Baath.[12]

The clash which erupted in Iraq after July 1958 was different from earlier Communist–Arabist disputes in its intensity, its scope and its duration. It was notable also because it poisoned relations between Communists and pan-Arabists in most parts of the Arab world, provoking ideological attacks from both sides, and from their partisans inside and outside Iraq, which went far beyond the specifics of the struggle for power in that country. Arab Communist parties in Egypt and Syria, and Arab Communists in general, came to be depicted as disloyal not only to the Arab nation, but also to the specific Arab nation-states in which they were located. This was a particularly heinous sin in the United Arab Republic, which happened at that moment to be the incarnation of Arabism. On the other hand, in a reversion to heavy-handed ideological judgements worthy of a Zhdanov, Arab nationalism, whether in its Baathist or its Nasserist form, came to be described by the Communists as reactionary, and opposed to the social progress and the independent development of individual Arab countries.

Not all of this mud stuck, of course, and many of the more heated and exaggerated charges were eventually either retracted or forgotten. It was particularly easy for Egyptians, who were by far the least affected (and who shed far less of one another's blood), to put these polemics behind them when circumstances changed. But the bloodshed in Mosul and Kirkuk in March and July 1959, and later the far more horrible slaughter when the Iraqi Communists in their turn were hunted down and killed, left an indelible imprint on much of the Arab world. The enmities and some of the charges arising out of this conflict were hard to forget, not only for Iraqis but also for many others.

The end result was a deep estrangement of Arab Communism from other ideological currents in this period, particularly in Iraq, but in other parts of the Arab *mashriq* as well, and to a lesser extent in Egypt. In some measure, these differences between parties and ideologies were a reflection of conflicts between the distinct social groups in which they were rooted. But, tragically, this ideological dispute envenomed relations between social groups and classes in the Arab world whose interests could have been reconciled in other circumstances, and who faced far greater joint enemies elsewhere. The long-term consequences of this split – a profound residue of suspicion of Communism in a broad sector of the Arab political spectrum, and a deep distrust of nationalism among those Communists who survived – were to influence Arab politics into the 1970s. They were in some measure to lay the groundwork for the swing to the right which became so apparent in that decade and afterwards in many formerly radical Arab regimes, and also affected the Arab world's still inchoate attitude to the USSR.

(3) Neither Egyptian nor Syrian leaders entered into their new relationship with the Soviet Union in the 1950s without misgivings. Because of long-standing friction with the Communist parties in Cairo and Damascus respectively, and these parties' ties to Moscow, there was more than a little hesitation before the first approaches

were made to the USSR. Another restraining factor for Arab leaders was the cost to be expected in terms of the virulent Western hostility against any state entertaining close relations with the Soviet Union, a hostility which indeed played a major role in precipitating the 1956 Suez conflict.

Suez, however, helped many in the Arab world to overcome these fears, and enhanced measurably the standing there of the USSR.[13] The enhancement of Soviet prestige rubbed off on the Arab Communist parties in Iraq and Syria, and helped to lessen some of the suspicions of them which decades of anti-Communist polemics had helped to foster. But, as Batatu, Oles Smolansky and others have shown,[14] the struggle for power in Iraq after 1958, and the role played by the USSR in supporting, albeit at times lukewarmly, the Iraqi Communists against the pan-Arabists, reconfirmed all the old suspicions of the USSR, and kindled new ones.

After the Krushchev–Nasser polemics of early 1959, Arab states now had to consider their relations with the USSR in an entirely different light. The Soviet Union was still seen by many as a vital counterweight to the West and an indispensable source of aid and arms. But it came to be seen as motivated just as much by narrow national self-interest as were the Western powers, and as tightly linked as these powers to local clients who were potential rivals for power, and who had an agenda which often conflicted with that of the Arab regimes. Indeed, given the destruction through measures such as land reform and nationalization of the social and economic base of the power of the old social classes which had been linked to the Western Powers, and their resulting political eclipse, the Communist parties were in some cases left as the most formidable rivals of the ruling regimes and the pan-Arab parties. This made Soviet links with these parties all the more dangerous in their eyes. These conflicts were further envenomed as US policy-makers at the end of the 1950s and in the early 1960s began to see Arab nationalism and Abdel Nasser as potential tools against the USSR and local Arab Communist parties.

Some of these problems diminished in importance in the wake of the 1961 Syrian secession, which Nasser blamed on his foes on the right rather than those to the left, and after the Yemeni Revolution of 1962 and the resulting inter-Arab polarization, both of which pushed Egypt closer to the USSR. But the damage had been done. The Soviet Union would never be regarded in the same way by the Baath – at least by its right wing, factions of which were to hold power in Syria from 1963 to 1966, and in Iraq from 1968 onwards – or by the Arab Nationalist Movement, a group which provided the shock troops of Nasserism in several Arab countries until the 1967 débâcle. Here, too, can be found some of the roots of later shifts to the right in their international orientation by Arab leaders such as Sadat.

## IV

The Iraqi Revolution can thus be seen to have had a major impact on the rest of the Arab world. In the welter of events which followed, it was often forgotten that a variety of trends which have continued since the late 1950s were profoundly influenced by the Revolution and its aftermath. Hanna Batatu's book, although it is focused on developments inside Iraq itself, enables us to see the roots of this impact, locating them at one and the same time in the specificities of Iraqi society and politics, and in the regional system of which it formed a part.

It can thus be said of *The Old Social Classes* that in addition to being the standard work on Iraq, it gives us also an outstanding analysis of the composition and nature of the Baath Party, the Arab Nationalist Movement, and several Arab Communist parties, as well as of the interplay and interpenetration between Iraq and the rest of the region during a period which marked the height of Nasser's prestige and influence. Batatu's work is an outstanding example of how much can be learned about transcendent regional processes from an examination of a specific case, when this is done from a perspective broad enough to encompass such processes. Among its many merits, it never loses sight of the wider context, the Arab sub-system, even while maintaining a constant sharp focus on the specifities of Iraq.

### Notes

One of the best ways to learn about anything is to teach it. This was what I had to do in the autumn of 1976, when at short notice I was asked to fill in for Hanna Batatu (who was at the time finishing *The Old Social Classes* (see note 1) and teach his course on 'Modern Arab Governments' at the American University in Beirut. When classes started in October, West Beirut suffered occasional artillery barrages, but that was the least of my worries. I had never before taught or studied this topic. It was therefore with some desperation that I read the books in Batatu's syllabus, often only days before my students did so. I soon realized that I was following along lines laid down by someone who had thought very carefully about the modern Arab world. I would like to think that my approach to this subject since then owes something to what I learned in teaching that first course at the AUB.

1. *The Old Social Classes and the Revolutionary Movements of Iraq* (Princeton, 1978).

2. Hanna Batatu, *The Egyptian, Syrian and Iraq Revolutions: Some Observations on Their Underlying Causes and Social Character* (Washington DC, 1983), p. 12.

3. Ibid.

4. See R. Khalidi, 'Social Transformation and Political Power in the "Radical" Arab States', in Adeed Dawisha and I. William Zartman, eds., *Beyond Coercion: The Durability of the Arab State* (New York, 1988), pp. 203–19; and Malcolm Kerr and El-Sayed Yasin, eds., *Rich and Poor States in the Middle East: Egypt and the New Arab Order* (Boulder, 1982). Batatu points to this convergence in *The Egyptian, Syrian and Iraqi Revolutions*, p. 14, noting that: 'the tendency toward state dominance of the economy and the related trend toward big government are as characteristic of the traditionally-oriented as of the radical or quasi-radical Arab countries.'

5. Batatu uses the term 'particularism' to describe Qasim's political orientation (*Old Social Classes*, p. 818), and 'Iraqist' (p. 846) to denote some of Qasim's allies in the officer corps, and earlier to describe the leaders of the 1936 coup (p. 29).

6. See: Muhammad Y. Muslih *The Origins of Palestinian Nationalism* (New York, 1988), pp. 115–54; Philip S. Khoury, *Urban Notables and Arab Nationalism: The Politics of Damascus 1860–1920* (Cambridge, 1983), pp. 75–91; and Malcolm B. Russell, *The First Modern Arab State: Syria under Faysal, 1918–1920* (Minneapolis, 1985), pp. 67–92, 132–52 and 196–208.

7. Batatu, *Old Social Classes*, p. 815.

8. Ibid., p. 831.

9. *The Struggle for Syria: A Study of Post-War Arab Politics, 1945–1958* (2nd ed., New Haven, 1986).

10. Walid Khalidi, 'Thinking the Unthinkable', *Foreign Affairs*, 56, 4 (July 1978), p. 698.

11. *Old Social Classes*, pp. 864–65.

12. This can be followed in Seale, *The Struggle for Syria*, pp. 307–26.

13. For more details, see R. Khalidi, 'Consequences of the Suez Crisis in the Arab World', in Roger Louis and Roger Owen, eds., *Suez 1956: The Crisis and its Consequences* (Oxford, 1989), pp. 377–92.

14. Oles Smolansky, *The Soviet Union and the Arab East under Krushchev* (Lewisburg, 1974).

# 7

# The Social Classes and the Origins of the Revolution

MARION FAROUK-SLUGLETT and PETER SLUGLETT

Over thirty years after the event there are still numerous unanswered questions about the nature and social character of the Iraqi Revolution of 1958. This is partly because our empirical knowledge of Iraqi society at the time – and indeed at the present time – is still much too general, and relies heavily on aggregate and quantitative statistics. This kind of data, though undoubtedly useful, tells the social historian very little about the way in which various strata or groups within society were affected by the overall processes of social transformation taking place around them, and how they reacted, adjusted or recreated their existence within this new and rapidly changing context.

In what follows we shall give an historical outline of the main political conjunctures, both national and international, and the overall social and economic context of the Revolution of 1958. We shall show that the timing of the Revolution and the particular course which it took cannot be 'deduced' from the material conditions existing during the decades immediately preceding it, although these were obviously important. The course and timing of the Revolution were also deeply affected by the political and ideological atmosphere in Iraq and the rest of the Middle East at the time.

This will be followed by a brief discussion concerning our lack of knowledge about the processes of social evolution within Iraq. The focus of this section will be the pioneering work of Hanna Batatu.[1] While recognizing the immensity of Batatu's achievement, we shall suggest that his concentration on the *polarization* between the very rich and the poor has led him to assign less than due weight to the emergence, and perhaps even more importantly to the persistence, of the 'traditional' urban middle strata active in commerce, services and small-scale manufacture.

We shall conclude with a discussion of some of the broader methodological issues raised in attempting to analyse the 'pre- and post-revolutionary' societies of the Middle East in the middle years of the twentieth century. Historians need to bring out the extreme and often bewildering fluidity of these societies before arriving at a more nuanced analysis of their social and political evolution.

## The Role and Influence of Britain in Iraq

Although the Iraqi Revolution of 1958 had numerous and multi-faceted causes, one of the objectives most widely shared among the population was the securing of unconditional political and economic independence from Britain, as well as the abolition of the monarchy and the rest of the political system which Britain had imposed on Iraq since 1921. Under the mandate and monarchy Britain fundamentally influenced if it did not always determine in detail, the course of events. Hence a brief description of the role played by Britain during these years is appropriate.[2]

As applied to the former Arab provinces of the Ottoman Empire, the mandate system was intended by its originators as a form of indirect colonial rule, carried out under the auspices of the League of Nations, which would prepare the various new nation-states for independence.[3] In Iraq the system was underpinned by a small but powerful corps of British 'advisers' whose advice had to be taken; in addition Britain controlled the country's foreign relations and had what amounted to the right of veto in military and financial matters. This involved the defence of Iraq from external threats and the maintenance of internal security.

The national government introduced in 1921 was headed by an outsider, Faisal the son of Hussein of the Hijaz. His selection and election as king had been stage-managed by Britain, a factor which was to stand against him and perhaps more particularly against his successors in the years which followed. Relations between Iraq and Britain were regulated by a treaty, which embodied the terms of the mandate without actually using the word. In fact Faisal did not prove quite as pliant as the British had expected; the logic of his position meant that he and his circle were constantly involved in a delicate balancing act, attempting to muster enough credibility not to be rejected entirely by their countrymen while simultaneously having to remain quietly 'loyal' to Britain.

By 1925, however, the Mosul boundary dispute showed the Iraqi government the true extent of its dependence on Britain. Only British aid, both diplomatic and military, could secure the area for Iraq, keep the Turks out and restrain the Kurds. In consequence the last seven years of the mandate formed a period of close co-operation between the British and Iraqi governments, and reflected a gradual loosening of the formal ties between them. In September 1929 Britain agreed to recommend Iraq for League membership in 1932, and in 1930 a new Anglo–Iraqi treaty was drawn up, designed to come into force when Iraq entered the League. In fact, the country's passage from mandated territory to independent state in October 1932 occasioned little excitement since, however disguised British power and influence might be, it was clear to most Iraqis that they were not the masters of their country. Nevertheless, the end of the mandate gave the ex-Sharifian officers around Faisal a freer hand to exercise control.

In the 1930s the Iraqi Army came into its own as an alternative locus of political power, although, once again, it was free to act only within the parameters which had been defined by Britain. A period of quasi-military rule inaugurated in 1936 came to a head with the formation of a pro-Axis ministry by Rashid Ali in May 1941. The Regent, Abdulillah, and his Prime Minister, Nuri Said, fled the country; Iraqi troops loyal to Rashid Ali made a somewhat quixotic attempt to defy a British invasion force, but were defeated after thirty days. The monarchy was duly restored and another period of British occupation followed.

In addition to the influence they exerted on Iraqi politics, British policies also penetrated deeply into social and economic life. From the beginning of the Mesopotamia Campaign in 1914 the British had consciously bolstered the powers of tribal shaikhs and landlords, both by creating a separate system of jurisdiction for the tribes (which was to remain in force until the Revolution) and by appointing 'suitable' tribal leaders as 'government shaikhs'. Similar policies were pursued by the Iraqi government throughout the mandate and monarchy; in particular, political and tax-levying powers were given to individuals selected for their likely loyalty to the authorities. As early as the mid-1920s informal arrangements had grown up between the government and the larger landowners in many parts of Iraq. In return for their support, the landowners were virtually exempt from taxation and left to their own devices as far as the administration, taxation and policing of their local area was concerned.

Britain's historical links with Iraq derived 'naturally' from the latter's geographical location on the land mass between the Mediterranean and British India. Its strategic interests derived originally from the British Empire in India, so that Iraq also became an important staging-post on the Empire air route and part of the chain of British imperial communications. In the inter-war years Iraq was also an important peace-time training ground for the infant RAF, which proved its worth as a cheap and effective method of maintaining internal security in the southern marshes and the northern mountains of Iraq.

Britain continued to dominate the bulk of Iraq's import and export trade until after the Second World War. Of primary concern to the British was Iraqi oil, which they controlled by a majority holding in what became the Iraq Petroleum Company (IPC) in 1925. By the end of the 1940s the Iraqi government had become substantially dependent on its income from oil, which it received from the IPC on a royalty basis; the fact that the government had not been allowed to acquire any of the equity in IPC came to constitute one of the major grievances of the national independence movement.

The occupation of Iraq by British forces in 1941 brought a series of restrictions and regulations in its wake, but the Second World War itself brought new influences to bear upon the political climate, especially after the entry of the United States and the Soviet Union on the Allied side. Among the population at large political consciousness was heightened by 'the avalanche of declarations, broadcasts, and propaganda literature extolling [the] merits of the democratic way of life and promising improvements in the internal conditions of the country if the democratic Powers won the war'[4], all of which raised expectations which were not to be fulfilled. For a few months (February–May 1946) a more liberal and tolerant cabinet under the premiership of Tawfiq al-Suwaidi held office, but al-Suwaidi was soon forced out of power, and repressive measures were reintroduced under the governments of Arshad al-Umari and Nuri Said.

Although a number of British officials and some British ministers began to have serious doubts about the wisdom of relying too exclusively on Nuri and his close associates ('with the old gang in power this country cannot hope to progress very far'[5]), there were inevitably limitations on the extent to which Britain could bring significant pressure on the 'old gang' to mend its ways. It was a cardinal feature of British policy that vital imperial communications, in terms of bases and other military facilities, as well as access to Iraqi oil, had to be maintained. British official anxieties were temporarily allayed when Iraq's first Shi'i prime minister, Salih Jabr, took office after the elections of 1947. In particular, it was believed that Jabr would be more keenly aware than Nuri Said of the importance of implementing some of the more urgent social reforms.

This optimism was not to last long, as Salih Jabr presided over one of the most repressive regimes to come to power in the Middle East in the first half of the twentieth century. Some of the worst violence took place in January 1948, in the aftermath of the negotiations between the British and Iraqi governments which sought to 'extend the treaty [of 1930] in the guise of revising it'.[6] Popular opposition to the renewal of the treaty exploded in enormous demonstrations in Baghdad, during which several hundred people were killed and injured. Jabr's government resigned, and the treaty negotiations were suspended indefinitely.

## Iraqi Politics under the Mandate and the Monarchy

In theory, Iraq was to function as a constitutional monarchy, with a king, a written constitution, a bicameral legislature and full democratic rights. In fact, and inevitably, given the previous history of the country and the sheer novelty of the system, Iraq was a dependent semi-colonial state, in which the influence of Britain and Britain's local servants, proxies and sympathizers was paramount. Britain and her agents effectively controlled the political arena, whose ground rules always included the maintenance of the status quo and of the British connection. In such circumstances formal political life soon became sterile, and such political parties as were allowed to function amounted generally to temporary combinations between fortuitously like-minded individuals. 'Official' politics became largely divorced from the immediate concerns of the great bulk of the population, so that by the end of the 1940s, if not before, many Iraqis had lost confidence in their government. In consequence, the emerging opposition parties and movements were effectively driven underground. They aimed to bypass or to supersede, rather than to transform, the existing system.

We shall now consider the nature and style of these new organizations. Although the 'rediscovery' of a secular Arab ethnic identity had its origins in the latter part of the nineteenth century, Arab nationalism in the sense of a movement of opposition to Ottoman domination emerged only in the years immediately preceding the First World War. The objectives of the movement ranged from local autonomy for the Arab provinces of the Ottoman Empire to the setting up of an independent Arab state or states, possibly under the aegis of the European powers.

There is a certain limited sense in which the emergence of the Iraqi state after 1920 can be seen in terms of the partial fulfilment of the second of these objectives. It is clear that some of the Iraqis around Faisal, such as Nuri Said, his brother-in-law Jafar al-Askari, Jamil Midfai and the Suwaidis, could claim with some justification in the early 1920s that their service in the new state was not incompatible with the ideals they had advocated before 1914. Of course, as their participation in the administration and politics of Iraq came to require almost total subservience to Britain, the credibility of the nationalism which they professed rapidly began to decline.

With the end of the Ottoman Empire and the division of the former Arab provinces into a number of separate states, a new ideology began to emerge in the Arab world, which was supported in its main essentials by almost all actors on the political stage, ranging from the 'conservative' figures previously mentioned (and their counterparts and contemporaries in other Arab countries) to liberals and Communists. This included a rediscovery of the common Arab heritage and a recognition of the existence of an 'Arab nation' of which Iraq (or Syria, or Palestine) formed an integral part.

In the particular case of Iraq, this was accompanied by the promotion and reiteration of the theme that twentieth-century Iraqis were the direct descendants of the Mesopotamians and Babylonians. The purpose was to promote feelings of loyalty and pride in the new country. As both of these two streams – Arab nationalism and Iraqi patriotism – were widely expressed in the schoolbooks of the time, a new feeling of patriotic consciousness or awareness came into being that gradually developed into a common ideological denominator around which all political actors were obliged to orientate themselves. When 'genuine' political parties emerged, they could attract widespread support only if they succeeded in merging their political programmes with the wider concepts and aspirations of either Arab or Iraqi independence.[7]

Of course the aspirations of Arab nationalism underwent important changes with the passage of time. In the period before the Second World War, and before the emergence of the Iraqi Communist Party as a major, if not *the* major, force in the organized opposition to the regime, the mainstream of Arab or Iraqi national awareness began to pass away from the first generation of Arab nationalists (although many of them remained politically active until the fall of the monarchy) and to crystallize around two main trends, a combination of social reformism and Iraqi nationalism on the one hand, and pan-Arabism on the other.

The social reformist tendency was most predominantly represented by *Jama'at al-Ahali*,[8] a group that had been established by Iraqi students at the American University of Beirut in the late 1920s. Its founder members were Muhammad Hadid, Abdul Fattah Ibrahim, Abdul Qadir Isma'il and Husain Jamil, all of whom were to have substantial influence in Iraqi politics in various capacities both in the opposition to the monarchy and briefly after the Revolution of 1958. As young men, they were all active in student politics and participated in demonstrations against the mandate. Their newspaper, *al-Ahali*, soon became popular as a forum for progressive opinion after first appearing in January 1932. The political principles of *Jama'at al-Ahali* were drawn largely from British Fabianism (Muhammad Hadid went on to study with Harold Laski at the London School of Economics) and amounted to demands for a combination of political and economic independence with democratic social reform, all of which, it was thought, could be achieved through the ballot box. These beliefs were shared by many educated members of the middle classes, but any attempts on the part of the members of *al-Ahali* and their supporters to use it to forward their views were always checked by those with more powerful vested interests in the maintenance of the status quo. Nevertheless, *al-Ahali's* essentially bourgeois democratic ideals were respected by a constituency extending far beyond its actual membership. After the military coup in October 1936, Hikmat Sulaiman, the civilian whom the army leader Bakr Sidqi had chosen as prime minister, invited three prominent members of the group to join his government, but it became clear that Sidqi was either unwilling or unable to allow free elections or a free press, and was also prepared to intimidate his opponents. These soon came to include the *al-Ahali* ministers, who were forced to flee the country the following year.

The second influential political tendency of the period before the

Second World War was pan-Arabism, a set of notions associated with the educationalist Sati' al-Husri, whose ideas influenced several generations through his contributions to the school textbooks of the time in Iraq and other Arab countries.[9] Al-Husri developed a new form of Arab nationalism which held that although the Arab countries had been liberated from Ottoman rule, the post-war Arab world simply saw the substitution of one form of alien rule for another. He also argued that the Arab world was essentially a single geopolitical entity that had been divided artificially and arbitrarily by the Western powers after the First World War. The regeneration of Arab society could be achieved only through the reunification of the 'Arab nation', of which Iraq was an integral part. These ideas appealed particularly to Sunni Muslims, in Iraq and elsewhere, who would form the great majority of the population of a united Arab state.

In fact, the heterogeneous nature of the new state of Iraq, with its preponderantly Shi'i population and its important Kurdish minority, meant that these ideas did not enjoy such widespread popularity in the inter-war period as they did in Syria, where the notion of Arabism had originated in Ottoman times, and where the sense of division and separation was compounded both by the separation of Palestine from the rest of the geographical Syria and by the internal divisions which the French had imposed upon the state itself. However, as Iraq was at least nominally independent, it had its own army, whose senior officers had all served in either the Ottoman or Sharifian armies (or both in some cases), and were Sunnis almost to a man, with the result that the Iraqi officer corps was particularly receptive to such ideas, and considered those of *Jama'at al-Ahali* excessively 'regionalist' or 'Iraqist'.[10]

In the years between 1937 and 1941 the principles of pan-Arabism were particularly influential in Iraqi politics, since they formed the core of the beliefs of the small group of officers who were effectively running the country. By this time two important additional factors had entered political calculations. In the first place, events in Palestine began to have greater impact, particularly after the Round Table Conference in London in January–March 1939 and the arrival of the Mufti of Jerusalem in Baghdad in October of the same year. Secondly, and even more significantly, the outbreak of a war in which a victory for Britain (and France) did not seem a foregone conclusion appeared to open up a new range of possibilities to those who had already been seduced by the new forms of nationalism in Nazi Germany and Fascist Italy, two countries that were perceived as having emerged as strong and united nation-states after long periods of destructive disunity, and could thus be taken as models for the future development of the Arab world.

We have already made brief mention of the reforms initiated in the first half of 1946, when some of the opposition demands for political and trade union rights were briefly conceded. The prime movers in the organization of the labour movement, and subsequently of the massive demonstrations of 1948, were the Communists and their sympathizers. Founded in 1934, the Iraqi Communist Party had a brief period of public activity in support of *al-Ahali* and Hikmat Sulaiman's government in 1936–37, but was suppressed after the army strong man, Bakr Sidqi, moved against it in March 1937. A number of prominent Communists were sent into exile, and the party largely disappeared from view until 1941, when it gave its enthusiastic support to Rashid Ali's attempted defiance of Britain.[11]

As well as inaugurating a brief era of cautious democratization, the circumstances of the Second World War had important and far-reaching effects upon the Iraqi economy. The presence of the Allied armies of occupation caused a sudden influx of a large body of newcomers with substantial purchasing power, while the absence of normal supplies of manufactured goods from abroad gave local firms and industrialists an obvious incentive to expand or initiate production, and thus facilitated capital accumulation on a larger scale than had previously been possible.

At the same time, the doubling of the population of Baghdad between 1922 and 1947 and the concomitant growth in the size of the labour force, combined with the gradual growth in political awareness, created conditions that favoured the development of a labour movement. A number of political parties were licensed by the al-Suwaidi cabinet in the first half of 1946, including the National Democratic Party, which inherited some of the mantle of *Jama'at al-Ahali*, and the *Istiqlal* (Independence) Party, which favoured a milder form of the militant pan-Arabism of the late 1930s. Sixteen labour unions were also licensed in 1946, twelve of which were controlled by the Communist Party; the largest of these were formed in the country's most important industrial undertakings, Basra Port and the Iraqi Railways, which were both under British management.

However, al-Suwaidi's period in office represented an isolated flush of liberalism rather than the beginning of a general trend, and a major clampdown on political activities of all kinds soon followed. In July 1946, a strike took place in the Iraq Petroleum Company, where permission to form a union had been refused; a strike meeting in Kirkuk was suddenly charged by armed police, and ten people were killed. In June 1946, under the premiership of Salih Jabr, three prominent Communists were sentenced to death; in addition the National Democratic Party leaders, Kamil al-Chaderchi and Abdul-Fattah Ibrahim, were brought to trial in September, and the party itself was banned. Such measures naturally had the effect of further undermining confidence in the political system.

The killings at Kirkuk in July 1946 were a foretaste of the terrible violence of 1948, the year of the great national uprising known as *al-Wathba*, the leap. The immediate cause of this massive disavowal of the status quo was the Portsmouth Agreement, the outcome of the Anglo–Iraqi treaty negotiations which have already been mentioned. When its terms were announced in Baghdad on 16 January 1948, the tide of popular discontent became a flood and the opposition political parties put out a united call for the 'immediate abolition of the Treaty, the dissolution of parliament, a new, free election and a prompt supply of bread'.[12]

The hatred revealed in the dreadful scenes in Baghdad on 26–27 January, so graphically and movingly described by Batatu, was a portent of the wrath to come. Jabr's ministry was replaced by a caretaker cabinet under another Shi'i, Muhammad al-Sadr, who had been active in the Revolution of 1920. Al-Sadr's main task was to organize new elections in the summer, which, as usual, were rigged in favour of the 'old gang'. During the spring and summer, violent opposition spread outwards from Baghdad. In what became the best-known uprising of that period, the IPC pumping station near Haditha was brought to a standstill in April and May 1948 by a strike of the 3,000 workers and clerical staff, organized by the Communist Party. After two and a half weeks, the government and the IPC cut off supplies of food and water to the strikers, and after three weeks the latter decided to march to Baghdad, a distance of some 250 kilometres. This act of defiance, known as *al-Masira al-Kubra*, the 'great march', was a major expression of popular determination to stand against the political order, even in the face of overwhelming odds. Almost all manifestations of opposition by organized labour during the 1940s and 1950s combined claims for higher wages and better living conditions with demands for national independence. The strikes and demonstrations were often directed against British-owned or British-controlled concerns. This made the labour movement both more articulate and more effective than either its numbers, its cohesion or its apparent lack of economic muscle might suggest, and it also ensured its full integration into the national movement.

The elections in 1948 coincided with the beginning of the war in Palestine, which aroused further strong anti-British (and hence anti-regime) feelings, to the extent that martial law was introduced in the autumn. Nuri took over the premiership again in January 1949; his crude answer to all opposition, which was to crack down upon it with an iron fist, was given savage expression in mid-February, when Fahd, the Secretary-General of the Communist Party, and two members of the Politbureau, who had all been in prison since 1947, were hanged in public. The party took some time to recover from this blow; a large number of senior cadres had either been arrested with Fahd in 1947, or between then and 1949, with the result that many of the most experienced members of the party spent much of the last decade of the monarchy in prison. On the other hand, Fahd and his two colleagues became martyrs and their own supreme sacrifice, as well as the draconian punishments meted out to other Communists for their political activities, ensured that the party would achieve an almost legendary status in the opposition movement.

The last ten years of the monarchy saw some twenty cabinets in and out of office and represented the peak of Nuri's personal power; if he or his close associates were not actually running things, it was only a matter of months before they had to be called back in again. At this stage, another important factor began to emerge: oil income began to grow rapidly, from ID 2.3 million in 1946 to ID 49.9 million in 1953 and eventually to ID 79.9 million in 1958.[13] The opportunities suggested by this sudden access of revenue gave rise to a certain optimism in British official circles. Although well aware of the unpopularity of the Iraqi government and of the corruption and venality of many of its members, British officials expressed the general view, at least at the beginning of the 1950s, that both British interests and the monarchy's survival might be ensured by the possibilities now being opened up by 'development', in which Nuri seemed to be taking a lively interest.

The activities of the Iraq Development Board, established in 1950, were quite insufficient to hold back public discontent. The board concentrated mainly on flood and irrigation control, communications and construction, the kind of large-scale projects that, however sensible, would take several years to materialize. It was also widely believed that whatever the ultimate benefits of industrial, agricultural or irrigation projects, the most obvious spin-offs were the rich pickings which went to those who had had the good fortune to be awarded the contracts.[14]

The mood of the country was also profoundly affected by the expressions of defiance against Britain on the part of the opposition movements and in time by the governments of some neighbouring states. In particular, the successes of Nasser in the 1950s gave rise to widespread confidence and optimism among the political opposition in Iraq, which was now dominated by the Communist Party. At this stage, in the period leading up to the 1958 Revolution, the dividing lines between Nasserists, Baathists and Communists were less distinct than they would become later. In the first place, the Nasserists were never properly organized into a group and neither they nor the more formally organized Baathists had more than a few years' experience of underground political activity. Secondly, neither group was ever able to gain the level of support in Iraq that their counterparts had attracted in the neighbouring Arab states. Finally, no detailed blueprint for the future had been worked out by any of the parties, beyond very general programmes of social reform, liberation from Britain and the abolition of the *ancien régime*. The question of power and of how this was to be gained and maintained had never been prominent on the political agenda. In striking contrast to the deep divisions that emerged in 1958 and 1959, a certain amount of fellow feeling still existed between members of the three clandestine groups.

The Partisans of Peace, a Communist front organization whose members came mainly from the professional and middle classes, began to be active in the early 1950s. The Communist Party itself began to revive under the leadership of Baha al-Din Nuri. He and his associates led and organized the massive demonstrations in Baghdad in November 1952 known as the *Intifadah*, originally sparked off by student discontent. In response, martial law was declared and General Nur al-Din Mahmud was appointed to head the government. Eighteen people were killed as a result of military action; political parties were banned, and some 300 political leaders arrested, including Siddiq Shanshal and Faiq al-Samarrai of the *Istiqlal*, Kamil al-Chaderchi of the National Democrats, and Ali Mahmud of the Partisans of Peace.[15]

In 1953, Faisal II, then aged eighteen, came of age. The Regent, evidently unwilling to lose the control he had exercised on the boy's behalf since 1939, did not step into the background but continued to act as if nothing had changed. In Nuri's absence in Europe in the spring of 1954, Abdulillah planned to hold a relatively free parliamentary election, which he hoped might produce a chamber of deputies where his arch-rival's influence would be diminished. In May, the three main political parties, the National Democrats, the *Istiqlal* and the Communists, agreed to join together in a national front, a unique and potentially influential political alliance, which actually won eleven out of 135 seats in the elections in June. As the Anglo–Iraqi treaty of 1930 was about to expire however, Abdulillah thought it prudent to bring Nuri back for the negotiations. Nuri returned in August to form the twelfth of his fourteen cabinets and began to rule by decree after proroguing parliament.

During the intense clampdown that followed, unparalleled in the previous history of the monarchy, all opposition parties were banned and a totally servile parliament assembled. Although Nuri's diplomatic activities resulted in the conclusion of the Baghdad Pact in February 1955, they were out of tune with national feeling. But the response was less co-ordinated than it had been in 1948. In Egypt, the revolutionary government's reaction to a new Western-sponsored defence agreement for the Middle East was predictably hostile. Nasser's vigorous denunciation of the pact, and his emergence as an international figure at the Bandung Conference in 1955, strengthened his claim to the leadership of a vigorous pan-Arabism that was rapidly gaining support from a wide range of 'anti-imperialist' opinion in Iraq and in other parts of the Middle East.

In this heady atmosphere, the Suez crisis put the 'old gang' in a particularly difficult position. There were large demonstrations in Baghdad and other cities, most notably in Hayy and Najaf. The government itself was obliged to make a face-saving statement of protest to Britain, but it stamped down heavily on demonstrations and imposed martial law once more. Increasingly, as in Egypt at the beginning of the 1950s, there was a sense that it could be only a matter of time before the regime fell. By the end of 1956 Iraq was out of step with the governments of almost all the other Arab states, and the humiliation brought about by this isolation was compounded by almost universal dissatisfaction with the slow rate of material progress and the absence of civil liberties.

Perhaps most ominously for the *ancien régime*, and in spite of considerable improvements in status, pay and conditions, discontent was spreading in the army, where, as might have been expected, Nasser's pan-Arab doctrines were reaching a ready and appreciative audience. The Iraqi Army had expanded substantially after its foundation in 1920 and the rapid growth of the officer corps provided an important means of advancement for those without fortune or family. Although most of the more senior officers in the late 1950s were still closely associated with the regime through ties of family, friendship or material interest, the younger generation came from more disparate social backgrounds and their views reflected the variety of political trends in circulation, including Communism, Nasserism and Baathism.

The year before the July Revolution was fairly uneventful in comparison with the turbulence of the early 1950s, but the disfavour in which the regime was held made a profound impression on observers at the time.[16] A second national opposition front was formed in February 1957 which included the National Democratic Party, the *Istiqlal*, the Communists and the Baath Party. The latter founded in 1953, had almost 300 members at the time.[17] Given the profoundly volatile circumstances that have been described, the powerlessness of the opposition politicians in the face of the government's monopoly of the means of coercion, and the fact that it was impossible to bring in a government with fundamentally different (that is, anti-British) policies through the ballot box, the overthrow of the regime could be carried out only by force.

## Social and Economic Conditions before the Revolution

There seems to be almost unanimous agreement among writers on Iraq that the social and economic conditions that emerged under the mandate and monarchy created such severe social tensions as to make the Revolution of 1958 almost inevitable. Most of the contemporary British archival material now available reflects this sentiment and much is made in the diplomatic reports[18] of the political dangers arising from Nuri's apparent inability to carry out any kind of social, particularly agrarian, reform. It is therefore not surprising that much of the discussion of the causes of the Revolution has emphasized the desperate conditions in the countryside and among the urban poor, and the deeply-felt need for economic development for which sufficient resources were becoming available. But what were the principal social factors underlying the Revolution, what do we know about them, and what is Hanna Batatu's approach?

Batatu describes a highly diverse society and its transformation through the incorporation of Iraq into the international market under the particular conditions of dependence on Britain. He describes how large shaikhly landownership was created under the mandate, the effects of imports on the expansion of trade and commerce, and the increase in the accumulation of industrial capital in the two decades immediately preceding the Revolution, largely as a result of Iraq's enforced isolation between 1939 and 1945. He characterizes these years as: 'an era of growth and upward mobility for the trading people [in which] the number of traders with yearly incomes of more than 150 dinars rose from 1,862 in 1932/33 to 5,445 in 1942/43'.[19] While part of this increase could be explained by the decline in the purchasing power of the dinar, this kind of expansion continued, particularly after 1953, so that:

Retail shops numbered no fewer than 36,062 and wholesale establishments 1,576. Their 1956 annual turnover, partly estimated, amounted to 82.6 and 53.6 million dinars respectively. From the aspects of national production, the estimated value added by them and by hawkers, street sellers, and open-air markets increased from 17.3 million dinars in 1953 to 28.8 million in 1957 at current prices. (262–63)

The rate of commercial expansion was reflected in the increase of 'first class' members of the Baghdad Chamber of Commerce from 13 in 1927/28 to 190 in 1957/58; total membership increased from 288 to 2,812 in the same period. Merchants were assisted by a number of favourable fiscal policies, such as income tax exemptions, and most importantly by the 'vast flow of oil money after 1951' which 'set in motion capital development schemes, and pyramided the wealth of a growing number of mercantile families' (266). The amount invested by Iraqi companies in industry reached ID 27.2 million by 1957, exceeding the ID 20.7 million of corporate capital invested in commerce.

Industrial enterprises, however, were concentrated in the hands of only 23 rich families, many of whom had controlling shares of stock in several often functionally unrelated enterprises (274), owning some ID 30–35 million between them. These families stood 'at the pinnacle in the realms of trade, finance, and industry' in 1958 (312), and possessed between them 'assets amounting to the equivalent of not less than 56% of the whole private corporate commercial and industrial capital of the country – a concentration enhanced by the pattern of marriage alliances' (312–14). Nevertheless, since the 'lion's share' of the economic benefits generated by oil and trade found its way into the bank accounts of foreign firms, especially British ones, the potential for the accumulation of capital and profit remained relatively restricted (266–67).

Although Batatu emphasizes the plurality and persistence of ethnic, religious and other divisions within Iraqi society, he constantly draws our attention to the profound socio-economic polarization which had developed in town and country during the monarchy, of great extremes of wealth and poverty. As for the social groups between these two extremes, Batatu and other writers have pointed to the emergence of a new stratum including intellectuals, professionals and army officers who had benefited from the new opportunities for social advancement through the expansion of the state educational system and of the army and were often at the forefront of the movement for national independence.

Here the main omission is a broad spectrum of social groups, in both town and countryside, standing somewhere 'in the middle', who are never adequately taken into account, although they must have been very much affected both by the transformations of Iraqi society at the time and by their ability or inability to take advantage of the new opportunities. There is a whole group of 'invisible social classes', medium to small property-owners, wholesale and retail merchants, manufacturers, owners of workshops and repair shops, petty traders and so on, who formed a very substantial and often interrelated stratum. They are 'invisible' in the sense that they have not usually been taken into account by historians. As a result, we have very little knowledge about how the new political and social environment affected their lives or how they reacted and adapted to these new conditions.

We shall use some of Batatu's own findings further to develop the point, although the terms of reference will have to be quantitative rather than analytical. If, as Batatu states, 56% of the 'whole of private corporate commercial and industrial capital' was confined to the richest 23 families, the remaining 44%, which are not accounted for, must have been controlled by those who were somewhere 'in the middle'. While they were also differentiated internally and included relatively poor as well as richer families, the distance between the upper and lower strata of these 'middle groups' was not, of course, as great as that between the whole group and the very top families at the 'pinnacle' of wealth. Yet in emphasizing the polarization of wealth between a small number of very wealthy merchants, industrialists and landowning families and 'the poor', the huge gap which also existed between the wealthy *and most of the rest of the population* has tended to be overlooked. In the same way, it was not just the mass of the poor who had little or no access to the state or to state decision-making.

This relative lack of differentiation among the majority of the population – the lines have been simplified here in order to make the point – may give a partial explanation of why the country was so unanimously behind the Revolution of 1958.[20] A striking feature of societies of this type – in which the gap between the small numbers of very rich at the top and the whole of the rest of society is extremely wide – is that it is relatively easy to expropriate large landowners, the few wealthy industrialists and the richer business-men,[21] without severely upsetting the existing socio-economic system. But what this situation also highlights is that although business was thriving and Iraq experienced rapid capitalist penetration, this was largely confined to the sphere of exchange in trade and commerce and began only gradually to undermine the pre-capitalist relations of production which continued to prevail elsewhere. The majority of the active population (including those working in the countryside) seems to have continued to work within the traditional and largely pre-capitalist sphere.

## Towards a New Agenda for the History of Twentieth-Century Iraq

The factors that facilitated the gradual incorporation of the region into the international capitalist market in the late nineteenth and twentieth centuries are well known: the opening up of facilities for commerce, the expansion of trade, the improvement of roads, railways and river transport, and the introduction of the telegraph. Some of these had already begun to make an impact by the turn of the century, but they became even more important after the First World War, with the simultaneous establishment of the state of Iraq, the British mandate and the Hashemite monarchy.

For a variety of reasons, including competition from European, particularly British, consumer goods, the consolidation of large landownership and the general subordination of the economy to British interests, capitalist relations of production developed only slowly. Modern industries were, as we have seen, primarily confined to those owned by a very small group of families and to public utility companies providing infrastructural services, such as the railways, electricity and water companies, Basra Port and the Iraq Petroleum Company, which were all foreign controlled. Agriculture was still run on pre-capitalist lines; few landowners became agricultural entrepreneurs.

Nevertheless, the gradual penetration of the capitalist market set in motion dynamics and processes that, although uneven both in time and space, had the *general* effect of undermining existing pre-capitalist relations of production. Nevertheless, as indicated earlier, it was only in a few relatively limited economic spheres that pre-capitalist relations and forms of production were *replaced* or *superseded* by new class structures and social relations.[22] One important reason for this was the way in which and the speed at which the market expanded, under conditions that were essentially external in origin. These conditions of domination and dependency maintained the persistence of pre-capitalist relations of production, especially in the countryside, where the majority of the population lived.

The polarity between the small class of some two thousand very large landowners and the vast mass of poor, almost entirely landless, sharecropping *fellahin*, and the severity and injustice of the sharecropping system[23] are sufficiently appreciated to need no further description. On the other hand little is known about the way in which production was managed or adapted by the *fellahin*, and no analysis has been made of the social and economic implications of the fact that sharecroppers continued to work 'their land' not as individual landless labourers but in family or household units. For example, if the household continued to constitute both the unit of production and consumption and its most important target remained subsistence or survival and not the market or profit, this meant not only that the bulk of the *fellahin* was excluded from the internal market, but also that traditional pre-capitalist attitudes and norms of conduct persisted among them. In other words the patriarchal nature of household production was largely sustained, and social relations and value systems were not yet determined or thought of in terms of market relations.[24]

As well as continuing to be reproduced in the countryside, these values were also brought to the cities with the wave of rural to urban migration that began at the end of the Second World War. In the decade immediately before 1958 the urban population increased by about three-quarter of a million to form just under half of the total population of the country. The impact of this rapid influx can hardly be underestimated, because it meant that the value system accompanying patriarchal relations was imported into the city almost 'unscathed', even if the family as a unit of production was being replaced by employment providing wages or a salaried income.

State investment was largely confined to the country's major infrastructural undertakings (and some irrigation projects). As there were still very few industries of any size, the process of proletarianization was checked in the absence of wider employment opportunities. Those streaming into the reed and mud shanty towns on the outskirts of the larger cities (and into the inner cities after the departure of the traditional middle class from the city centres) were rarely able to find permanent employment in industry or manufacture, and sought temporary work in building and construction, as hawkers or porters in the markets, or as *farrashin* (watchmen) in government offices, schools and hospitals.

Again, very little is known about the way in which the expansion of market relations affected existing pre-capitalist social relations and forms of production in the city, or the degree to which these relations were transformed or replaced, or whether and to what extent they merely adapted themselves to the new socio-economic conditions while retaining many of their original features. There is little information about the changes (or absences of changes) within the family unit of production, either on the land or in the workshop, that has always been organized and managed on patriarchal lines, relying primarily on unpaid family labour, or the degree to which traditional norms and values persisted up to or beyond the period of the Revolution. Even less is known about the various 'middle' social groups or strata to which reference has already been made; those engaged in production or the retail and wholesale trades, or small-scale services, many of whom continued to live in the old parts of the cities of Baghdad, Basra, Mosul and the smaller towns.[25]

In an important sense, these social groups were 'invisible' politically as well as economically, because, apart from their general support for the idea of national independence, their aspirations were not expressed directly in any of the political movements or parties of the time. From our own contacts with individuals of this social background it is clear that their way of life continued to be embedded within the value system of the 'Muslim family' and that religion and the mosque still played an important part in their lives.

It is only a slight exaggeration to say that social scientists either ignore the existence of these groups entirely or lump them together with all others who are neither owners of the means of production nor workers. Matters such as relations between the sexes, and the situation of women, as well as attitudes towards work, money, status, time and so on were still regulated largely by pre-capitalist norms and values.

Few writers on Iraq apart from Batatu have ventured beyond presenting a picture, developed almost *ad absurdum*, of a bewilderingly atomized, highly heterogeneous and undifferentiated society composed of a 'mosaic' of separate ethnic and religious communities. Although it will be difficult to obtain satisfactory or accurate answers, it is important to pose certain basic questions about the kind of capitalism that developed in Iraq: which socio-economic groups were incorporated into the system and the nature of their responses, and in what manner and to what extent did capitalist relations of production – as opposed to capitalist market relations – penetrate the socio-economic system as a whole. To bring the inquiry up to date, such questions must be related to the different stages or watersheds within recent Iraqi history, including, ultimately, the role of the 'socialist' state as a vehicle for – or impediment to – a more thoroughgoing process of capitalist penetration.

## The Causes of the Revolution Reconsidered

Although historians seem to agree that the causes of the Revolution of 1958 were, like most other revolutions, both social and political, it seems appropriate at this stage to try to recapitulate the principal factors that contributed to it and led to the violent overthrow of the monarchy. To do this, emphasis will be shifted somewhat from the social question, which is usually considered to be its primary cause, to the shortcomings of the political system itself and to the external and internal political atmosphere. Analyses of the Iraqi political system before the Revolution have emphasized that the Iraqi state was weak and 'external' to the society on which it was imposed;[26] more important, they have also stressed its lack of social and political integration.

When reconsidering the immediate causes of the Revolution, however, it is possible that abstractions on this level of generality may obscure the degree to which the shortcomings of the political system itself affected the political atmosphere over the years. To put it more precisely, since the day-to-day running of Iraqi politics allowed a lot of room for manoeuvre, it is questionable whether the authoritarian and repressive policies pursued by Nuri and his circle were the only options open to them. Or to put it another way, did the political system, despite its essentially subservient nature, really have to be so inflexible as to prevent the inclusion of wider interest groups such as the nascent national bourgeoisie or broader sections of the population?

Reports from the British Embassy in Baghdad during the 1950s show that British officials do not seem to have given serious consideration to the possibility of improving the political system and establishing more truly democratic forms of government by such means as the holding of proper elections. They were much more concerned with the severe social imbalances that they thought would constitute the most important threat to the status quo. In fact Roger Louis's chapter in this volume shows that apart from Michael Ionides, a British member of the Iraq Development Board who lamented the absence of proper elections and of meaningful political discussion,[27] more liberal forms of government were never even considered. The overall concern was internal stability and stronger government. In fact, in 1958, the British Ambassador, Sir Michael Wright, contemplated the possibility of 'a more authoritarian régime based on the Army with a soldier as the strong man behind a civilian figurehead . . .' if and when 'the time comes for Nuri to leave the political scene'.[28]

Apart from British officials' apparent inability to imagine that the political system could be run on more democratic lines, their attitudes were greatly influenced by the cold war atmosphere[29] and the obsessive fear of Communism that informed much of the thinking at the time. This in its turn accentuated the one-dimensional authoritarian approach on the part of the Iraqi authorities (and their British advisers) in the face of demands for political and economic change. It is probably true to say that if some form of representative government and more democratic procedures had been adopted by the Iraqi government and its British sponsors, it is at least conceivable that the violent and chaotic course of events of the Revolution and its immediate aftermath might have been modified.[30] The failure and abuse of the parliamentary system, the lack of democratic liberties, the constraints on political expression, the execution and imprisonment of political opponents and the censorship of the press had the effect of discrediting the parliamentary system, with the result that the opposition, which the system had radicalized and driven underground, came to seek its abolition rather than its reform.

By the mid-1950s major economic and social imbalances had developed that urgently needed to be changed,[31] and the national independence movement, which took up the question of social change and economic development, continued to gain in strength. The Iranian defiance of the oil companies in Iran in the early 1950s, the rise of Nasserism in Egypt and Nasser's own 'insurbordination' over the Suez Canal combined to create a contagious mood of self-confidence and a sense that the government and its 'imperialist' allies were not invincible;[32] they would either be defeated now or in the near future, and political independence would bring social justice, social change and economic development in its wake.

In sum, therefore, the main causes of the Revolution were the international and regional political conjuncture in the 1950s, which gave tremendous confidence to the national independence movement; the inflexibility of the political system, its inability to respond to the new needs of the country and its failure to ameliorate the material grievances and impoverishment of the mass of the urban and rural population. The combination of these factors with the organization and seizure of the initiative by the Free Officers brought about the coup that became the Revolution of 1958.

### Notes

1. Hanna Batatu, *The Old Social Classes and the Revolutionary Movements in Iraq* (Princeton, 1978).

2. This section is based on our *Iraq since 1958: from Revolution to Dictatorship* (London, 1987), pp. 1–45.

3. See Peter Sluglett, *Britain in Iraq 1914–1932* (London, 1976), *passim*.

4. Majid Khadduri, *Independent Iraq 1932–1958: A Study in Iraqi Politics* (2nd ed., London, 1960), p. 253.

5. Chancery, Baghdad, to Eastern Department, Foreign Office, 16 July 1946, FO 371/52315/E2217, quoted in Wm. Roger Louis, *The British Empire in the Middle East 1945–1951: Arab Nationalism, The United States and Postwar Imperialism* (Oxford, 1984), p. 309.

6. Batatu, *Old Social Classes*, p. 546.

7. Note that [Troutbeck] 'believed that the Communist movement in Iraq and elsewhere in the Middle East was essentially nationalistic' (Wm. Roger Louis, 'The

British and the Origins of the Iraqi Revolution', p. 40 above.) If we substitute 'anti-colonial' for 'nationalistic' this assessment seems perfectly accurate.

8. See Mudhaffar Amin, 'Jama'at al-Ahali: Its Origins, Ideology and Role in Iraqi Politics 1932–1946', Durham University Ph.D. thesis, 1980.

9. Al-Husri's career and influence have been studied in Bassam Tibi, *Arab Nationalism: A Critical Enquiry* (London, 1981), pp. 90–172.

10. Out of a sample of 61 senior officers in the Iraqi Army and Air Force in 1936, 58 were Sunnis, 2 Christians and 1 Shi'i. See Mohammad A. Tarbush, *The Role of the Military in Politics: A Case Study of Iraq to 1941* (London, 1982), pp. 80–82.

11. Although the Communists were subsequently accused of opportunism in supporting Rashid Ali, because of the latter's evidently pro-Axis sympathies, it would have been impossible, given the widespread public acclaim for his action at the time, for them not have done so and still to maintain their credentials as patriots and their integrity as fighters for national independence. The contradictions inherent in such situations and the perceived necessity on subsequent occasions to enter into alliances with other broadly 'anti-imperialist' forces often served to damage the Communists' standing in the years to come, but in 1941 the situation did not seem to pose such a dilemma. For the Communists, as for the vast majority of their fellow countrymen, the most immediate and burning issue was the struggle for independence from Britain; hence the enemies of Britain were 'bound' to be the friends of the Iraqi independence movement.

12. Phebe Marr, *The Modern History of Iraq* (Boulder, 1985), p. 104.

13. The increase between the end of the 1940s and the beginning of the 1950s is accounted for by the conclusion of the '50–50' agreement between the IPC and the Iraqi government in February 1952 which provided for an equal division of the profits between them. The IPC had long refused to change from a royalty rate to profit-sharing, but was evidently influenced by the 'developing crisis in Iran'. See Louis, *The British Empire in the Middle East*, pp. 590–603.

14. Ibid.

15. Batatu, *Old Social Classes*, pp. 666–70; Marr, *Modern History of Iraq*, pp. 112–13.

16. See, for example, E. and E. F. Penrose, *Iraq: International Relations and National Development* (London, 1978), pp. 199–201; Marr, *Modern History of Iraq*, p. 120; 'Caractacus', *Revolution in Iraq* (London, 1959).

17. Batatu, *Old Social Classes*, p. 743. The figure (actually 289) is based on a membership list seized by the police in June 1955.

18. For the quotations from the despatches of Sir John Troutbeck and Sir Michael Wright see above, Louis, 'The British and the Origins of the Iraqi Revolution' in this volume.

19. Batatu, *Old Social Classes*, p. 262. Page references hereafter given in the text.

20. In addition to the widespread influence of the radical ideas of Communism, Arab socialism, and 'development' as such, which cannot be discussed here, this also explains why the social and economic reforms advocated by the various nationalist governments which came into power after the revolution were in some way or another responding to popular demands and needs. Those social groups whose economic interests as smaller or larger entrepreneurs were linked to the acquisition of private property – and this might include the very poorest – were usually not attracted to programmes of radical social change or to the establishment of Communism in Iraq and were therefore – as well as for other reasons, such as their Islamic belief – often

profoundly anti-Communist.

21. Many of the larger and more modern industries owned by the richest Iraqi families had not grown organically from the indigenous socio-economic system, but were based on imported capital goods and were therefore to some degree extraneous in character. It would be interesting to look at the industries which these families owned and to analyse their local content.

22. What we are referring to here is not simply the phenomenon of 'uneven development' or the emergence of a 'dual' economy, in which pre-capitalist and capitalist sectors exist more or less side by side, but rather to the very complex processes and dynamics set in motion by the rapid expansion of the market in a newly created nation-state. We use the term 'forms of production' in the sense used by Harriet Friedmann, who has influenced our analysis. See her 'World Market, State and Family Farm: Social Bases of Production in the Era of Wage Labour', *Comparative Studies in Society and History*, 20 (1978), pp. 545–86, and 'Household Production and the National Economy: Concepts for the Analysis of Agrarian Formations', *Journal of Peasant Studies*, 7 (1980), pp. 158–184.

23. See Robert A. Fernea, *Shaykh and Effendi: Changing Patterns of Authority among the El Shabana of Southern Iraq* (Cambridge, Mass., 1970); A. P. G. Poyck, 'Farm Studies in Iraq (an Agro-Economic Study of the Agriculture in the Hilla–Diwaniya Area in Iraq)', *Medelingen van de Landbouwhogeschool te Wageningen*, 62 1 (1962), pp. 1–99; Shakir M. Salim, *Marsh Dwellers of the Euphrates Delta* (London, 1962). In addition to Batatu see Ronay Gabbay, *Communism and Agrarian Reform in Iraq* (London, 1978).

24. A clear illustration of this is that after the implementation of agrarian reform and the establishment of co-operatives in the 1960s and 1970s the *fellahin* generally ignored the new administrative regulations which had been designed to encourage them to work their land as individual members of a co-operative, and cultivated the plots they had been allocated in the kinship or tribal units to which they belonged. See K. S. al-Nasiri, 'Landlords, Lineages and Land Reform in an Iraqi Village', Ph.D. thesis, University of Durham, 1978. For a fascinating account of similar processes in other geographical context, see Michael T. Taussig, *The Devil and Commodity Fetishism in South America* (Chapel Hill, 1980).

25. Although, as Batatu has shown, many of the members and supporters of the Communist Party originated from this background, it is unlikely that the majority of those involved in such occupations were in favour of the sort of radical social change advocated by the Communists.

26. Sami Zubaida, 'Community, Class and Minorities in Iraqi Politics', in this volume, and our *Iraq since 1958*, chaps. 1–2.

27. Louis, 'The British and the Origins of the Iraqi Revolution', p. 44 above.

28. Ibid., p. 53 above.

29. Ibid., p. 39 above.

30. After having written this chapter we found that Henry Munson Jr. has argued on similar lines about the Iranian Revolution of 1979. See *Islam and Revolution in the Middle East* (New Haven, 1988).

31. Louis, 'The British and the Origins of the Iraqi Revolution', pp. 34–40.

32. At the present time the savage repression that has become the hallmark of Saddam Hussein's regime seems to have created the widespread conviction among Iraqis that his rule is invincible, which partly explains the prevailing mood of acceptance and acquiescence.

# 8

# State and Tribe in Southern Iraq: The Struggle for Hegemony before the 1958 Revolution

## ROBERT A. FERNEA

The hegemonic struggle to which my title refers was between and within tribalism and statism.[1] In 1958, developments in rural Iraq constituted a conflict in the way people were to think and to act. I am not writing about tribal social organizations, nor about the political significance of the tribes. I am concerned with knowledge of how things are done, the common sense of social behaviour and expectations – which is confirmed in daily conversations and underlies the criteria by which a person is judged. What order of punishment was to prevail in a world full of tribal feuds and government jails? What was to take social precedence in human encounters, education or age? What I witnessed in southern Iraq was a vacillation between one way of seeing things and another, day-to-day situations marked by a series of contradictions. On the one hand there was the state, already impossible to live without by 1958, imposing new disciplines, inscribing the lives of rural people with new forms of control. On the other hand and concurrently, there were the older ways – the things always said, the judgements always made, the time-sanctioned techniques for resolving problems between and among blood kin – in short, the strategies of power employed through traditional discourses.[2] Did the Revolution of 1958 resolve this struggle for hegemony over the minds and bodies of the people I knew then in southern Iraq?

By the time of the 1958 Revolution, the presence of the Iraqi governmental administration was part of life throughout all but the most remote marshes and windswept mountains of rural Iraq. In each province, officials were distributed in the cities and smaller towns. Police enforced the law. Schools, though still inadequate in number, had begun to educate rural children. Many of the government administrators were young men, themselves removed from a tribal life only by education and employment. Expectations of a better life were high, but there was great disappointment with the Nuri Said government. Roads were not being built fast enough to suit either the wealthier farmers with market surpluses or young people who wanted to go on to school. The government health clinics were too few in number and inadequately staffed. Canals needed to be cemented, new ones needed to be dug. Much land was rapidly becoming salinated through lack of proper drainage. Although reports spread by the newly ubiquitous transistor radio encouraged the belief that there were new technological solutions to these and other problems, little was being done. Rural administrators were demoralized by the poverty and ignorance of the country people as well as by the failure of the government to carry out its promises of social reform. They dreamed of going to Baghdad, where they could live the good life, the civilized life, among people like themselves, and be more likely to be promoted. Some also joined the Communist cells which formed among the educated young men in the rural areas. These were the conditions I observed when I knew men in the party, and when I was the guest of a shaikh.

In *The Old Social Classes*, Hanna Batatu devotes a chapter to the 'Shaikhs, Aghas, and Peasants' in which he paints a picture of the appalling social conditions in the Iraqi countryside in the last decades before 1958. There were shaikhs in southern Iraq who by then had become greedy absentee landowners, their inequitable holdings poorly developed through lack of investment, and their methods of extracting agricultural labour providing only starvation levels of return for the peasants. He argues that this situation came about primarily as a result of British policy during the mandate and was sustained by the monarchy according to their interests.[3] In Batatu's view, the 'shaikhdoms', had by 1958 become instruments of exploitation and one of the most destructive remnants of the British colonial legacy in the Kingdom of Iraq.[4]

Though Batatu does not go into great detail, he concedes that the Iraqi shaikhs were once active as part of a system that maintained some form of peace and that this was needed when the cities of Mesopotamia were weak and unable to administer the countryside.

In the late eighteenth and early nineteenth centuries the shaikh in the river valleys and the agha in the mountain belt served a social function. They were needed ... But when the cities stood again on their feet and began themselves to provide the needed security, and the shaikh, once a protector, became an economic burden, there arose the question of whether this remnant of a past and different age had not become an historical irrelevancy.[5]

No one could take issue with the charges of exploitation levelled against the shaikhs if one thinks of the Kut–Amara region – or any area where they owned enormous estates. It is more relevant to my interests here, however, to ask where, and among whom, arose the question of the 'historical irrelevancy' of the shaikhs. Did they intend this to refer to *all* shaikhs, or just to some of them? People were starving and many were migrating to the thousands of reed-mat shelters on the outskirts of Baghdad, as Batatu describes, but this was largely from the Kut–Amara region, where the farms were run by thugs, hired by the absentee landlord-shaikhs. Where I lived, in the Middle Euphrates area, a wider, though still unequal, distribution of landholdings prevailed. Some of the shaikhs lived fairly modestly. For instance, the shaikh I lived with had a 1952 Oldsmobile in 1956, a two-man entourage who travelled with him, and he lived in a mud-brick house. Still, I do not intend to argue with Batatu's description of the great economic and social inequities in southern Iraq. It is noteworthy, however, that the belief that *all* shaikhs were anachronistic petty tyrants was shared by most younger, educated Iraqis. Shaikhs and tribal life in general were identified with the reactionary Nuri Said regime and the perceived 'backward' qualities of national life. In fact, among the progressively minded, the very existence of tribes and shaikhs was a source of embarrassment and to bring up the subject among Baghdad intellectuals was to invoke a generally negative response.

As a fledgling cultural anthropologist, I lived and conducted research from 1956 until 1958 in a tribal settlement on the edge of the small town of Daghara, on a bifurcation of the Euphrates near the provincial capital of Diwaniyyah. My view of life in southern Iraq is based on a fairly good knowledge of a small community, whose lives were caught up in two very different but interesting ways of coping with the struggles of daily existence. One way involved government bureaucracies, to which they were obliged to go for certifications of birth and death, registrations of land, identity cards, medical care, irrigation water, to enroll their children in school, to lodge complaints and receive punishments. The other part of their lives centred around the shared understandings of tribal knowledge and practices – identities ascribed by genealogical descent, hierarchies which were constantly contested, preoccupations of peacemaking and revenge, obligations to each other based on marriages and common blood. These two very different ways of thinking and acting, the ways of the state versus those of the tribe, involved the same people in very different discourses of power and knowledge. The struggle between these two ways of organizing and of thinking about the world was still part of everyday Iraqi life in the 1950s.

The men referred to as shaikhs were not only found among wealthy landlords, but also among impoverished tenant farmers, where traditional rites of mediation and rituals of hospitality were also present. The honorific term 'shaikh' was the community term for whomever was fulfilling traditional responsibilities of leadership. It was a title that shifted among the lineages of settled tribal communities and even emerged among new groups of men brought together as migrant labourers. Often this title was contested, used as a term of address by some men but not by others, for the question of who was a shaikh was tied to the issue of which descent group was equal to another, where the cleavages between groups should be and what their proper ranking was, as well as the personal history and reputation of the man who would be shaikh.

Among tribal peoples a certain tension always existed between the doctrine of equality, predicated on the 'natural' grounds of common blood through shared ancestry, and the way in which individuals and groups always looked for an advantage in their relations with each other. Some individuals and some groups, I quickly learned, were always more equal than others. Lineages struggled for predominance even while their members proclaimed the equality of all tribesmen.[6] Indeed, by the 1950s it seemed as if the creation of new tribes with new shaikhs was in favour. In the past, warfare favoured alliances between large numbers of men, giving them advantages against their foes. But since internecine fighting had been forced to end, the possibility of proclaiming an equal and independent status for smaller tribal groups had advantages. The following note, taken while listening to petitioners in the irrigation engineer's office, suggests one reason why:

The upshot of this complaint is that the al-Ghannaniim people want an independent pipe from the South Branch canal, rather than sharing their outlet with the al-Zillawaat group, and they are arguing that they are not a lineage [*fukhuth*] but a tribe [*ashira*] and so should have a right to their own water supply.

The discourses of tribalism were dispersed throughout the fabric of human relations in the Daghara community. Marriages and divorces were matters of communal concern as they established, repaired or destroyed alliances within and between families, which were always looking for marginal advantages in the struggles of daily life. Even within the same family, brothers struggled with each other for their father's favour; younger men listened to older men, and men's superiority over women was unquestioned. Membership in a descent group was the basis of one's identity in the tribal context and the core of an individual's reputation.

In provinces such as Kut and Amara, where the British had registered enormous amounts of tribal land as the private property of incumbent tribal leaders, the processes of contestation were undermined, for rank had become tied to economic advantage. The shaikhs of Kut–Amara were really caricatures of the traditional tribal leader as they travelled about in tribal robes and limousines, for their great wealth placed them outside the processes of tribal life and their coercive power had turned their dispossessed fellow tribesmen into peasant-slaves. It was largely because of them that all shaikhs were regarded as wealthy, reactionary and powerful left-overs from British colonialism. Much of the literature about the period gives the same impression. Batatu, however, does indicate some variation in the wealth and power of the shaikhs, based largely on the differences in the size of their landholdings.[7] In the Kut–Amara region, the role played by government administrators was totally under the direction of the estate-owning shaikhs. In the Middle Euphrates region, where there were numerous small landowners, however, this was not the case. In this region, the government administration was a largely independent force, and it was the district engineer from the Ministry of Irrigation, not wealthy landowners, who controlled distribution of the water supply.

Abdul-Karim, the young irrigation engineer in Daghara, shared the urban view that shaikhs and tribes were an unfortunate remnant of the past, but he also knew they were not all wealthy and powerful and gave some their due as honest, even if reactionary, men. It was he who controlled the life force of the area. Every morning men came to petition for more water or complain about its loss. Abdul-Karim's office was arranged much like the guesthouses of tribal settlements. Men sat along the walls, waiting to speak to the engineer, and to win his favours. They rose, in turn, hands across their chests, the phrases of formal greetings on their lips. They petitioned for larger discharge pipes from the government canals, for different arrangements in water distributions, for independent, rather than shared, allotments. Abdul-Karim's reasons for granting or refusing such requests were phrased in technical terms, but to the cultivators his rulings were judgements which were subject to endless discussion and renegotiation in his office. In the past, water distribution problems had been settled by tribal negotiation or warfare. Now *al-hakuma*, the government, made the essential decisions. Even the fairly wealthy shaikhs in this region were obliged to stop by the engineer's office for a visit, their demands becoming part of the polite conversations. If this did not work, they could try to go over the engineer's head and appeal to the provincial governor or someone in Baghdad, but only rarely did this result in a change of mind by Abdul-Karim.

Did the new technical considerations prevail in disputes over water – or did the old strategies of threats and favours, obligations and compromise, so familiar to the diplomats of the tribal guesthouse, prevail over bureaucratic rules? The outcome varied from situation to situation and from case to case (as I have shown elsewhere).[8] However, it was often not a clear-cut matter, as one decision frequently impinged on another and a history of water distribution impacted on present practices. Some farmers took their water directly from government canals; others shared canals on land which had never officially been divided between them. The shaikh and the engineer were often involved in contingent problems.

Thus Shaikh Mujid, the village tribal leader in Daghara at the time we lived there, often made his way to the Administrators' Club, down the canal from the tribal settlement, where the teachers, clerks and other administrative officials gathered for board games, cards and tea after work. The shaikh would make his rounds of the tables, meeting and greeting local officials there, visitors from the provincial capital or even from Baghdad, shaking hands, exchanging remarks, smiling, attempting to smooth the paths of official business. Here the etiquette was different from in his guesthouse, and the shaikh tried to adapt himself to the more informal amenities. In fact, he deplored the morals of many of the *muwadhifiin*, the government employees – they drank too much and were lazy and in some cases corrupt – but he had to do business with them. The government employees, in

turn, treated the shaikh with friendly greetings, but the younger men
(including Abdul-Karim) considered him a symbol of the political
system they secretly despised, what with his Baghdad connections
and his position as one of Nuri Said's hand-picked and obliging
senators.

However, in the 1950s, before the Revolution, it was still
important for the local administrators to be on good terms with the
shaikh if they were to do their jobs effectively. In this Shi'a
community, on religious holidays such as the celebration of
Muharram, the district supervisor, engineers, medical personnel and
teachers, paid visits to the shaikh in his guesthouse. Even the female
school-teachers visited the shaikh's wives in their harem. He had
helped overcome local opposition to an elementary school for girls so
that his own daughters could learn to read and write. The police
chief also called on the shaikh to send out a call for tribesmen for
questioning in criminal investigations, just as the shaikh would
sometimes go to him at the behest of tribesmen to ask about their
imprisoned relatives. (One night he got the Daghara telephone
operator out of bed to open the switchboard so that he could call the
provincial capital and arrange to get his son and myself out of police
custody.) Thus, on ceremonial occasions and sometimes for business
reasons government officials in their Western-style suits would sit on
the rugs of the guesthouse, looking almost as awkward and
uncomfortable as British officials once did, judging from old
photographs. However, many of the Iraqi administrators were
themselves of tribal origin and their upbringing and personal ties
sometimes led them into contradictory situations.

One day I travelled on muddy roads to a remote hamlet several
miles from Daghara. My companion was a man in his late twenties
whose personal achievement was remarkable, but not unique. Born
to a poor tribal farm family, he had gone to public school, received a
fellowship to study in America, became a civil engineer and lived in
Baghdad. (Engineering was perhaps the most respected profession in
Iraq at this time.) We were visiting his natal home, a small mud-brick
house with a small guesthouse near by. As soon as we got out of our
Landrover he rushed to kiss his seated father's hand. But his father,
who appeared to be in his seventies, stood up as soon as he saw his
son and made him sit down, serving him (and myself) our meal,
waiting on us in every way. My friend appeared to be deeply
embarrassed, but though he changed into his tribal robes and tried to
resist this reversal of paternal–filial roles, he had to let his father

serve him and accept, in front of his tribal kinsmen, the position of honoured guest rather than that of respectful son.

Inter-personal decorum was a very powerful aspect of tribal discourse in the tribal guesthouse, as has been so well demonstrated by S. M. Salim.[9] All arrivals greeted the shaikh first, attempting to kiss his hand. They would then take their places at the greatest distance from the seated shaikh unless he called them forward and bade them sit closer to him. They rose when he rose, and spoke when he asked them their business. Shaikh Mujid sat just to the right of the entrance in the summer, closer to the fire pit during the winter. He was always the focus of attention, just as was the irrigation engineer in his setting.

The shaikh was believed to have special influence with the government and his help was often sought by men having problems with the administration. However, many of the problems were brought to him as an alternative to going to the police. As often as not, lodging a complaint with the police brought on as much or more trouble than had the problem which provoked the visit in the first place. Never go to the government for anything if you can possibly avoid it, was the general sentiment, which I heard expressed over and over again, and illustrations of the dire outcomes of taking such a reckless step were a favourite source of conversation. The irrigation engineer was the one possible exception in this regard; it was impossible to avoid his office when one's supply of water was in his hands. However, going to the police or district supervisor with problems was usually out of the question for the humble tribesman.

The following problems were discussed before the shaikh in his guesthouse on one afternoon in 1957: (1) A man complained because another man was putting out more animals to pasture than were agreed on at the time when a field was rented to him. (2) A man asked Mujid's help because his paternal uncle had forced his way into his house and taken his gun. (3) Mujid's brother (who often sat in for him) settled a problem between tenant farmers involved in a fight with gun butts. (4) A faulty registration of land, in which a poor Sayid[10] had consolidated his landholdings by incorporating a piece of Mujid's land, was discussed. (5) A man protested against the return of his wife to her parental home; her people asserted that he did not support her as well as he claimed he did. The shaikh was expected to do something about each of these matters, and render some kind of judgement after discussions had taken place involving many of the men present.

The most frequent and difficult of the problems which were discussed in the tribal guesthouse was that of the *fasl*, the settlement or terms of settlement of a feud. This ancient institution was the basis for the symbolic restitution of honour after a killing, accidental or deliberate, among tribesmen. Settlement was of two kinds: compensating the family of the dead man with a payment of money was called 'black' *fasl*; the giving of women in marriage from the offending to the offended group without a payment of dower to the bride's family was a 'white' *fasl*. The latter was considered to have a much better chance of preventing future bloodshed than had a 'black' *fasl*. To negotiate such settlements was a very difficult matter, full of passions, rejections and denials. It was the prestige of the shaikh which could best oblige the contending parties to submit their quarrel to his arbitration. Accepting the hospitality of the shaikh's guesthouse meant that the parties involved had agreed to accept a negotiated settlement. Traditional settlements between opposing kin groups, however, had no bearing on the transgressor's punishment in the governmental courts. State law stressed individual responsibility; that of the tribe conceived of offence and retribution as a group affair. If *fasl* was not arranged, revenge was usually taken no matter who was in prison or for how long and feuds could continue for generations. For example, an old man, uncle of a tribesman who was in jail for a murder, was stabbed to death by the murdered man's young paternal cousin as he lay sleeping in his yard, a few yards from where we lived.

More general levels of tribal violence in this region were not likely by 1958, though a real tribal uprising had occurred in the Middle Euphrates region as recently as 1936. There seemed to be more concern on the part of the Nuri Said government about the possibility that public demonstrations, fired by religious fervour, might get out of hand. The tribesmen of southern Iraq were Shia Muslims; the government of Nuri Said was predominantly Sunni. There is a long history of Shia martyrdom at the hands of the Sunni into which the people of southern Iraq could easily have fitted their impoverished condition. Many of the tribesmen did own old rifles which were worn daily and were fired into the air during festive occasions. In 1957 the local processions of *ashira* (tribes), which involved most of the population, were all cancelled by government order. So the shaikhs of southern Iraq before the 1958 Revolution were still regarded by the Nuri Said government as instruments of law and order. A man like Shaikh Mujid learned to play his role in ways which helped him retain some of his prestige and authority among his own people.

After a conversation with an old shaikh of a small lineage in January 1957, I wrote as follows:

One of the subjects to which he gave most weight was the decline of authority in the sense of someone having the ability to deal directly with wrong-doers. As has Mujid, he spoke of the days when the Shaikh could wipe out a whole clan if they transgressed. If a man lied he could be beaten and then thrown out or killed directly for a serious crime. He said, 'Now, there is the *hakuma*' [the government], and his emphasis on 'hakuma' was full of contempt as he pointed out that it now took months under the government to accomplish what used to be done in a few minutes.

The state in southern Iraq, at least the part I knew, was still an unwelcome imposition as it had been during the British mandate. Though the state dominated the region, the procedures it presupposed, the attitudes and support it expected from its citizens, were still not willingly given. Nowhere was this more clearly expressed than in the failure of its attempt to punish individuals to settle what were in local thought and practice the claims and responsibilities of the group. The Tribal Code, rescinded immediately after the 1958 Revolution, attempted to accommodate tribal customs as the British had conceived them, but it did not recognize the collective responsibility which was at the centre of tribal practice in matters of personal injury.

Most of the issues I have discussed above presumably have become irrelevant since the 1958 Revolution, as the power of government administration has become so absolute and as the basic attitudes of rural as well as urban people have changed. Before 1958, most of the younger men were working for a regime they despised and against which many were plotting. In this sense, they were the natural allies of the poorer tribesmen. But the differences between themselves and the rural tribal people, the significant differences of formal training and a devotion to what they called the 'higher life', undermined a sense of common cause. After the revolution, nothing stood in the way of an enthusiastic employment of the full range of state tactics and technology for the modernization of 'backward tribal people'. No shaikhs could stand as arcane obstacles to the execution of modern bureaucratic authority. The power of the state has found new expressions through the post-revolutionary administration of land reform programmes, resettlement schemes, co-operatives, rural education, medical care – and internal security forces.

The great technical improvements and innovations in communication of the last few decades have surely increased administrative efficiency many times over since 1958. No longer is the state run by an ex-colonial collaborator such as Nuri Said. Instead, most of the rulers of post-revolutionary Iraq have exercised a total monopoly of state power and have exhibited the very characteristics once admired in tribal shaikhs – fearlessness towards one's enemies, swift punishment to those judged to be wrong, and loyalty to kinsmen and supporters. The Revolution of 1958 made it possible for the Iraqi administration to establish for itself the very conditions of decisive, unobstructed rule which were then sometimes nostalgically recalled as part of the tribal past. As to the contemporary existence and relevance of the local practices I studied long ago in Daghara, this is a matter that awaits future research.

### Notes

1. Raymond Williams on hegemony: 'It is not limited to matters of direct political control but seeks to describe a more general predominance which includes, as one of its key features, a particular way of seeing the world and human nature and relationships ... depend[s] for its hold not only on its expression of the interests of a ruling class but also on its acceptance as a 'normal reality' or 'common sense' by those in practice subordinated to it.' *Keywords: A Vocabulary of Culture and Society* (New York, 1976), p. 118.

2. 'Tradition, it is important to reaffirm, in tribal and class-divided societies is a source of legitimacy: daily social practices, and the *durée* of experience itself, are moralized through their antiquity (although not through that alone ... ). The 'meaningfulness' of the day-to-day organization of social life is a taken-for-granted feature of human existence, and guaranteed by tradition.' Anthony Giddens, *A Contemporary Critique of Historical Materialism* (Berkeley and Los Angeles, 1981), p. 93.

3. 'Political behavior is rarely unicausal. However, the compliancy of the tribal chiefs to British policies or their subservience to the king or regent, or their participation in nationalist endeavors, were often at bottom no more than bids for the support of their private ambitions in land, that is, of their desire to preserve or add to their holdings or to pull down land rivals, or to reverse unfavorable land decisions, or to secure preferential treatment in land revenue, or to escape revenue all together.' Hanna Batatu, *Old Social Classes and the Revolutionary Social Movements of Iraq* (Princeton, 1978), p. 116.

4. Ibid., p. 87.

5. Ibid., p. 73.

6. See Robert A. Fernea, *Shaykh and Effendi: Changing Patterns of Authority*

*among the El Shabana of Southern Iraq* (Cambridge, Mass., 1970), 'The Shaykhship and the Dominant Lineage', p. 105.

7. See Batatu, *Old Social Classes*, chap. 6, 'The Shaikhs, Aghas, and Peasants'.

8. See Fernea, *Shaykh and Effendi*.

9. Shakir M. Salim, *Marsh Dwellers of the Euphrates Delta* (London, 1962), pp. 72–83.

10. Some Sayids, or descendants of the Prophet, lived with the tribe. They were given land in exchange for their services as mediators in tribal disputes.

# 9

# Class and Class Politics in Iraq before 1958: The 'Colonial and Post-Colonial State'

ROGER OWEN

Hanna Batatu's mighty work has served us all as a model of historical research, a mine of information and a powerful interpretation of the twentieth-century transformation of Iraqi society. Like all such works it constitutes both a formidable influence and a formidable challenge. We can be dazzled by it, or we can try to use it as a basis for asking new questions and for providing a larger and more satisfying set of explanations for the major social and political processes involved.

It is in this spirit that I would like to return to the two major arguments which lie at the heart of *The Old Classes*. The first is that while in the 1920s and 1930s elements of the socially-dominant landed classes vied with each other for power, prestige and property, in the 1940s and 1950s they combined together in defence of the existing social order.[1] The second, sometimes stated explicitly, sometimes implied, is that the rural class conflict was displaced from the countryside to the towns by peasant migration, forcing the regime to continue to rely on the political support of shaikhs and other large landowners.[2]

While I generally agree with both of these arguments, I am less happy about Batatu's attempts to explain the underlying processes at work, particularly the almost total absence of reference either to the state or to day-to-day class politics. Major political actors such as the 'British', the 'Monarchy', the 'Army' are present, it is true, but in almost every case they appear as persons or collectivities without reference to the structures and institutions which they controlled and through which they were forced to act. By the same token, there is only occasional mention of the arenas in which groups, classes or institutional interests bargained with one another or came into conflict.

In the following discussion I would like to see how it might be possible to augment Batatu's explanations by 'bringing the state back in'. To do this I will make use of the notion that there is no single definition of the state but at least three, each with its own vocabulary and its own angle on political practice. These are: (1) the state as a territorial unit with a capital, boundaries, and its own laws; (2) the state as a set of institutionalized practices for rule-making and rule-enforcement; (3) the state as a necessary condition for the creation of what Sami Zubaida has called a 'national political field' which constitutes the primary arena for political competition between various organizations, classes and groups.[3]

## The Colonial State and its Legacy

It is a truism to assert that the British created the Iraqi state in all three of the above definitions even if, as can be easily argued, the three Ottoman provinces of Basra, Baghdad and Mosul contained various properties of 'stateness' and modernity long before the occupation. It was the British who first negotiated, and then patrolled and defended, the boundaries, who obtained international recognition for the new entity and who created the centre of political administration in Baghdad with a monarch, a constitution, a bureaucracy and an elite drawn mainly from former Ottoman army officers and officials. This arena soon came to constitute the competitive area within which all significant Iraqi politics took place, with most groups organizing themselves to seek influence in Baghdad or through the new local administration. The speed at which this happened was quite remarkable. Already by the early 1920s the most politically active groups within both the Shi'i and Kurdish populations had accepted the realities of the new order and focused their attention on trying to exert pressure on the power centre in Baghdad. A good example of this is the issuance of the *fatwa* (religious decree) by certain Shi'i *ulama* (Mulsim clergy) in 1923 condemning the forthcoming elections to the Constituent Assembly, a move which may have seemed to some as atavistic, but which, in reality, was clearly designed to assert their own claims to leadership of their co-religionists within the framework of the Iraqi state.

Just as important, the British instituted an important set of policies and practices which were to provide an influential legacy for those who governed Iraq after the official end of the mandate. These, of course, represent the play of imperial necessities formed by administrators who owed their allegiance to institutions in Britain and India and whose primary concern was with security and, to a slightly lesser extent, with finance. One of the most important of such practices was management of the tribal areas which extended from the support of the shaikhs and the special regime established in the Amara *liwa* (sub-province) to the division of the country into two separate legal systems as a result of the Tribal Criminal and Civil Disputes Regulation first issued on a temporary basis in 1916 and finally confirmed by royal decree in 1924. Another was the creation of a two-tier electoral system which allowed maximum control by the central authorities over who was elected to the lower house of parliament. A third was the establishment of various mechanisms for maintaining law and order – the military, the Ministry of the Interior and the *mutasarrifs* (provincial governors), the tribal shaikhs – and the institutionalized conflict between those interested in order and those interested in either maximizing revenues or imposing a common system of administration and justice on the whole country. A fourth was a notion of economic development based on flood control, irrigation and the encouragement of the use of pumps.

In addition, the British took certain important steps to safeguard essential features of their order before the end of the mandate. These included the ratification of the Anglo–Iraqi Treaty of 1930, the oil concession agreement of 1931, the management of the currency (with the dinar pegged to sterling and managed by a British-controlled currency board in London) and the placing of advisers in key positions within the Iraqi administration. This clearly gave Britain a predominant influence in independent Iraq, although just how this continued to affect the country's politics and its economic development remains controversial. For example there has been no serious study of the role of the British Embassy and, just as important, the British advisers after 1932. Moreover, the country was, in effect reoccupied in 1941 and the structure of British influence was placed on quite a new footing. Just as important, there does not seem to have been any consensus among those concerned as to the degree to which British interest required day-to-day involvement in Iraqi affairs or how it ought properly to be exercised.[4] Once again there were obvious differences of institutional opinion reflecting the different responsibility of the major British ministries involved.

With this in mind, I would like to pass on to an examination of those features of the Iraqi state in the early 1930s which relate most directly to Batatu's points about the formation of a ruling class.

## Institutions, Structures and Politics in the 1930s

The main components of the Iraqi state as it existed in the early 1930s are well known and do not require repeating.[5] Nevertheless, there are certain aspects which need underlining for the purposes of my argument. Of these the most important is the significance of the transition from a mandatory (or colonial) to a post-independent state. This is not a subject which has received very much attention by historians so far, perhaps because it was accompanied by little change of personnel among Iraqi's major political actors (the King and the small group of politicians encouraged by the British), perhaps because the colonial power still retained such a dominant position for itself by treaty and in so many other ways. But, in fact, the change was of considerable importance. Instead of a state which obtained its coherence and sense of power from external authority in the metropolis, it was now necessary to find a new basis for unity and, if possible, legitimacy based on a marshalling of internal resources such as loyalty to the person of the monarch and to a putative sense of Iraqi nationalism.

That this was consciously attempted at the time there is little doubt, whether by organizing a competition to find a national anthem or by signing treaties with Arab neighbours such as Saudi Arabia as a way of stressing Iraq's sovereignty over its own territory. Nevertheless, the problems involved in state creation were enormous. Some stemmed from an underdeveloped administrative structure and an obvious lack of resources. Others were the inevitable consequence of earlier British practice by which the colonial power had deliberately brought about the entry of a number of social groups into the political arena without providing a set of satisfactory mechanisms by which their various interests and demands could either be reconciled with one another or contained within some overall national framework of accepted political practice. Moreover, no social class existed which was strong enough to monopolize power and to play a hegemonic role by universalizing its own claims on the basis, say, of private property and the development of capitalism. Meanwhile, the British, as elsewhere in the colonial world, had started a process of constructing fixed, singular, communal identities for Iraqis (as Sunnis, Shi'is and so on) by means of their censuses and other methods of categorization, leaving their successors the difficult task of coping with the divisions and the strains imposed by the new political practices which this entailed.

Some of the consequences of this situation can now be sketched in. The first was the fluidity at the centre where relationships between King, cabinet and the fledgling bureaucracy were all highly politicized and in a constant state of flux. As we know, few cabinets lasted more than a couple of years,[6] and, as Yasin al-Hashimi noted as early as 1934, each new one would proudly announce a lengthy and complex programme of legislation which no one took very seriously or actually expected it to carry out.[7] In these circumstances it might be expected that the role of the permanent civil servants would consequently be enhanced, particularly in those technical ministries such as finance and irrigation where medium- to long-term planning was often required. However, we also know that government service was not well protected from political interference and that, by the end of the 1930s, it was common for incoming ministers to replace many of their senior officials with their own friends and supporters.[8] In this context, there is no simple answer to the question of where rules were drawn up or policy made and no alternative to the difficult task of tracing each particular piece of legislation to its own particular sources.

A second aspect which I would like to underline concerns the way in which the major institutions of government in Baghdad acted as a focus for political competition around which developed what seems like a modern form of national political activity. This can be demonstrated most forcefully in relation to the tribes, as I will try to show. But it can be seen just as clearly in the growing use of extra-parliamentary methods of influencing political decisions: press campaigns, strikes by professional groups such as lawyers, demonstrations or the 'General Strike' of July 1931. This, in turn, aroused the government of the day to counter with a growing armoury of new methods of control: press censorship or laws to allow the banning of public meetings or to prohibit 'Malicious Propaganda'.

The third aspect concerns the relations between state and tribe. To over-simplify, state policy was based on two seemingly contradictory sets of practices: the isolation of the tribes from the rest of society by means of the Tribal Criminal and Civil Disputes Regulation and yet the political incorporation of the shaikhs at the centre by means of their membership of the Senate, the lower chamber and other national institutions. Some of the administrative anomalies which this produced were well appreciated at the time. The successful appeal by Falih Bey al-Sadun to be tried under tribal law for his murder of a former Director-General of the Ministry of the Interior in 1931, and the use of the same regulations to banish inconvenient political opponents, excited much contemporary comment and encouraged the obvious criticism that they created two types of legal system and two types of Iraqi citizen. Again, officials of the Ministry of Finance were constantly complaining that tribal policy placed political considerations above those of increasing rural revenue.

The structure of relations between state and tribe also allowed a particular type of politics in which shaikhs were encouraged to find new ways to make their influence felt in Baghdad rather than by threatening violence in their own tribal lands. A trivial but none the less telling example of such a process of adaptation took place in May 1933 when, after eighteen months in jail, the same Falih Bey received a royal pardon fromn King Faisal as the result of a persuasive series of interventions by members of his influential family. At first, as the American Minister, Paul Knabenshue, reported, they talked openly of an uprising. But then 'more rational pleas' were employed including the erection of a statue to Sir Abd al-Muhsin Bey al-Sadun, Falih Bey's cousin and a distinguished former prime minister. The ploy of having this statue unveiled on the same day as one of the King (and also on Faisal's birthday) seems to have been enough to prompt the needed display of royal clemency.[9] More seriously, almost every aspect of the tribal risings of 1935–6 can be seen as part of an orchestrated political event, encouraged by opposition politicians and then closely controlled by these same men, now in office, with some of its major leaders, such as Shaikh Wahid, constantly visiting Baghdad for negotiations.

One interpretation of this new pattern of politics is that suggested by Batatu, and also by David Pool, to the effect that it constituted the basis for an alliance between the tribal leadership and the small group of ex-Sharifian officers turned politicians without large popular followings who vied with each other for control of the central state apparatus.[11] This is certainly one of the possible ways to read logic into the situation. But I prefer to leave this question open and to proceed with an examination of the nature of the Iraqi state through analysis of the relationship between the political centre and the rural population. I will look at this briefly under four heads: taxation, rules and laws, the army and conscription, and the politics of development.

## Taxation

The first attempt to create a uniform, national tax system on agricultural land was made in 1929 with Law No. 40 which aimed to impose a single consolidated figure encompassing a land tax, a water tax and a rent for the use of state land on every dunum (0.618 acres) according to the quality of its soil.[12] The timing of such a move makes sense in terms of British colonial policy elsewhere in the Middle East. A similar reform was designed to replace the Ottoman system (tithe) was introduced in Palestine in 1928. But it is not clear to me how the officials at the Iraqi Ministry of Finance had come to the conclusion that such a measure could be made to work in a country with such enormous disparities between different types of land and where the process of survey and classification (on which the new tax depended) was clearly going to be an enormously difficult, expensive and lengthy process. As it was, the onset of the world depression combined with other factors to produce a sharp revenue crisis and led to the introduction of the 'Istihlak' in1931, a return to one of the ways of collection used under the previous system – in other words, the appropriation of a proportion of any agricultural crop brought to market. The reasons for this change had probably much to do with expense, but there is no doubt that it benefited the large landowners in at least two ways: it was regressive in that it was levied at the same rate on rich and poor cultivators alike and it was easy to avoid.

The 'Istihlak' was supplemented by another law of the same year which attempted to place a water tax on all lands irrigated by flow and a rent on most *miri* (state-owned) land. This was amended in 1936 and finally phased out after 1939 on the grounds that it brought in too little revenue. Once again, the new system benefited the rich more than the poor. But the larger point still to be determined is whether this was a conscious act of favouritism or simply the result of the fact that the state bureaucracy was unable to introduce a system of uniform taxation in the context of natural geographical conditions which were extraordinarily diverse compared with, say, those found in Egypt.

*Rules and Laws*

The two major laws affecting agricultural relations were the Land Settlement Law (No. 50) of June 1932 and the Law Governing the Rights and Duties of Cultivators (No. 28) of July 1933. The first, passed just before the official end of the mandate, established the main legal categories under which agricultural land could be held, including three types of *miri*: *miri tapu, miri lazma* and *miri sirf*.[13] Of these, *miri tapu* was simply a recognition of Ottoman practice but *miri lazma* was a new category designed to fit tribal conditions and to protect tribal solidarity by giving the government the right to veto the transfer of such land if it would 'disturb the peace' by passing into outside hands. As commentators have pointed out, this law contained several significant variations from the recommendations of the British expert, Sir Ernest Dowson, on which it was largely based. Two of its basic categories, *miri tapu* and *miri lazma*, were very much closer to private property than he had suggested. And responsibility for registration and settlement was assigned not to one Central Lands Office but divided between a number of separate departments and ministries thus making its provisions more open to manipulation by interested parties.[14]

The Law Governing the Rights and Duties of Cultivators contained fifty-two articles defining the right and duties not just of the peasant cultivators but of two other categories of persons as well: the landlord and a set of people described as 'managers' and legally defined as 'persons who regulate tribesmen on a share-tenancy basis'. Once again the importance of regulating certain forms of practice to be found in the tribal areas of the irrigated zone in the south is obvious. In addition, the law contained a notorious Article 15 which gave the landlord the right to prevent a peasant tenant from leaving his estate so long as he owed him money. In origin, this latter clause may have represented a generalization of an earlier, 1924, prohibition preventing a *sirkal* (landlord's agent) who owed money to one shaikh from moving into the service of another, a measure which Sir Henry Dobbs, the second British High Commissioner to Iraq, believed had been introduced at the request of the shaikhs themselves.[15]

Both laws are excellent examples of the rule-making, category-creating activities of the state. Moreover, their impact was so significant that it is important to know more about the way in which they were drafted, the amendments they were subject to in parliament, and the input of some of the leading politicians of the day. As far as David Pool is concerned, the main initiator of the 1933 law was Yasin al-Hashimi, the Minister of Finance who was also the owner of sixteen estates which he had managed to create out of government domain.[16] He also suggests that al-Hashimi had built up a personal following by, among other things, the grant of land, tax concessions and tax remissions to his followers.[17] Further evidence of al-Hashimi's agricultural interests (and his concern to find the capital needed to develop his estates) comes from the fact that he was on the organizing committee for a project to establish an Agricultural Credit Bank in 1934 and was assumed to be anxious to become one of its directors.[18]

Nevertheless, it is important to note that Yasin al-Hashimi was not alone in trying to promote the interests of the large landowners. A British report of 1925 suggests that Naji al-Suwaidi, then Minister of Justice, had become a large landowner himself and that he and other ministers were then engaged in trying (successfully) to obtain dismissal of the Head of Survey at the Tapu and Land Survey Department after he had incurred their hostility by trying to stop various abuses.[19] It would also be interesting to know more of the role of the tribal shaikhs in the drafting of this legislation. A reasonable assumption would be that many of them had initially preferred a situation in which there were no rules and regulations governing survey and registration, and so might give them greater freedom to accumulate land and to manage it as they wished. But it is also possible that membership of the Chamber of Deputies and the Senate was enough to convince them of the advantages of protecting their interests by legislation. Some of them had certainly become sufficiently confident in the advantages of the new system to heckle Hikmat Sulaiman in the Chamber of Deputies when, as Prime Minister after the 1936 military coup, he tried to argue the need to distribute state-owned land to the peasants.[20] The way in which they joined with other members with landowning interests in trying to undermine him by calling him a 'Communist' points in the same general direction.

A last difficult question concerns the effectiveness of the two laws and the way in which they were implemented and interpreted. Here the conventional wisdom about the 1932 Land Settlement is that it led directly to the registration of large areas of land by a few powerful persons, either as *miri tapu* or *miri lazma*. It has also been argued that a key role in all of this was played by Dowson's concept of 'beneficial use', which, despite its intention to put lands in the hands of the actual cultivators, was actually employed to justify its award to shaikhs and those who owned pumps and who obtained full title after a much shorter period of time than the law actually allowed.[21] According to Warriner, 13.22 million acres of land (21.42 million dunums) were subject to settlement of title between 1933 and 1945, of which 2.67 million acres (4.33 million dunums) were granted as *miri lazma* and 2.22 million acres (3.60 million dunums) as *miri tapu*.[22] By 1958 the settled areas are said to have increased to 32.15 million dunums, two thirds of which were held as *tapu* and *lazma*. This seems a very large growth, particularly as the amount categorized as *miri sirf* remained more or less constant over the same period. However, as Batatu points out, it can probably be accounted for by the fact that the work of settlement by the state commissions was continued much more energetically after 1945 and that as much as one-third of the land in question was still uncultivated.[23]

There are other problems as well. Some land registered as *miri sirf* in 1943 seems to have been held as what was virtually private property, notably by the few large landowners whose estates dominated the area of Amara *liwa*.[24] It would appear that it was much the same picture in 1958. Lastly the question of who was to be given title to lands in the Muntafiq *liwa* claimed by the Sadun family on the basis of an Ottoman concession remained unresolved until 1958, in spite of two attempts at an official solution (in 1929 and the 1950s). However, what does seem possible to state with confidence is that a large proportion of the land in cultivation in 1933, and even larger proportion of lands brought into cultivation after that, passed, legally, into the hands of large landowners and that Warriner is perfectly correct to suggest that, as of 1955, peasants could no longer expect to be given title to land as a right (which was the import of the Dowson report) but only as a rare and special privilege.[25]

Discussion of the impact of the Law Concerning the Rights and Duties of Cultivators also presents problems. There is no doubt that, from a legal point of view, it not only tied the indebted tenant to the land but also gave his landlord complete power to decide what crops he grew and what times they were sown and harvested.[26] This was also backed up by the landlord's (legal) control over the system of irrigation as well as, in tribal areas, by his authority under the Tribal Disputes regulation. How all this worked out in practice is less clear. Was it the case, as Sir Kinahan Cornwallis (then Adviser to the Ministry of the Interior) asserted, that the 1933 law was 'incapable of universal application throughout Iraq'?[27] In the event, its impact seems to have depended on a variety of local factors, including the density of the agricultural population, the relationship between landlord and 'manager', and the role of local officials. Evidence for this comes from the fact that rents, or the proportion of the crop taken by the landlord, varied widely from one area to another. There is also a Second World War report that in areas where agricultural workers were scarce, as in the Muntafiq *liwa*, owners or sirkals could entice them from nearby estates by giving them advances to pay off their debts.[28] And even in Amara, many tenants were able to migrate to the towns (albeit at the risk of punishment to their families) well before the mass evictions which followed the failure of attempts to provide peasants with title to half the land under the 1952 Law for Granting Lazma Rights to Miri Sirf Land in Amara. Nevertheless, it would be reasonable to assume that the 1933 law played some role in maintaining the power of the landlords over a poverty-stricken rural population.

## The Army and Conscription

To make only the most obvious point, the role of the Iraqi Army after 1932, as well as its expansion under the National Service Law of 1934, was intimately connected with the relations between state and tribes. Not only was the army used to suppress tribal revolts in various parts of the country, it also contributed to some of these same uprisings by its efforts at conscription in the rural areas after June 1935. This in turn played a significant role in the military coup of October 1936. Senior officers were inevitably resentful at the way in which they were commanded by politicians to put down risings when the latter had done so much to stir up the trouble in the first place. The military officers felt also that they had not been given enough rifles to do the job properly, while General Bakr Sidqi himself complained that the government showed too much leniency towards tribal offenders.[29] In an important sense the coup represented the culmination of a classic case of the tension which can arise between the military and civilian institutions of a state. It might also be noted that the coup itself was greatly facilitated by the fact that the bulk of the army was either on duty in the tribal areas of the south or on its autumn manoeuvres – signs of its growing organizational maturity.

## The State and the Politics of Development

According to the 1931 agreement with the Iraq Petroleum Company, the Iraqi government was to receive a minimum annual payment of £400,000 (gold) for the next twenty years. This was at once seen as the basis for a capital works development programme which was to be passed into law in June of the same year. Schemes specifically included in this law were the Habbaniyah escape (to assist flood control) and two projects to provide extra water for cultivation, the Abu Ghuraib canal and the construction of a barrage at Kut to divert part of the Tigris down the Shatt al-Gharraf. As it transpired, the complete programme was beyond the country's immediate technical, as well as financial, resources. Nevertheless, the several items soon became the source of political and administrative controversy. Reference to new works of irrigation became, *de rigueur*, an essential feature of the programme of each new cabinet. And the fact that the more northerly of the schemes (for example, the Habbaniyah escape and the Abu Ghuraib canal) could be said to benefit mainly Sunni cultivators, while in the south the Shatt al-Gharraf canal affected mainly Shi'i-controlled land, played a role in a number of fierce disputes leading, *inter alia*, to the resignation of the cabinet in February 1934 after the Minister of Economy and Communications, Rustum Haidar (a Shi'i), was accused of publishing notices concerning contracts for the Abu Gharraf project without consulting the Minister of Finance.[30] In the end it was the Abu Ghuraib canal which was completed first (irrigating 120,000 dunums between Fallujah and Baghdad). Work on the Kut barrage was finished just before the outbreak of the Second World War, and led to an immediate increase (estimated at 1.5 million dunums) in the cultivated area to the south.

Just as important from the point of view of my argument, technical and financial controversies had become inextricably mixed up with questions of politics and of state policy. While the state as bureaucracy was concerned to spend money in ways which would develop the economy and, just as important, encourage nomadic tribes to settle down (a constant theme), the state as political arena witnessed a continuous struggle for control of development policy on behalf of various rival political constituencies.

## Institutions, Structures and Politics in the 1940s and 1950s

From the point of view of the relations between state and large landowners, the British re-occupation of Iraq and the restoration of the monarchical regime in 1941, had three main consequences. Firstly, the shaikhs were rewarded *en masse* for their support against Rashid Ali by increasing their representation in parliament in 1943. This gave them an even more powerful position from which to defend the advances they had made in the 1930s. Secondly, there was a renewed interest in schemes of flood control and economic development, later to be stimulated still further by the huge increase in oil royalty payments from 1950 onwards. In these circumstances, the British attempted to protect their own economic and political interests by pressing for the establishment of a Development Board containing a British representative and insulated as much as possible from local political currents.[31] This suggestion was first made in 1947 and came to fruition in 1950 with Sir E. Miller – followed by Michael Ionides – as the single Briton. Thirdly, many of the Iraqi governments of the period tried to use development policy to defuse social tension in the rural areas which some politicians were beginning to see as a threat to the status quo. That state policy towards the land, taxation and the tribes was always controversial, and played such an intimate role in the lives and fortunes of important classes and groups, meant that different political points of view were forcefully represented at the centre – even if only a few such groups were able to affect policy directly or to further their interests by way of new legislation. In addition, the bogey of rural Communism, once raised, tended to have a life of its own, referred to regularly by the British and Iraqi governments alike and made ever more frightening by the impact of outside events such as the onset of the cold war and the Egyptian Revolution of 1952.

In these circumstances, the relationship between state and tribal landowners began to change, although still subject to certain obvious constraints. On the one hand, the ruling class was forced to face up to some of the consequences of its alliance with the shaikhs as a result of continuing unrest in the rural areas (as well as its spill-over into the towns as a result of migration) and the fact that it was the police force rather than the tribal leaders who now mainly responsible for keeping control. There was also continuous pressure for some kind of agricultural reform from outside, whether from the World Bank mission or from foreigners, such as Lord Salter, who acted as advisers to the Development Board. On the other hand, the shaikhs themselves remained influential, both in their own lands and in Baghdad, and could usually manage to insure that their interests were protected, or even enhanced, when new legislation was proposed, as well as when it was actually implemented. Warriner makes an obvious point when she refers to the fact that there was no other social class with the same power to propose an alternative political strategy (for example, an industrial bourgeoisie as in Egypt).[32] The huge increase in oil revenue after 1950 must also have played a part as it removed the necessity for having to try to raise more money in taxes from the land.

The main lines of development policy are well known. They were to concentrate efforts on flood control (finally achieved in 1956) and on schemes which would bring new land into cultivation while paying little attention to raising the productivity of the already cultivated land.[33] This is explained, in part, by a natural bias towards big projects. But its main rationale seems to have come from the inevitable intrusion of powerful political arguments which can be summed up in this formula: new land could be given to poor peasants as a substitute for a thoroughgoing land reform, while improvements to old land would benefit only those who were already rich. The latter point was further underlined in 1954 by the Senate's rejection of a draft law aimed at allowing the state to recover from the landowners themselves the cost of any drainage improvements which stemmed from Development Board activity.

The result of these policies was predictable. Schemes to distribute new land to small cultivators provided (sometimes deliberately) large landowners with plenty of opportunity to increase their own holdings to a great extent. Such was the case with the Miri Sirf Lands Development Laws of 1945 and 1951 which resulted in the distribution of 140,000 acres (225,000 dunums) to 3,434 settlers in six schemes while allowing the Shaikh of the Shammar and other shaikhs with lands along the new Dujaila canal to increase their own estates by even larger amounts.[34] Furthermore, some at least of those who benefited from the schemes were not peasant cultivators at all but nomads who had little experience of farming yet who nevertheless obtained plots of land as part of the general state policy of tribal settlement.[35] Meanwhile, failure to tackle the problem of salination and soil-exhaustion due to faulty drainage not only reduced agricultural productivity but also led to a further acceleration of rural–urban migration.

Two other aspects of government policy toward the tribal landowners are also significant. One is the policy of removing the distinctions which had been erected between the tribes and the rest of Iraqi society by such measures as replacing the shaikhs in the rural judicial process by the courts and by subjecting agricultural revenues to the income tax (in 1956). These moves can probably be taken as a sign that the economic position of the shaikhs was secure enough, and strong enough, to allow them to pay the tax and to look after their own interests without special legal protection. Another pointer in the same direction was the decision to change over to a single-tier electoral process, which relied more on shaikhly influence over the rural voters to ensure the election of pro-government candidates than on official manipulation by the mutasarrifs.

The other important aspects of government policy were the attempt, finally, (1) to remove the anomalies inherent in the special status of the Amara and the Muntafiq *liwas* and (2) to arrange matters so that landlords, sirkals and tenants all obtained title to some land. The former provoked widespread disturbances when it was realized that it gave the landlords enormous advantages over the peasant cultivators in the event of land registration, and it had to be amended in 1954/55.[36] The latter aimed at compensating the Sadun family and others for their possession of old *tapu* titles while giving the actual occupants secure rights of possession after they themselves contributed half of the compensation. But this involved beginning the long deferred process of land valuation by local committee, a procedure which was subject to considerable administrative delay.[37] In the case of both the Amara and the Muntafiq land settlements it seems unlikely that either was completed before 1958.

## Conclusion: The Revolution of 1958. What state? Whose state?

I feel that any attempt to dot the 'i's and to cross the 't's of Hanna Batatu's great work runs the risk of being entirely misguided. Nevertheless, an effort to present many of the same facts from a somewhat different perspective, using somewhat different concepts, may be of value in bringing to light new comparisons, provoking fresh discussion and adding more factors to the existing range of explanations. The advantage of bringing back the state, as I see it, is that it forces us to confront the problem that before we can ask the question of whose state was it (in Batatu's case, the alliance between the landowning politicians, other persons of property and the shaikhs), we have first to ask what type of state was it which the various social forces were struggling to control? This is not as self-evident a question as it might at first seem. States are not just abstractions, however much we may have been taught to think of them in this way.[38] At the very least they have to be seen as collections of institutions and sets of practices with no necessary coherence between them and divided off from what is commonly thought of as society by often quite arbitrary boundaries. Furthermore, whatever they are, they have to be constructed in history, and this is a process which is always contested and always incomplete.

One of the interesting features of the Iraqi case before 1958 is that the processes in question are much more open to inspection than they were afterwards when greater secrecy prevailed. No group had, as yet, succeeded in dominating the state apparatus in such a way as to be able to impose that degree of coherence necessary to make the majority of Iraqis believe that it was something set apart from society, something abstract and non-particular, to which they owed their undivided loyalty and allegiance. Looked at from this viewpoint, one of the possible ways of trying to make sense of the processes at work is to characterize them, as Batatu does, in terms of the creation and consolidation of a particular class bent on dominating the state and on controlling it for its own interest. It then follows, of course, that the 1958 Revolution has to be seen, in large measure, as the work of forces seeking to challenge this same class and to replace it by some other coalition of interests.

But another way of reading logic into the same situation would be to define it in terms of a logic of failure. Try as they might, Nuri and his colleagues were unable to create a sense that they were at the centre of a single, unique, coherent entity with an unchallengeable claim to universal allegiance. Nor were they able to base their control on a universalization of their own class interests in terms of an order based on private property and untrammelled capitalist development. The result was a continual challenge to their position and, finally, their replacement by a coalition of military and civilian political interests temporarily united behind a project to monopolize an increasingly large share of Iraq's resources in order to create the powerful, unified state apparatus thought necessary for promoting national development under the new banners of independence, anti-imperialism, anti-feudalism and social justice. In this sense 1958 was the beginning not only of a process of political and social revolution but also the construction of a new type of Iraqi state based on a model of unity, coherence and a monopoly of power, such as to give it the capacity to impose itself on society and to reconstruct it in a variety of modern ways.

## Notes

1. Hanna Batatu, *The Old Social Classes and the Revolutionary Movements of Iraq* (Princeton, 1978), pp. 11–12.

2. Ibid., pp. 31, 110, 132.

3. Sami Zubaida, *Islam, the People and the State: Essays on Political Ideas* (London, 1989), pp. 145–52.

4. Joseph Sassoon quotes the views of one British official, Chaplin of the Foreign Office, who gave what must have been one of the most restricted definitions of British interests in Iraq in 1944 when he stated: 'I cannot see an efficiently run Iraq is of great strategic or economic importance. We are concerned to safeguard our communications and our oil supplies, both in the country and across the Shatt al Arab. It is surely less necessary to ensure that trains run on time, that the roads and bridges are properly maintained and that the "fellahin" get a square deal from the "effendis" than that the Iraqis are friendly disposed to us . . . Conditions may be chaotic at times; there may be coups d'état, but temporary inconveniences are surely better than uniting effendi and fellah against us.' *Economic Policy in Iraq 1932–1950* (London, 1987), pp. 27–28. Other Britons with other interests preached a more interventionist line.

5. For example, Stephen Hemsley Longrigg, *Iraq 1900 to 1950: A Political, Social, and Economic History* (London, 1953), chap. 5.

6. There were 45 cabinets formed between 1932 and 1958 lasting an average of 7 months each. Cf. Batatu, *Old Social Classes*, Table 7–2, p. 176.

7. Yasin al-Hashimi's speech to the Chamber of Deputies on 24 February 1934 is quoted in Knabenshue to Secretary of State, Baghdad, 23 March 1934, Records of the Dept. of State Relating to the Internal Affairs of Iraq (Hereafter US), Microfilm, Reel 2. (Copies can be found in the Private Papers Collection, Middle East Centre, St Antony's College, Oxford.)

8. In an interview in January 1939 Nuri Said asserted that 'all officials in key positions' were changed by each new cabinet. Knabenshue to Secretary of State, Baghdad, 16 January 1939, US Reel 2.

9. Knabenshue to Secretary of State, Baghdad, 31 May 1933, US Reel 2.

10. The US Minister also asserts that, at this same time, Shi'i tribesmen were advised not to attack the railway by Rashid Ali al-Gailani acting on the advice of the British Ambassador who argued that this might cause the British to intervene under the terms of the 1930 Treaty. Enclosure No. 2 in Knabenshue to Secretary of State, Baghdad, 21 March 1935, US Reel 2.

11. David Pool, 'From Élite to Class: The Transformation of Iraqi Political Leadership' in A. Kelidar, ed., *The Integration of Modern Iraq* (London, 1978), pp. 63–87.

12. Still the best historical account of the Iraqi land tax system is Guzine A. K.

Rasheed, 'Development of Agricultural Land Taxation in Modern Iraq', *Bulletin of the School of Oriental and African Studies (BSOAS)*, XXV, pt. 2 (1962), pp. 262–74.

13. *miri tapu* = land where ultimate ownership was retained by the state but with usufruct rights acquired by a holder as well as right to sell, mortgage or bequeath. *miri lazma* = land held under almost the same conditions as *miri tapu* but government retained the right to veto its transfer, particularly if this involved tribal land passing outside the tribe. *miri sirf* = land over which state retained legal ownership and actual possession.

14. For example, Doreen Warriner, *Land and Poverty in Middle East* (London and New York, 1948), pp. 110–11.

15. Peter Sluglett, *Britain in Iraq 1914–1932* (London, 1976), p. 321.

16. Pool 'From Élite to Class', pp. 81–3; Knabenshue to Secretary of State, Baghdad, 28 November 1934, US Reel 2.

17. Pool, 'From Élite to Class', p. 83.

18. Knabenshue to Secretary of State, Baghdad, 28 November 1934. The bank was finally created when al-Hashimi was in office again in 1936, but as an Agricultural and Industrial Bank with an initial capital of ID 150,000 provided by the government.

19. Quoted in Mohammad A. Tarbush, 'The Role of the Military in Politics: A Case Study of Iraq to 1941 (London, 1982), p. 28.

20. Interview between Hikmat Sulaiman and the British Ambassador described in Knabenshue to Secretary of State, Baghdad, 10 June 1937, US Reel 2.

21. Sassoon, *Economic Policy in Iraq*, pp. 161–3.

22. Warriner, *Land and Poverty*, pp. 110–11.

23. Batatu, *Old Social Classes*, p. 53, and personal correspondence.

24. Doreen Warriner, *Land Reform and Development in the Middle East: A Study of Egypt, Syria and Iraq* (London, 1957), p. 142.

25. Ibid., p. 161.

26. Report by H. D. Walston on 'Land Tenure in the Fertile Crescent', quoted in ibid., p. 137.

27. Sassoon, *Economic Policy in Iraq*, p. 169.

28. Warriner, *Land and Poverty*, p. 115.

29. Tarbush, *The Role of the Military*, p. 128; Knabenshue to Secretary of State, Baghdad, 18 June 1936, US Reel 2.

30. Knabenshue to Secretary of State, Baghdad, 23 February 1933, US Reel 2.

31. The policy of pushing for the establishment of Development Boards with British membership was widely employed by the British Middle East Office.

32. *Land Reform and Development*, p. 174.

33. Michael Ionides, *Divide and Lose: The Arab Revolt of 1955–1958* (London, 1960), pp. 120, 206–07.

34. Warriner, *Land Reform and Development*, pp. 158–61.

35. British Middle East Office, 'Visits to the Miri Sirf schemes at Hawija, Shahrazoor and Latifiyah', by M. C. Wordsworth (Co-operatives Advisor), *mimeo* (May 1956).

36. Warriner, *Land Reform and Development*, pp. 150–54.

37. Ibid., pp. 155–56.

38. On this point see the very useful analysis by Philip Abrams, 'Notes on the Difficulty of Studying the State', *The Journal of Historical Sociology*, I1 (March 1988), pp. 58–89.

# 10

# The Struggle for Cultural Hegemony during the Iraqi Revolution

## ABDUL-SALAAM YOUSIF

The 14 July 1958 Revolution, however one looks at it, marked a veritable turning-point in Iraq's modern history. As the culmination of the struggles that had pervaded all aspects of life in Iraq, it erupted as a social, political and cultural revolution – a truly genuine revolution. This explosive rupture in the very fabric of Iraqi society was preceded by intellectual ferment and a process of unremitting cultural criticism, as symbolized by the sculptor Jewad Selim's creation of the figure of the 'Imprisoned Thinker' immediately before the 'Soldier' in 'The Monument to Liberty'. For in Nuri Said's Iraq, all was not quiet on the cultural front. Indeed, an intense struggle for cultural hegemony[1] permeated the literary and artistic domains as well as education and the press, in effect smoothing the way for the ideas of change, progress and revolution.

In post-independence monarchical Iraq three schools of thought were contending in the cultural terrain: the *tabi'i* (dependent, official nationalist), *qawmi* (pan-Arab) and *watani* (national or democratic).[2] *Tabi'i* intellectuals monopolized the state cultural instruments of radio and television (introduced around 1934 and 1956, respectively), as well as censorship, but by no means did they have uncontested control over the press, the educational system and the various forms of cultural production. Newspaper editorials, for instance, were often critical, explicitly or obliquely, of Iraq's internal policies and of its ties to Britain; pan-Arab nationalist ideology permeated the school texts;[3] and democratic intellectuals published journals, cultural reviews and literary works that were vocal in their criticism of prevailing social conditions. Not only was this last group at the forefront of the social struggle, it was concurrently most prolific and innovative in the cultural terrain. Whereas the official and pan-Arab cultural groups tended to be tradition-conscious and conservative in social outlook, the democratic element drew its poetry from the future, questioning the sanctity of tradition, the subordination of women and the disparities in the social system. Thus it played a prominent role in the elaboration of cultural politics of opposition.

The impact of the democratic cultural movement can be gleaned from Hanna Batatu's seminal study of Iraq's social classes (*The Old Social Classes and the Revolutionary Movements of Iraq*), which draws on internal party documents and police archives to reconstruct hitherto repressed aspects of Iraq's modern history. While primarily focusing on the politico-economic aspects of the struggle which both preceded and accompanied the July Revolution, Batatu also provides cogent insights into the intellectual ambience of literature and the process of cultural change, as in his treatment of Husain al-Rahhal and Mahmoud Ahmad al-Sayyid and his discussion of *al-Sahifa* and *Jama'at al-Ahali* groups. Unfortunately, he does not extend this kind of cultural analysis to the post-Second World War period, to the important cultural review *al-Thaqafa-al-Jadida*, for example, and to Nuri Said's 1954 anti-intelligentsia campaign. Still, his verse quotations, his references to cultural figures who were prominent in oppositional politics, and his remarks on Marxist inroads among the intelligentsia point to the nexus of culture and leftist politics, as they also do to the cultural aspects of the struggle for hegemony.

The pursuit of hegemony meant that succeeding governments were not oblivious to the advantages of winning the consent of the governed. King Faisal I, in particular, was skilful in orchestrating cultural hegemony, as evidenced in his overtures to the poets Maruf al-Rasafi and Muhammad Mahdi al-Jawahiri.[4] But, especially after the Second World War, the sailing was rough, for the gap between the *tabi'i* and *qawmi* groups widened, and the impact of the *watani* group on the cultural sphere became more pronounced. Looking back upon the period, a historian of culture notes the impact of such figures as Aziz Sharif, Kamil al-Chaderchi, Abdul-Fattah Ibrahim, Husain Jamil, Yusuf Matti, al-Jawahiri, Muhammad Salih Bahr al-Ulum and Dhunun Ayyub.[5] Batatu sketches Dhunun Ayyub's Communist background, but Ayyub's cultural output is of greater note. Besides their status as literary landmarks, his collection of short stories *The Emissaries of Culture* (1937) and his novels *Doctor Ibrahim* (1938) and *The Hand, the Earth, and the Water* (1948, the first Iraqi peasant novel) were works of social criticism in their own right, laying bare the educational structure and exposing the exploitation embedded in the social and semi-feudal systems.

Such works were a prelude to the vital post-Second World War writing that emerged as a subversive articulation of discontent. It is only appropriate at this juncture to start with al-Jawahiri, the poet whose life spans Iraq's modern history. In his poem 'The Martyr's Day' he proclaimed a few weeks after the *Wathbah*:

> Woe to a State run by incompetents who fancy
> that the Government can be maintained by the whip![6]

A government by whip! The phrase captures the government's insecurity and its constant recourse to coercion, the kind of coercion that hit the poet when his brother Ja'far was shot dead by the police during the *Wathbah*. Al-Jawahiri thundered back. The poet delivered an august public reading of 'My Brother Ja'far', which begins with one of the most memorable lines in modern Iraqi poetry:

> Do you know or do you not know
> that the wounds of victims are a mouth?[7]

There are prolific examples of further opposition poetry. One readily thinks of Bahr al-Ulum's 'Ayna Haqqi' ('Where is my right?'), which was committed to memory by not a few Iraqis and is remembered for such powerful lines as:

> How can the majority continue to see these comedies,
> People toil without reward for a few individuals,
> And millions of victims between peasant and worker,
> Are still stricken by injustice – calling:
> 'Where is my right?'

Affectionately called the 'People's Poet', Bahr al-Ulum recited his protest poetry at workers' meetings (he founded and led a number of workers' unions), at religious ceremonies and at street demonstrations. His poems enthused the masses during the *Wathbah*.[8]

Poetry, the art of Iraqis, became a vehicle for social protest, a harbinger for the Revolution:

I can almost hear Iraq husbanding the thunder,
Storing lightning in the mountains and plains,
So that if the seal were broken by [able] men
The winds would leave in the valley not a trace of Thamud.[9]

Thus did Badr Shakir al-Sayyab invoke the oncoming revolution in the famous poem 'Song of the Rain' (1953). Another young poet, Abdul-Wahhab al-Bayati, commemorated the 1952 *Intifadhah* in the following lines:

Our slogans were like the sky!
Drenched with the blood of comrades
And we were demanding, in the name of children,
In the name of life,
In the name of Iraq,
Demanding the land for the peasants
And bread and salt for the hungry.[10]

Demonstrations, workers' strikes, peasants' uprisings and the massacres of political prisoners supplied the literary and artistic communities with leitmotifs that figured prominently in their works. In the mid-1940s a specific topos of the *munadhil* (militant) arose and inspired the narratives of Dhunun Ayyub, Shakir Khisbak (a pioneer of prison literature), Abdul-Malak Nuri (well-known for his collection of short stories *Song of the Earth*, which depicts the life of the dispossessed), Gha'ib Tu'ma Farman (presently Iraq's foremost novelist), Abdul-Haq Fadil and Abdul-Razzaq al-Sheikh Ali.[11] These writers raised the social question and stamped Iraqi fiction with its hallmark of critical and social realism. At the popular level the giving of names began to assume a decidedly political significance, as seen in the examples of Munadhil (Militant), Nidhal and Kifah (Struggle, given to both sexes), Wathbah (Uprising) and Naseer (Partisan). Even moustaches modelled on Stalin's were not uncommon at this time.

The post-war years witnessed the cultural ascendancy of the democratic faction, with the Communists playing an active role in organizing and disseminating opposition writing, giving shape to an alternative culture in the process. The party's leader, Fahd, attached great importance to the unmasking of patterns of cultural colonialism, exposing the cultural politics of the successive governments, and calling for the democratization of culture and education.[12] Fahd, moreover, encouraged Jewish members of the Iraqi Communist Party to form the League Against Zionism and to issue its organ, *al-Usba*, both of which attracted a considerable number of Jewish intellectuals.

The Iraqi Communist Party's advances among the intelligentsia are delineated in Batatu's study and need no further exploration here. In addition to contributions to *Atard, Venus, al-Rabita, Alam al-Ghad* and other progressive magazines, the Iraqi Communist party was the motive force behind such cultural reviews as *al-Majallah, al Muthul al-Ulya* and *al-Thaqafa al-Jadida* ('New Culture', issued in late 1953 and banned in 1954). Though short-lived because of censorship, these reviews left their mark. Pierre Rossi, director of the French Cultural Centre in Baghdad during the 1950s, holds that the progressive movement clustering around *al-Thaqafa al-Jadida* signalled the second stage toward the July Revolution, the first stage being the 1952 *Intifadah*.[13] This review featured poems by al-Sayyab and al-Bayati, short stories by Fuad al-Takerli and Abdul-Malak Nuri, translations by Khaled al-Saleam and Nehad al-Takerli, and articles by such prominent leftist university professors as Faisal al-Samir (author of *Thawrat al-Zanj* – 'The Zanj [Negro] Revolution' – and translator of Shaw's *Arms and the Man*, later a Minister of Guidance under Qasim), Ibrahim Kubba (the Minister of Economy in Qasim's first cabinet and later the Minister of Agrarian Reform), Safa al-Hafidh, and Safa Khalis who served on the editorial board. In the 1940s the Iraqi Communist Party managed to establish a publishing house, Dar al-Hikma. It, too, had a short life span. Even in prisons, however, the Communists produced journals, held poetry recitals and conducted classes, virtually turning their jails into cultural institutions and giving rise to the genres of prison literature and prison political songs. They also used their own resources to combat illiteracy.

In post-Second World War Iraq, Batatu affirms, Communism became 'a factor in the life of Iraqis' and a passion among many of the youth.[14] This is undoubtedly true; its cultural inroads prompted Khalil Kannah, the Minister of Education, to declare rancorously: '*Ummi mukhlis khairun min muthaqqafin haddam*' ('a loyal illiterate is far better than an intellectual saboteur' – 'saboteur' being a code word for Marxist or Communist). Better for whom? Better for what? And loyal to whom and to what? The question is not rhetorical; it points to the heart of the social struggle which was overflowing in the minister's own backyard. Colleges and teachers training institutions became Communist hotbeds, 'real nurseries of revolution'.[15] Nevertheless, a 'loyal' intellectual was in practice a rare animal at the time, one is even tempted to say a contradiction in terms. By then the word *muthaqqaf* (intellectual) to many Iraqis had come to signify 'democrat' or Marxist, displacing *effendi*, an appellation which began to acquire conservative overtones.

Equally resentful of 'intellectual saboteurs' was Muhammad Fadil Jamali, another *tabi'i* educationalist–politician. During his premiership in 1954 he closed down *al-Thaqafa al-Jadida*. Its fourth issue was confiscated and the journal was not distributed until the Revolution. Jamali, Kannah and Kannah's successor Abdul-Hamid Kadhim tried to curb the influence of the 'democratic' group by inviting an American cultural presence, especially in the educational field.[16] Organs promoting the 'American way of life' in the Arab world were available in Iraq: *al-Mukhtar (Reader's Digest)*, *al-'Alam (The World*, which sold for a penny), and some glossy publications distributed without charge by the American Information Center. Free copies of anti-Communist writings such as Arthur Koestler's *Darkness at Noon* were distributed to college and to high-school students.[17] The different, more passive approach of the British Council and the French Cultural Centre made it possible for leftist intellectuals to initiate art exhibitions and literary gatherings. Some, like Buland al-Haidari, also contributed to the sole cultural magazine in Iraq at the time, *Ahl al-Naft* ('The Oil People'), which, though financed by the oil companies and engaged in public relations, acquired cultural credibility under the able editorship of the accomplished writer and critic Jabra Ibrahim Jabra. Jabra introduced texts from world literature and literary journalism and featured prominent Iraqi writers. Reading became an obsession with the Iraqi intelligentsia, as Lebanese and Egyptian publishers were quick to realize. Chosen books ranged from European detective fiction and historical novels, Egyptian popular romances, to the latest available translation of romantic, realist and existentialist texts. The more conscious elements among Iraqi readers showed keen interest in Egyptian, French, and Russian realist writings[18] and in the English and American writers Ernest Hemingway, John Steinbeck, Jack London, Erskine Caldwell, Charles Dickens, G. B. Shaw, John Keats, Lord Byron, Percy Bysshe Shelly, Walt Whitman and T. S. Eliot. The latter influenced the emergence of the 'Free Verse' movement.[19]

During the 1950s the intellectual milieu in Iraq teemed with cultural activity. By now socialist realism had permeated Iraqi poetry, especially the poems written in free verse, the new mode (itself a dramatic revolution in Arabic poetry) which so prevailed among the committed poets that it was not uncommon for their adversaries to brand it 'crimson'. In addition to *qalaq* (a sense of uneasiness and anxiety) and railing at the city, the new poetry was characterized by rebellion against authority, traditional ways and the old order, whether it was written by the committed, the romanticists or the existentialists. The short story attained renown in the hands of Abdul-Malak Nuri, Abdul-Majid Lutfi and Fuad al-Takerli, all of whom identified with Marxism and explored topics from the life of the poor and the underprivileged.[20] The same ideology influenced the discourse of the *Ahali* journalist Abdul Majid al-Wandawi and the *Bilad* journalist Selim al-Bassoun, among others. Marxist interpretive models were applied in the scholarly articles published in *al-Thaqafa al-Jadida*, and prominent academics and intellectual figures such as Abdel Jabbar Abdullah, Muhammad Salman Hasan, Ibrahim al-Samarrai, Mahdi al-Makhzumi, Mahdi Murtada, Akram Fadil, Taha Baqir, Ali Jewad al-Tahir and Ali al-Shouk sympathized with socialist ideas and French humanist thought. The Palestinian poet Ma'in Bsisu and the Lebanese thinker Husein Muruwwah, who were residing in Iraq at the time, were caught up in this cultural ambience.

In tandem with the literary revolution, profound changes were under way in the abundantly creative visual and plastic arts. Jewad Selim, Faiq Hasan, Kadhim Haydar, Khalid al-Jadir, Khalid al-Rahhal and Mahmoud Sabri effected a shift from portraits, still-life and landscape paintings to the depiction of scenes from popular life: demonstrations, peasant women and prostitutes in the case of Sabri, and unemployed workers in the case of Selim. In 1953 a miniature by Selim won a distinguished prize in a contest in Rome. Its theme was the unknown political prisoner. Drama, too, developed with a clear orientation toward social realism and local colour, best noted in the works of Yusuf al-'Ani, whose penchant for critical humour often led to the censoring or even banning of his plays. Edmond Sabri's narrative *Quarrel*, which presented episodes from the life of a petty-bourgeois intellectual, was adapted as a successful film, *Sa'id Effendi* (directed by Kameran Husni) in 1957, its release marking a milestone in the history of the Iraqi cinema. Its veiled criticism of the social order was not lost on the audience, who read Sa'id Effendi's use of the popular proverb 'the fish rots from the head first' as an allusion to the regime. Such searches for hidden meaning were encouraged by the fact that both Yusuf al-'Ani and Zainab, who played the leading roles in the film, were known for their leftist tendencies. So, too, was Mahmoud Sabri, who designed the film's promotional poster. These literary and artistic figures helped to shape the norm for cultural producers and consumers, both of whom use culture as an ideological weapon.

The flourishing of cultural productions inimical to the state and antithetical to 'official' culture by no means suggests that artists and intellectuals enjoyed full freedom. They did, however, make maximum use of the limited liberties granted in the Constitution. Nevertheless, the clustering of so many leftist cultural figures did not escape the watchful eyes of the authorities. When Nuri Said assumed the premiership in 1954, one of his first acts was to clamp down hard on the intelligentsia. Nuri's minister of education, Khalil Kannah, first expelled seven university professors known for their leftist views: Rose Khadduri (Red Rose), Ibrahim Kubba, Faisal al-Samir, Safa al-Hafidh, Safa Khalis, Abdullah al-Bustani and Tal'at al-Shaibani. This act was followed by the dismissal of more than four hundred intellectuals, many of whom, to use US Ambassador Waldemar J. Gallman's expression, were 'inducted' into isolated military camps and forced to undergo military training.[21] Among the 'inducted' were the aforementioned Professors Faisal al-Samir, Safa al-Hafidh, Safa Khalis and Tal'at al-Shaibani; the playwright and actor Yusuf al-'Ani; the short-story writer Abdul-Malak Nuri; and the poets Abdul-Wahhab al-Bayati, Abdul-Razzaq Abdul-Wahid and the now famous Mudhaffar al-Nawwab. The writer Aziz al-Hajj, the 'People's Poet' Bahr al-Ulum and the prominent Kurdish poet Abdullah Goran were already in prison and had to await the 1958 Revolution to be released. Earlier, in 1953, the musician Krikor Badrosian, a Communist, had been expelled to Lebanon. A year later, leading members of the Communist front organization Partisans of Peace, Tawfiq Munir and Kamil Qazanji, together with a few other 'subversive' intellectuals such as Aziz Sharif, were stripped of their Iraqi nationality. Munir and Qazanji were actually deported to Turkey. Veteran Communist Abdul Qadir Ismail, meanwhile, who also was a short-story writer and a journalist, had lived in exile in Syria for more than a decade. In the period between Nuri's notorious decrees and the July Revolution, exile became the lot of scores of writers, notably the poets Abdul-Wahhab al-Bayati, Kadhim al-Simawe, Kadhim Jewad, Sa'di Yusuf, and the fiction writers Dhunun Ayyub and Gha'ib Tu'ma Farman.

Nuri Said revoked press licences and enforced censorship and (indirectly) self-censorship on publications. Only seven newspapers, less than a quarter of the total, were given permission to reappear.

The flow of publications from Arab countries was restricted and, to a greater extent than at any time in the past, 'subversive' books became incriminatory evidence against detainees. So relentless was the campaign against the intelligentsia that, as Pierre Rossi relates, police investigations stripped the libraries, theatrical performances were censored, La Fontaine's fables were expurgated, the name Jean-Jacques Rousseau became taboo, the film *Les Misérables* was banned shortly after the first showings, and Victor Hugo's novels were banished to the black market.[22] In addition, students were not to be admitted to colleges and educational institutions unless they had their fingerprints taken and obtained a certificate of 'good conduct' (*husn al-suluk*) from the police; the Ministry of Education, meanwhile, intensified its efforts to monitor the teachers. Informers, of course, infiltrated the high schools, colleges and coffee-houses. Not surprisingly, such figures became the subject of scathing denunciations in Iraqi literature. Al-Sayyab, for instance, devoted his poem 'The Informer' to sketching this type, as did Ayyub in an earlier short story, 'The Tower of Babylon'.

To the unwary observer the cultural terrain seemed clear for such official luminaries as Fadil Jamali, Khalil Kannah, Ibrahim al-Wa'idh, and a number of university professors such as Abdul Aziz al-Duri, Nasir al-Hani and Safa Khalusi, whose conservative brand of pan-Arabism allied them with 'official' culture. Bland journalism reigned supreme. Jamali's launch in 1957 of his newspaper *al-'Amal* ('Action', dubbed 'al-'Ameel', 'the Agent', by the opposition) added another stale medium to official propaganda. It is worth noting that in a secret memorandum in May 1958, Bahjat al-Atiyyah, the Director of Security, recommended that the media and the radio in particular enlist the services of prominent intellectuals and university professors in order to present in a palatable way the official standpoint, *'regardless of its conformity to truth'*.[23] Little did al-Atiyyah realize that the official propaganda machine was bankrupt precisely because, for many Iraqis, its messages did not conform to the truth. The *tabi'i* legacy in literature and the arts fared no better. In the words of the aforementioned keen observer Pierre Rossi: *'La classe dirigeante irakienne ignorait la culture et s'en méfiait.'*[24]

Unlike the *tabi'i* cultural element, the *qawmi* group was closer to the sentiments of the masses. Thus Hilal Naji and Adnan al-Rawi, among others, wrote odes on the *Wathbah*. The Palestine débâcle and the outbreak of the Algerian Revolution generated a plethora of anti-colonial pan-Arab texts. *Qawmi* figures such as the poets Khalid al-Shawwaf and Nu'man Mahir al-Kan'ani, the lawyer Faiq al-Samarrai and the journalist Qasim Hammoudi wrote on pan-Arab concerns in a tone hostile to Iraq's pro-Western stance and its estrangement from revolutionary Egypt. Nuri's cultural assault did not spare the vocal *qawmi* poet-journalist Adnan al-Rawi, who fled to Cairo and was stripped of his Iraqi nationality.

In 1956 Fuad al-Rikabi, the Secretary of the Iraqi Region of the Baath Party at the time, was 'inducted' into a special military camp. Though new to the Iraqi political scene, by the mid-1950s the Baath Party had attracted a number of students and men of letters, including the Iraqi poets Ali al-Hilli and Shafiq al-Kamali, the Syrian poet Sulaiman al-Isa, the Tunisian poet Abu al-Qasim Qarou and the Saudi writer Abdul-Rahman Munif, of whom the last three attended Iraqi colleges. Before Nuri's crack-down on the press, the Baath had propagated its doctrines in the *qawmi* newspapers *Al-'Amal*, under Adnan al-Rawi and *al-Afkar*, under Ismail al-Ghanim, and in the *Liwa' al-Istiqlal* of the right-wing *Istiqlal* (Independence) party. The Baath also prevailed upon Qasim Hammoudi of the *Istiqlal* to issue *al-Hurriyah*, which became in essence a public organ for the party.[25] After the crack-down this situation changed and Baathist men of letters such as Shafiq al-Kamali and Abdul-Rahman Munif faced Nuri's courts and were, in most cases, either acquitted or fined.[26] The entry of the Baath into the political arena, however, had added new vigour to the pan-Arab camp. For the first time in Iraq a *qawmi* group adopted 'socialism' as one of its ideological planks, however vague this 'socialism' may have been.

On the heels of the Baghdad Pact and Gamal Abdel Nasser's anti-Nuri campaign, the mass of Iraqis had become so alienated from the government that Nuri's stance on the Suez crisis prompted criticism from a number of pan-Arab lawyers and academics such as Abdul-Rahman al-Bazzaz, Muhammad Nasser, Jaber Umar, Khalid al-Hashimi, Muhammad Ali al-Bassam and many others who hitherto had been, to a greater or lesser degree, within the confines of 'official' culture. Nuri responded by placing al-Bazzaz and a few of his colleagues under police surveillance and by banishing them temporarily to Takrit. Evidently the regime had lost the little credibility it had enjoyed.

Meanwhile, and especially after the tripartite aggression against Egypt, *watani* and *qawmi* forces began taking genuine steps to close ranks. There had been joint action in the past and the political situation necessitated its renewal. Thus the Front of National Unity came into being. From different ideological perspectives, both cultural groups now worked to undermine the authority of the regime. Previously, democratic and pan-Arab poets had composed odes on the *Wathbah*, Palestine and Algeria. Now they wrote fiery odes in support of Egypt, heralding Nasser as the hero of Arabism and anti-imperialism. On the eve of the Revolution pan-Arab intellectuals joined their democratic counterparts in forming the 'Committee of Litterati' (*Lajnat al-Udaba' al-Tabi'a lil-Jabhah*) which was attached to the Front of National Unity.

To many an outside observer, such as Lord Birdwood and Anthony Nutting, Iraq seemed indeed an island of stability in the region.[27] Did not Nuri Said himself, having weathered the 1956 storm, boast that 'the house of the master is secure' ('*dar al-sayyid ma'muna*')?[28] The Chamberlain Tahsin al-Qadiri, however, did not share his master's confidence. 'If only the people of this country could go to sleep for ten years and then wake up', confided al-Qadiri to Gerald de Gaury.[29] A few years earlier, in 1951, al-Jawahiri, as if in anticipation of al-Qadiri's wish, had exhorted the people to 'go to sleep'. In the tradition of political irony started by al-Rasafi, al-Jawahiri exclaimed in 'Tanwimat al-Jiya' ('Lullaby for the Hungry'):

> Sleep, you hungry people, sleep!
> The gods of food watch over you.
> Sleep, if you are not satiated
> By wakefulness, then sleep shall fill you
>
> [. . .]
>
> Sleep, you hungry people, sleep!
> For sleep is more likely to protect your rights
> And it is sleep that is most conducive
> To stability and discipline.[30]

Sleep or no sleep, a deceptive calm settled during the last year of the monarchy; deceptive because the forces that would undermine the monarchy were at work.

In the remote village of El Nahra in the Diwaniyyah province, the district engineer Jabbar, a Marxist, persisted in using the expression 'When the revolution comes' in his discourse.[31] The Revolution did, in fact, come.

The day of 14 July 1958 shook the world. The long-awaited Revolution, often invoked by the opposition, broke out, overthrowing the monarchy and proclaiming the Republic of Iraq. For many, indeed for the mass of Iraqis, the Revolution signalled the dawn of a brave, new world. Popular enthusiasm expressed itself in the display of violence against the pillars of the *ancien régime* and in overwhelming outbursts of jubilation that marked the first weeks of the Revolution. The mood was euphoric, one of intoxication with the newly-found 'freedom', a word which became the catchphrase of the day.

> The sun shines in my city
> The bells ring out for the heroes.
> Awake, my beloved,
> We are free![32]

So exclaimed al-Bayati from exile. Indeed, such was the atmosphere of the time that 'Hurriyah' (Freedom), 'Thawra' (Revolution), and 'Jumhuriyyah' (Republic) were given as names to newly-born girls. 'Tha'ir' (Revolutionary), Abdul-Karim and Abdel Salaam to boys. Three days after the Revolution the doyen of Iraqi poets, al-Jawahiri, recited on Baghdad Radio an ode celebrating the dawn of freedom. Almost to a man, democratic and *qawmi* poets dedicated odes to the Revolution, giving expression to the general mood and investing it with a festive aura. In an obvious retort to Nuri's famous statement quoted earlier, the leftist vernacular poet Zahid Muhammad mused, in 'The House of the Pasha':

> Oh house of the arrogant Pasha!
> Have you seen how the world turns?
>
> [. . .]
>
> Oh house, you're in such a desolate state!
> Never have you considered that the people would revolt.
> Oh house of the arrogant Pasha!
>
> Oh 'secure' house of the Pasha!
> Where is the Pasha, and where his craft?
>
> [. . .]
>
> Vast Iraq did not shelter him.
> In an hour he crumbled, together with his rule.[33]

*　*　*　*　*

Making the Revolution itself 'secure' would prove just as difficult. For while the thrill of triumph was still palpable, cracks in the edifice of the revolutionary movements that united to destroy the Pasha's defunct era *(Al-'Ahd Al-Ba'id)* began to surface. The drama that earlier had unfolded during the Bakr Sidqi reign was now reproduced. The dispute between the democratic and pan-Arab forces over the immediate merger with the United Arab Republic was in essence an argument over the social course of the Revolution. The ensuing deadly struggle is aptly documented in Batatu's work. How it was played out in the cultural domain will now be touched upon briefly in the discussion of the cultural transformations that attended upon the Revolution.

The July Revolution occasioned an explosion in all aspects of the social and cultural life of Iraqis, unleashing pent-up desires and exposing latent tensions. The first months of the Revolution witnessed an active revival of the Iraqi press. Among the first newspapers to be launched was *al-Jumhuriyyah* ('The Republic') – edited by Sa'dun Hammadi: Abdul-Wahab al-Ghireri, one of its writers, was later accidentally shot by his comrades during the Baathist attempt on Qasim's life). Although a number of democratic journals were licensed *Ittihad al Sha'b* ('People's Union'), the organ of the Iraqi Communist Party, had to delay publication until January 1959. Restrictions on the flow of Egyptian and Lebanese journals and books were lifted and translations of works by Gorky, Mayakovsky, Lorca, Neruda, Elouar, Aragon, Jorge Amado and Nazim Hikmet were no longer prohibited. Now that the Revolution it had heralded was a reality, the democratic cultural cluster of pre-revolutionary Iraq re-emerged with a vengeance in the cultural arena, effecting a veritable cultural revolution. *Al-Thaqafa al-Jadida* resumed publication, to be joined by the new cultural reviews *al-Muthaqqaf* (The Intellectual) and *al-Adeeb al-Iraqi* (The Iraqi Writer, the latter featuring a supplement in Kurdish). A large number of Iraqi works, notably poetry collections in free verse by young talent, flooded the bookstores and pavements. Equally notable were the flourishing Kurdish literary works. A considerable number of newspapers in the Kurdish language appeared, poems and short stories published, and writers such as Goran and Ma'ruf al-Barzanji became known to the larger Arab audience.

The Revolution, moreover, precipitated the emergence of a new feminine identity, reflected in the rise to prominence of women poets and actresses and the growing number of women who ventured into the political and public spheres.[34] To the chagrin of the conservative elements, the statutes of the Civil Law were modified to be more equitable to women. Perhaps the appointment of Naziha al-Dulaimi as Minister of Municipalities reflected, in part, this new status.

Other aspects of the cultural revolution are worth noting. The songs, for example, became markedly political, and the monologists (the monologue refers to a humourous, often satirical, sketch song) Aziz Ali and Fadil Rasheed spared no occasion to poke fun at the 'enemies of the Revolution'. New theatre troupes sprang up, with Yusuf al-'Ani emerging as Iraq's leading playwright and actor. Political posters abounded, as did political cartoons. Art exhibits by various artists such as Kadhim Haydar, Mahmoud Sabri and Faiq Hasan on the theme of the Revolution drew a large number of people. The noted sculptor Jewad Selim was commissioned to produce a monument to the Revolution, 'The Monument to Liberty'. Erected in the very centre of Baghdad, this grand mural – designed to look like a huge banner, reminiscent of those used in the mass demonstrations – celebrates in fourteen figures, inspired by 14 July, major themes in Iraq's history. One such figure, the 'Imprisoned Thinker', mentioned at the beginning of this chapter, is a tribute to the struggle of the revolutionary intellectual. It is believed that the sculptor had in mind the National Democratic Party leader Kamil al-Chaderchi, who had spent some time behind bars in Nuri's prisons.[35]

It is no exaggeration to claim that the Revolution triggered a democratization of culture. Not only were monuments such as the 'Monument to the Unknown Soldier', Jewad Selim's 'Monument to Liberty', Faiq Hasan's peace mural and Khalid al-Rahhal's sculpture 'A Mother and her Child' erected in public places, but many unprivileged people could now have access to culture, attending theatrical performances and art exhibits, for example. So popular were the televised proceedings of the People's Court that some viewers at home or in coffee-houses would join the applause when al-Mahdawi (popularly known by many as *lisan al-Sha'b*, the people's tongue) uttered a cutting epithet or Wafiyyah Abu Klam recited a revolutionary poem. The people, moreover, drew from their reservoir of popular practices: composing poems and *hausas* (rallying chants) in the vernacular, transforming love songs into political songs, using words of abuse in the chant rhymes and infelicitously superimposing pictures of belly dancers and donkeys on those of the 'enemies of the Revolution', Nasser in particular (this following the deplorable rift among the revolutionary forces).

Batatu points to the rural character of the Revolution,[36], and the event indeed had far-reaching consequences for the peasantry, shattering, as it did, the political privileges of feudalism and launching an agrarian reform programme. Peasants' organizations dominated by the Iraqi Communist Party and the National Democratic Party sprang up in the country, and special radio programmes were transmitted. So popular was Abu Gat''s programme that it earned the malice of Iran's rulers, whose Arabic broadcasting service undertook the task of dissuading Iraqi peasants from listening to it. In one of its invectives it warned:

Don't believe in whatever news Abu Gueti' [diminutive form used here derogatorily] recounts
And be on your guard, O gallant, against communist treachery!

The irruption into the political life of the workers and peasantry was also reflected in the literary output during the period, in the abundance of vernacular poems celebrating Qasim and the Revolution. More importantly, the new vernacular poetry rose to the status of a legitimate literary medium, thus constituting a radical development analogous to the emergence of free verse.

When the counterrevolution ventured into the open, Mudhaffar al-Nawwab, who pioneered the new vernacular poetry, sounded the alarm. 'It's a shame', he warned, 'that the wolf's eye should sleep when the snake hisses.'[37] In an earlier vernacular poem, which was inspired by the assassination of the leftist Sahib al-Mulla Khassaf at the instigation of the feudal shaikhs, al-Nawwab stressed a note of defiance, underscored forcefully in the evocative refrain:

Don't gloat over our spilt blood, Oh feudal shaikh!
For when Swehib dies, the sickle claims [avenges his blood].[38]

Thus charged with the power of mobilization, it was only natural that the new vernacular poetry would be attacked as being vulgar (deviating from standard Arabic) and subversive.

The high point in the ascendancy of the democratic cultural movement came during the two 'red' months (March–April) in 1959, when its forces dominated the professional organizations (those of the writers, artists, journalists, teachers, lawyers, and musicians) and infiltrated the state's ideological agencies (the press, radio and television, the Ministry of Education, the Ministry of Guidance). The Partisans of Peace drew active support from some religious elements such as Abdul-Karim al-Mashta. In the meantime pan-Arab intellectuals had gone underground; some were imprisoned (for example, Khaldun Sati al-Husri, Jaber Umar and Adnan al-Rawi), while others, such as Faiq al-Samarrai, defected to Cairo or to Damascus. Books and journals from the United Arab Republic were again banned. Instead, Marxist classics, Soviet novels, Mao's writings and poems, Zhdanov's treatises on literature, Stalin's tracts, and even his pictures, were displayed prominently in bookshops and on pavements. Soviet movies, a novelty in Iraq, attracted enthusiastic audiences. *Ittihad al-Sha'b* became the leading paper in the country, attaining an average circulation of around 25,000, twice the circulation of *al-Bilad*. Democratic journalists like Abdul-Jabbar Wahbi of *Ittihad al-Sha'b* (better known by his pen name Abu Said), al-Jawahiri, editor of *al-Ray-al'Am*, Lufti Bakr Sidqi and Kadhim al-Simawe, editors of the weeklies *Sawt al-Ahrar* and *al-Insaniyya*, respectively, and Aziz al-Hajj advocated the Communist line in a number of articles and books. Other dailies such as *al-Bilad* and *al-Zaman* struck a sympathetic chord; the People's Court meanwhile became a public forum for voicing Communist demands. As the appellations 'Pasha', 'Bek' (Bey), and 'Effendi' fell into disrepute, *muwatin* (citizen) gained currency day by day. 'Bourgeois', in particular, became a favourite label of abuse, often used indiscriminately. 'Imperialism', 'colonialism', 'fascism', 'chauvinism', 'opportunism', 'conspiracy', 'the fifth column', 'counterrevolution', 'democrat', 'comrade', progressive', 'reactionary', 'the bourgeoisie', and 'the proletariat', among others, entered the daily vocabulary of Iraqis. 'Sole Leader, Dual Power' is Batatu's apt characterization of the period, for Communism, whose forces enjoyed cultural hegemony and dictated the mood in the streets, constituted a rival power base to Qasim and a spectre haunting Iraq.

But the 'ebb' was not far behind this Communist 'flow'. In May of 1959, Qasim, who was biding his time and exploiting the strife among political forces, began to curb the influence of the Iraqi Communist Party and to harass the democratic cultural group. He demoted and dismissed leftists from the state cultural agencies, at the same time easing press restrictions on the pan-Arabists, who launched a vehement campaign against the Left. Later on he appointed the anti-Communist military man Ismail al-Arif as Acting Minister of Guidance, then Minister of Education. Once again

Marxist classics were banned, and taken to the courts were such leftist journalists as Abdel-Qadir Ismail, editor of *Ittihad al-Sha'b*, and al-Jawahiri, editor of *Ray-al'Am* and head of both the Journalists' and Writers' Associations. In the meantime, official culture had become consonant with Qasimism (a blend of personality cult, populism and Iraqi particularism) and with the conservative wing of the National Democratic Party, which, alarmed by the Communist tide and the push for deeper changes in the social order, contributed, as the Communists had earlier done, to the cult of Qasim. Communists began sharing prisons with the pan-Arabs, increasingly replacing them as the latter were being released. Soon Yunis al-Ta'i's Qasimite newspaper *al-Thawra* began to acquire a pan-Arab political complexion; *Ittihad al Sha'b*, meanwhile, was finally supressed. Before long al-Jawahiri and al-Simawe chose voluntary exile abroad. The Revolution had run its radical course; it now started to eat its Jacobins.

As the cultural landscape was being forcibly redrawn to the disadvantage of the left, *qawmiyyah* (pan-Arabism) became the flag behind which paraded the shaikhs and notables who identified with the *ancien régime*. Similarly, the *tabi'i* cultural group resurfaced under this ideological banner and traditional intellectuals, notably the ecclesiastics, were to lend them support. 'Enemies of Communism, Unite!' (itself an example of subverting the Communist slogan) became the rallying-cry of counterrevolution. To the officially revived terms *al-afkar al-haddamah* (subversive ideas) and *fawdhawiyyah* (anarchy), the term *shu'ubiyyah* (an historical term meaning favouring non-Arabs over Arabs) was conjured up by the pan-Arabs and used in Nasser's speeches as a label for both Qasim and Arab Communism.

To counter the literary organization dominated by the Communists and their fellow travellers and headed by al-Jawahiri, their antagonists formed an association of their own, *Jam'yat al-mu'allifin wa-l-kuttab al-Iraqiyyin*, consisting mainly of poets and academics, such as Khalid al-Shawwaf, Shafiq al-Kamali, Muhammad Jamil Shalash, Hafidh Jamil, Yusuf Izz al-Din and Abdul-Razzaq Muhi al-Din. In the war of words and ideas poetry served as a convenient medium. The cultural battle swept the newspapers, too. The pan-Arab daily *al-Hurriyyah* serialized the anthropologist Shakir Mustapha Selim's satirical 'mudhakkarat shuyu'i muta'amir' ('Memoirs of a Communist Conspirator') and al-Sayyab's 'kuntu shuyu'iyan' ('I was a Communist').[39] It must be added that most polemical discourse by both democratic and pan-Arab cultural groups at the time resorted to sloganeering and baiting, such as the epithets which al-Mahdawi traded with the Egyptian Ahmed Said, chief announcer of 'Sawt al-Arab' (Voice of the Arabs') Radio, who incited Iraqis against Qasim and the Iraqi Left. The expression 'Qasim al-Iraq' (the 'divider' of Iraq) resonated from 'Sawt al-Arab', to which al-Mahdawi responded with 'Nasser al-Isti'mar' (the 'supporter' of colonialism). Egypt's leading journalist Muhammad Hasanain Haikal attacked Qasim and the Iraqi Communist Party in *al-Ahram*. Cairo, moreover, welcomed scores of Iraqis, including Salman al-Safwani, Jaber Umar, Fuad al-Rikabi, Sa'dun Hammadi, Hilal Naji and Adnan al-Rawi. The last two not only broadcast on the air and recited fiery poems against Qasim and the Communists, but also wrote books on the 'Red menace'. The Revolution's radical phase, it seems, had given birth to a host of Iraqi and Arab 'experts' on the Iraqi Communist Party, who published their tracts in Cairo, Damascus, Beirut and even Amman, thus providing an index of how frightened various quarters were of the ascendancy of the working class in Iraq.

The cultural war zone extended to the Arab world. At the Congress of Arab Writers in December 1958 in Kuwait, the Iraqi delegation, headed by al-Jawahiri, drew severe criticism, some of which was directed at Safa Khalis's discourse on the revolutionary aspects of the Qarmatian movement (*Qarmatiyyah*). The famous Lebanese cultural review, Suheil Idris's *al-Adaab*, became a platform for anti-leftist writing, such as that of Nazik al-Mala'ika, Shafiq al-Kamali, Hilal Naji, Shakir Mustapha Selim and the Arab writers Akram Zu'ayter and Muhammed Sa'b. In Israel the Palestinian poet Rashid Husain published a scathing attack against Iraqi Communists. On the other hand, Samih al-Qasim, Mahmoud Darwish and Tawfiq Zayyad wrote in support of the Iraqi Left. So did the Lebanese journalists Amin al-A'war and Husain Murruwwah. With the exception of a few accounts (for example, that by 'Caractacus'),[40] the People's Court was portrayed as a circus in the Arab and Western worlds. Little mention, however, was made of the First Martial Military Court (presided over by Brigadier Shams al-Din Abdullah), which 'specialized' in persecuting leftist elements on trumped-up charges such as burning copies of the *Quran*. The parallel existence of these two courts reflected, in effect, the polarization in Iraqi society, which, as Batatu explains, cut across *mahallahs* (city quarters) and districts. Social bandits like the pro-Communist Khalil Abu al-Houb and *shaqawat* (bullies) such as the pro-Baathist Jabbar Kurdi took sides in the political struggle. In short, violence and coercion became the order of the day. In the *qawmi* strongholds of

Ramadi and Mosul a red tie or a red dress was sufficient cause for
verbal abuse, if not physical assault. Even personal names reflected
the divisions in Iraqi society: 'Uruba' (Arabism), 'Jihad' and 'Wahda'
(Unity) became associated with the pan-Arabs, 'Kifah', 'Nidhal',
'Munadhil', 'Yasar' (Left) and 'Tali'a' (Vanguard) with the Left.

Once the Iraqi Communist Party failed to take advantage of the
combativeness of the working class and of the favourable mood in
the country to translate the moment of cultural hegemony into a
moment of political domination, the initiative passed into the hands
of its enemies. Eventually, it was the barrel of the gun, not massive
popular support or cultural authority, that decided the issue in
February 1963, when a coalition of pan-Arab and conservative forces
toppled the first Republican regime, executed Qasim and launched a
reign of terror. One of the first acts of the new rulers was to display
Qasim's corpse on television, thus using the new medium as an
instrument of social control. They also directed their wrath against
cultural artifacts, smudging the figure of the peace pigeon in Faiq
Hasan's peace mural, a very symbolic act in light of the vengeance
that was meted out to the *watani* intellectuals, some of whom lost
their lives. The prison experience during the time is depicted vividly
and in a quasi-documentary fashion in Shakir Khisbak's novel *al-
Hiqd al-Aswad* ('Black Malice', Beirut, 1966), which underlines the
spite felt by opponents of the Left towards the *muthaqqaf*
(intellectual) and *katib* (writer).

Pan-Arab culture, now promoted as official culture, soon began to
reflect the divisions between Baathists and various *qawmi* groups. No
cultural work of note was produced in the mid-1960s, for the bloody
terror campaign against the democratic intelligentsia, far outweighing
that conducted by Nuri, had resulted in the impoverishment of
Iraqi culture.[41] Many cultural figures fled the country. Those who
were already in self-imposed exile abroad, like al-Jawahiri and Faisal
al-Samir, formed a committee for the defence of the Iraqi people.
Bertrand Russell and Ethel Mannin, among other world cultural
figures, spoke against human rights abuses in Iraq. During 'the
Bitterest of Years' cultural texts, notably al-Nawwab's vernacular
poems (e.g. 'al-Bara'a' 'The Recantation') functioned to uplift the
morale of the Left and to help generate support for it. Thus began
another chapter in the struggle for cultural domination, a chapter in
which the July Revolution itself was contested. As recently as 1988
more than 700 Iraqi intellectuals in exile, members of the Rabita
(The League of Democratic Iraqi Writers, Journalists and Artists)

declared the 14 July week as the week of Iraqi culture, to be celebrated annually with various activities. Their tribute to the Revolution and the cultural flowering it gave rise to is in part a response to official revisionist history that ignores the anniversary of the 14 July Revolution and looks with nostalgia to the pre-Republic era. Today, some thirty years after the Revolution, there is a sense of the *déjà vu* in the fact that al-Jawahiri, Gha'ib Tu'ma Farman and Sa'di Yusuf are once more (indeed for the third time) in exile.

It emerges from this study that the cultural struggle within the Revolution reflected aspects of the tensions within Iraqi society. The ruggle, moreover, assumed a national and anti-imperialist character. During the monarchical era opposition by both *watani* and *qawmi* cultural groups was instrumental in demystifying the legitimacy of the ruling clique and in questioning its claim to represent the interests of the whole nation. This opposition acted as a catalyst of change, demonstrating the stark conditions of the dispossessed and projecting the utopia of a just society. To a large extent the democratic cultural group played a conspicuous role in opposition politics, acting vigorously to create a state of mental preparedness for the Revolution.

Characteristic of the cultural ambience on the eve of the Revolution was rebellion against authority and traditional norms as well as a commitment to the cause of social justice. Typical of the *muthaqqaf* (intellectual) of the time was Jabbar, who, according to Elizabeth Fernea, 'believed firmly that Iraq needed a revolution to throw out the Nuri Said government', and for whom 'socialism represented the application of science to the problems of society'.[42] Even educated youth from the shaikhly class, whose fortunes were definitely not declining, reflected Marxist intellectual trends. Thus Robert Fernea reported that Hadhi, a shaikh's son, 'sounds as if he has been given the treatment by the local Commies'.[43]

It seems plausible to argue that the attraction since the mid-1940s of so many intellectuals and cultural figures to Marxist ideology has as much to do with Batatu's observation about the origins of many oppositional intellectuals in the declining social classes as with his thesis about the impact of the Iraqi Communist Party on the life of Iraqis and its transformation of political into social discontent.[44] One may add that this new pattern had transformed ethnic and sectarian solidarities into class, national and international ones. The 'democratic' intelligentsia cut across class, gender, religion, sect and ethnic origin. It is not far-fetched to claim that it contributed to the shaping

of an Iraqi national identity. Using Batatu's categories of passive and
dynamic class feeling or consciousness, it can be maintained that
Marxist ideology succeeded in making the masses aware of the
possibility of changing their position of subordination, and alerting
them to the possibility of revolution. Indeed, one learns from
Batatu's work that economic factors alone cannot do full justice to
the complexity of the social reality, for in isolation they do not a
revolution (nor a revolutionary) make. The same applies to cultural
factors. The July Revolution sprang not from such a single cause but
rather from a convergence of economic, political and cultural forces.

On the cultural plane, Marxist ideology was not the sole
determining influence on Iraqi culture. Marxist thought was linked to
popular and native traditions and thus assumed a national-popular
character. To borrow Gramsci's formulation, it became a cultural
movement, a 'religion', a 'faith',[45] and its values permeated the
cultural sphere and saturated social relations. In other words, it
functioned to provide 'intellectual and moral leadership', in effect
establishing the cultural hegemony of the working class over allied
and kindred groups. This contention is borne out, I believe, in the
context of Iraqi politics and culture: 'democratic' connoted Marxist
and Communist; Communism by many was held to be the actualiza-
tion of Utopia, the embodiment of liberty, democracy, progress and
the elimination of all forms of discrimination; the word *muthaqqaf*
(intellectual) became almost synonymous with Marxist; Marxist
discourse inspired many literary and cultural writings; 'existentialists',
'romanticists' and 'rebels' like Buland al-Haidari, Abdul-Amir al-
Husairi, Husain Mardan, and Mahmoud al-Buraikan contributed to
this Marxist phenomenon. More pertinent to our discussion of
cultural hegemony is Batatu's verdict that 'Communism had provided
a whole generation of Iraqis with not a few of their categories of
thought.'[46] Certainly revolution is one such category. 'Its rhetoric, its
mood, its style of thinking', observes Batatu, 'affected even its
opponents.'[47] Taken together, these two statements, in essence, form
Batatu's guarded way of signifying the cultural hegemony of the
Marxist element. This contention is corroborated by al-Sayyab.
Several months after the 1963 *coup d'état*, al-Sayyab complained in
the American-sponsored *Hiwar* (published in Beirut) that 'although
Communism was crushed in Iraq, its outlook on literature is still
predominant: it has been adopted unconsciously by *qawmi* elements.'[48]

Ever since Husain al-Rahhal 'injected Marxist elements into the
thinking of an informal literary group',[49] Marxist ideology has
continued to captivate the Iraqi intelligentsia, to inform literature

and the arts, and to disseminate the concept of revolution. The two decades between the early forties and early sixties witnessed a flourishing of the arts and literature. Full of creative cultural energies, this period can justifiably be described either as the age of enlightenment or the Iraqi renaissance. Herein lie the intellectual origins of the Revolution. A truly genuine revolution, as I remarked at the outset, the Iraqi Revolution, like those of France and Russia, was preceded by intense cultural agitation. The chemistry is far from simple, but in the dynamics that eventually led to the Revolution, culture played a catalytic role.

The cultural legacy of the Revolution still exercises an incalculable influence on large parts of the Iraqi population. Iraq's current leading intellectuals, artists and writers are the children of the Revolution. The Revolution, in effect, changed the entire tenor of culture and education, throwing open the doors to large numbers of people and giving rise to new forms of cultural expression. At Liberation Square in the heart of Baghdad stands today Jewad Selim's grand cultural artifact, 'The Monument to Liberty', with which we began our discussion. Its fourteen groups of figures and symbols telling the epic of the Revolution provide a lasting memorial of the events of 14 July 1958.

## Notes

1. The term 'cultural hegemony' is derived from Antonio Gramsci, who conceives of it as a process that is produced and activated constantly. Being distinct from domination, cultural hegemony functions through the signifying systems to organize consent and to establish or maintain 'intellectual and moral leadership' of a specific social group over allied and kindred groups (Gramsci, *Selections from the Prison Notebooks*, trans. and ed. by Q. Hoare and G. N. Smith (New York, 1971), pp. 57–8, 80n, 161, 181–82 and passim.

2. Broadly speaking, the *tabi'i* formation consisted of 'official' intellectuals or intellectuals-in-power with ties to Britain and later the USA; they were endorsed by Ambassador Waldemar J. Gallman as representing 'a healthy, constructive Arab nationalism' (Waldemar J. Gallman, *Iraq Under Nuri: My Recollections of Nuri al-Said, 1954–1958* (Baltimore, 1964, p. 14). *Qawmi* intellectuals or intellectuals-in-uniform had strongholds in the officer corps and displayed a propensity for action, as seen in the Ikha Party and the para-military orientation of the Muthanna Club and the Futuwa organization. Some of their old leaders looked to the example of Germany for inspiration; later on revolutionary Egypt nurtured *qawmi* hopes of achieving Arab unity. In the main pan-Arabs were not excluded from the power apparatuses of the state, their ties to official culture becoming strained, though not totally severed, following the Anglo–Iraqi war of 1941. The last formation, the *watani*, or revolutionary intellectuals, refers to socially radical intellectuals (social reformists,

populists, Marxists and Communists) who imbibed socialist doctrines and French humanist thought. It remains to be added that despite the decline of religion, it was still a force to be reckoned with. Indeed, a streak of religious ideology coloured the cultural manifestations of the first two groups and was not totally absent in the case of the third. Similarly, it was not uncommon for some men of religion to lend support to this or that particular group.

3. This was due mainly to the pan-Arab policies of Sati al-Husri, who resisted British dictates in the educational field. Moreover, at the early stages of the monarchy official ideology tended to be pan-Arab in orientation.

4. Despite his outspoken criticism, al-Rasafi held several government positions in the educational field and became Deputy for the Muntafiq province. As for al-Jawahiri, King Faisal I appointed him in the Royal Palace, and both Nuri Said and Crown Prince Abdul-Ilah tried to patronize him.

5. To those must be added the *al-Thaqafa al-Jadida* writers, who will be mentioned later on in this chapter.

6. Muhammad Mahdi al-Jawahiri, *Diwan al-Jawahiri* ('Al-Jawahiri's Poetical Works') (Beirut, 1982), 4 vols. This quote from vol. 2, p. 143.

7. Ibid., vol. 2, p. 117.

8. In a number of previous poems, such as 'Buried Alive' and 'The Peasant Revolution', Bahr al-Ulum exhorted the peasants to rise against their oppressors, the shaikhs and the government. In 1935 one such poem, 'The Peasant', earned him a life sentence from a military tribunal (Yusuf Izzidien (Izz al-Din), 'Poetry in the Social and Political Development of 20th Century Iraq', Ph.D. Dissertation, School of Oriental and African Studies, University of London, 1957, p. 252). Although he was subsequently released, Bahr al-Ulum soon was to find his way to the Iraqi Communist Party, and consequently to become a veteran of prisons.

9. Salma Khadra Jayyusi, ed., *Modern Arabic Poetry: An Anthology* (New York, 1987), p. 429.

10. Khalil Shukrallah Rizk, 'The Poetry of 'Abd Al-Wahhab Al-Bayati: Thematic and Stylistic Study', Ph.D. Dissertation, Indiana Unviersity, 1981, p. 146. Translation slightly modified.

11. In a tragic example of how life imitates one's own fiction, the short-story writer al-Sheikh Ali himself was kidnapped in the early 1950s and has not been seen since.

For more details on those and many other *watani* writers, see Abdul-Majid's dissertation, which also provides instances of the textualization of the Iraqi Communist Party watchwords in poetry (Abdul-Latif Abdul-Majid, 'Al-Fikr al-Ishtiraki fi-l Adab al-Iraqi, 1918–1958' ('Socialist Thought in Iraqi Literature'), Ph.D. Dissertation, the University of Baghdad, 1976, pp. 59, 91 and passim).

12. Fahd, for instance, wrote:

[The colonial powers] have not forgotten to utilize to the utmost the communications and propaganda means, thereby flooding the market with their publications, hiring newspapers and writers, monopolizing printing material, and tightening the grip on liberal intellectuals. In addition, they possess other means of propaganda like news corporations, broadcasting stations, information centres, cultural institutions, and an army of foreign and dependent teachers in the national educatinal institutions.

Fahd (Yusuf Salman Yusuf), *Muallafat al-Rafiq Fahd* ('The Works of Comrade Fahd') (Baghdad, 1973), p. 228.

13. Pierre Rossi, '"La culture nouvelle," mouvement révolutionaire des intellectuels irakiens', *Orient*, 8 (1958), p. 59.

14. Hanna Batatu, *The Old Social Classes and the Revolutionary Movements of Iraq* (Princeton, 1978), p. 465.

15. Ibid., pp. 645–47.

16. Kannah told Rossi that he was not in favour of sending students on scholarships to France, since many, he believed, returned as doctrinaire Communists (Pierre Rossi, *L'Irak des revoltes* (Paris, 1962), p. 177). As for Kadhim, he secured American money and an American camp specialist to help launch his plan for student summer camps that would provide seminars and lectures on Communism (Gallman, *Iraq Under Nuri*, p. 124).

17. I am indebted to Aseel Muhammad Nasser from the University of Texas at Austin for drawing my attention to this point.

18. The Egyptian reviews *al-Risala* and *Kitabi* and the series *Riwayat al-Hilal* were great hits in Iraq. Also popular were the works of Victor Hugo, Alexander Dumas, Balzac, Tolstoy and Turgenev. Iraqi readers, moreover, were familiar with the works of Taha Hussein, Abbas Mahmoud al-Akkad, Ibrahim al-Mazini, Naguib Mahfouz, Khalid Muhammad Khalid, Muhammad Mandur, Mahmoud Amin al-Alim, Abdul-Adim Anis, Salama Musa, Amin al-Rihani, Raif Khouri, Umar al-Fakhouri and George Hanna, among others. 'Subversive' books, including novels, were smuggled into Iraq via the Syrian borders. One should also mention that the deliberate proliferation of pocket books, featuring detective stories, mainly the adventures of Arsène Lupin by Maurice Leblanc, created a vogue among the majority of the Iraqi readership. It must be said, however, that the enchantment with Lupin is not unrelated to the fact that he was a figure who assisted the helpless and outmanoeuvred the powerful and the police, a sort of social bandit.

19. The works of T. S. Eliot and of James Frazer (author of *The Golden Bough*) inspired the invocation of myths and mythical figures to suggest the inevitability of regeneration, of revolution.

20. Kishtainy's following passage recaptures vividly aspects of the intellectual currents prevalent among the educated youth:

[My] university years [were] the years of student idealism, high-pitched anti-imperialist struggle and dedication to the cause of the social revolution in Iraq . . . In the early 1950s, the old brothel ghetto of Baghdad, the historic Kallachia, became the haunt of the revolutionary intellectuals . . . We used to stroll into the nooks and crannies of the old lanes, reciting passages from the *Communist Manifesto* and verses from Bahr al-Ulum's poem on the prostitute's grave. There was the painter who paid a black whore only to sit for him. There was the story writer who invited a blind one to a meal of kebab only to hear her story . . . There was the real political writer who actually went to bed with Zahra and came out crying. (Khalid Kishtainy, *The Prostitute in Progressive Literature* (London, 1982), p. 10.

21. Gallman, *Iraq Under Nuri*, p. 94.

22. Rossi, *L'Irak*, p. 220.

23. Ja'far Abbas Hamidi, *Al-Tattawurat wa-l Ittijahat al-Siyasiyyah al-Dakhiliyyah fi-l Iraq, 1953-1958* ('Internal Political Developments and Trends in Iraq, 1953–1958') (Baghdad, 1980), p. 347.

24. Rossi, *L'Irak*, p. 220.

25. Hamidi, *Al-Tattawurat*, p. 215.

26. Ibid., pp. 222–25.

27. For example, Lord Birdwood stated: 'Only Iraq could be regarded as a focus of

stability, and for this, the Prime Minister could take his credit' (quoted in Rossi, *L'Irak*, p. 237). And Nutting wrote: 'By no means all other Arab regimes are as stable as Iraq' (quoted in Khaldun S. al-Husri, 'The Iraqi Revolution of July 14, 1958', Part 2, *Middle East Forum*, 41, 1 (winter 1965), p. 28). Al-Husri's article is a poignant rebuttal of al-Jamali's apologia of the *ancien régime*, published in an earlier issue of the same journal.

28. Speech of December 16, 1956 (Hamidi, *al-Tattawurat*, p. 178).

29. Quoted in al-Hursi, 'The Iraqi Revolution', p. 28.

30. Jayyusi, ed., *Modern Arabic Poetry*, pp. 80–81.

31. Elizabeth Warnock Fernea, *Guests of the Sheik: An Ethnology of an Iraqi Village* (New York, 1969), pp. 86, 285.

32. Abdul-Wahhab al-Bayati, '14 Tammuz' ('July 14'), in Salma Khadra Jayyusi, *Trends and Movements in Modern Arabic Poetry*, vol. 2 (Leiden, 1977), p. 702.

33. Akram Fadil, comp., *Al-Shi'r al-Sha'bi fi-l-Ahd al-Jumhuri* ('Vernacular Poetry in the Republican Era') (Baghdad, 1959), p. 20.

34. For example, the poets Lamia Abbas Imara, Sabriyya al-Hassu, Maqbula al-Hilli, Hayat al-Nahr and Wafiyya Abu Qlam, who were associated with the Left, and Nazik al-Mala'ika and Atika al-Khazraji, who were known for their pan-Arab stance. The leftist Na'ima al-Wakil issued the weekly *July 14*, the actresses Zainab and Nahida al-Rammah became household names, Rose Khadduri and Bushra Bartu delivered speeches and wrote articles in journals, and the pro-Communist Association of Iraqi Women boasted close to forty thousand members. *Qawmi* women, too, entered the world of politics, as in the case of Yusra Said Thabet, who defied al-Mahdawi in the People's Court.

35. Jabra Ibrahim Jabra, *Jewad Selim wa Nusb al-Hurriyah* 'Jewad Selim and the Monument to Liberty') (Baghdad, 1974), p. 148.

36. Batatu, *Old Social Classes*, p. 999.

37. Mudhaffar al-Nawwab, *Lil-Rail wa-Hamad* ('For the Train and Hamad') (Beirut, 1969), p. 43.

38. Ibid., p. 23.

39. Al-Sayyab left the Iraqi Communist Party in the mid-1950s, henceforth becoming a virulent anti-Communist. His defection may not be unrelated to a Zhdanovian spirit that had crept into the cultural apparatus of the Iraqi Communist Party and that perhaps later led to the estrangement of a number of other literati.

40. 'Caractacus', *The Revolution in Iraq* (London, 1959).

41. In1966 Mahmoud al-Abta complained in *al-Adaab*: 'Today there is not in Iraq a single magazine devoted to literature, thought, and art!' He added that the pan-Arab Association of Writers 'had closed offices . . . no longer existing as a moral entity or a physical body.' (Mahmoud al-Abta, 'Malamih al-Fikr al-Rahin fi-l Iraq' ('The Features of Contemporary Thought in Iraq'), *Al-Adaab*, 14, 1 (January 1966), p. 73).

42. Fernea, *Guests of the Sheik*, p. 282.

43. Ibid., p. 306.

44. See Batatu, *Old Social Classes*, pp. 293, 465–6, 470, 999, and passim.

45. Gramsci, *Selections*, p. 328.

46. Batatu, *Old Social Classes*, p. 466.

47. Ibid., p. 465.

48. Badr Shakir al-Sayyab, 'Risail Thaqafiyyah al-Iraq, min Badr Shakir al-Sayyab' ('Letters on Culture: Iraq, from Badr Shakir al-Sayyab'), *Hiwar*, 1:6 (Sept.–Oct. 1963), p. 105.

49. Batatu, *Old Social Classes*, p. 393.

# 11

# Community, Class and Minorities in Iraqi Politics

## SAMI ZUBAIDA

The communal fragmentation of Iraq along lines of tribe, religion, ethnicity and region is generally regarded as an essential factor in the politics of the country and an obstacle to its governability and, consequently, to the formation of a national entity. This is also a common explanation, sometimes a justification, of the excessive levels of political repression that have characterized the country for most of its modern history and that have reached a particular intensity under the current Baathist regime.

In this chapter I explore these themes critically, making distinctions between different ways in which communal factors enter politics. In particular, I distinguish between communalist politics as such, where the communal interests are represented in political struggles, and the ideological conditioning which communal perspectives bring into conceptions of the national entity and its destiny.

This analysis is particularly pertinent to the events leading up to the Revolution of 1958, to the nature of the Qasim regime and to the forces which led to its demise. Those were the years when Iraq came nearest to constituting itself as a national entity, when the main forces entering the political struggles could be identified in ideological terms, fighting over conflicting conceptions of the national entity and its destiny, and when the communalist forces fostered by the monarchical regime were on the retreat, able to function only through attachments to the ideological groupings.

These considerations constituted a crucial part of Hanna Batatu's project in tracing the hesitant formation of the Iraqi national entity in the face of the fragmentation of the population into a multiplicity of particularistic solidarities. There are moments of collective struggle which mark the formation of the nation:

> If this community in embryo will in future hold together and maintain its separate identity, the Uprising of 1920, the war of 1941, the *Wathbah* of 1948, the *Intifadah* of 1952, and the Revolution of 1958, though not free of divisive aspects, will be seen as stages in the progress of Iraq towards national conherence.[1]

The aspiration to this national coherence was certainly a powerful motive in the various, and often conflicting, political forces which participated in these events, but their respective visions of the shape of this national entity did not always coincide. Conflicting images of the nation to which they all aspired were, paradoxically, partly conditioned by their communal affiliation. But there is an important point to emphasize here (in line with the distinction made above): communal conditioning of political positions in the case of the national forces was not based on the pursuit of narrow communal interests as such, but on different aspirations for the national entity, different 'world-views' conditioned by communal perspectives.

## Communities and Minorities

The communal fragmentation of the Iraqi population is too familiar to recount here. The Shi'a are not a minority numerically but politically. When speaking of political minorities in the Iraqi context, we should make clear that they do not constitute a homogeneous phenomenon. There is a clear division between Kurds and Shi'a on the one hand, and the rest of the minorities on the other, in that Kurds and Shi'a are contenders for power in the political field while Christians, Jews and Turkomans are not. Kurds and Shi'a in turn represent asymmetrical sources of political formation. Kurds are a national minority openly campaigning for national rights; they do not hide their ethnicity behind other ideological labels. They have specific political organs, such as the Democratic Party of Kurdistan, and they also participate in Iraqi national parties, historically the Communist Party. In this latter case, their concern with Kurdish rights is made explicit.

The Shi'a, on the other hand, are not a national group; they are predominantly Arab. Shi'a have been represented in a wide range of

Iraqi political parties, mostly oppositional, few with any specifically Shi'i communal interests. The only exceptions were narrow sub-class interests in the case of the southern Shi'i shaikhs-landlords under the monarchy. The significant representation of Shi'is in the Iraqi Communist Party, like that of the Kurds, has often been explained in communalist terms: Arab nationalism would align Iraq with a predominantly Sunni Arab world, to the detriment of both the Shi'a and the Kurds, while the Communist Party (but also the National Democrats, with low Shi'i representation) were the main Iraqist alternative to Arab nationalism. Batatu occasionally takes up this theme,[2] but qualifies it in many important respects, such as by citing Shi'i representation in nationalist parties (Independents and Baath) and the fact that the Shi'a were not numerically overrepresented in the Communist Party. He also favours a class explanation of their oppositional positions: Shi'a and Kurds were amongst the poorest sectors of the population. I shall return to this question later.

## Forms of Politics

We may follow here the familiar distinction between the 'politics of notables' and the politics of ideologically-based political parties. The mobilization of political support through networks of kinship, communal or regional interests and patronage is a phenomenon familiar throughout the world (and not only the 'Third World'), and Iraq was no exception. The theoretical alternative is the political party based on a universalist ideological appeal, mobilizing support through organization of political constituencies among the people. Even though there is often some overlap between the two forms in practice, it is possible and useful to maintain this distinction. In Iraq, the National Democrats, the Communists, the Baathists and the Independence (*Istiqlal*) Party were primarily ideological formations, although regional and kinship networks may have played some part in the organization and support in some of them. On the other hand, the establishment parties under the monarchy were clearly parties of patronage, clientelism and tribalism, as is, in a different way, the Baath leadership currently in government.

What were the constituencies of support for these parties and how were they organized? Some of the ideological parties, particularly the Independents, appear to have been no more than political clubs of intellectuals and professionals (especially lawyers); they engaged in the mobilization of popular support only sporadically, in the context of elections, or in organizing demonstrations. On the other side of the spectrum was the Communist Party, which, from its inception, worked assiduously in the organization and mobilization of popular strata, often with great success, as demonstrated so fully in Batatu's book. The National Democrats combined the clubbish image of the Independents with a definite class orientation, in the identification of its leadership with modern-progressive bourgeoisie, mainly industrialists, who at the same time favoured social democracy. Ascertaining the extent of popular support for this party is complicated by the fact that, at various stages, it was infiltrated with Communist cadres. The Baath Party, a relative late-comer on the scene, was committed to popular mobilization, but lacked the numbers, the skills and the persistent hard work needed for grass-roots organization. At the level of popular organization and mobilization, the Communist Party was by far the most effective, and as such, a crucial force in the events of the Qasim years.

At this point, I shall digress to point out the crucial relevance of Iraqi politics in the decades between 1940 and 1970 for the themes and debates which have arisen concerning the Middle East in recent years. One idea is that political parties and ideologies in the region are but the games of intellectuals (when not thin disguises for ethnic and other particularistic interests), divorced from and irrelevant to the thinking and interests of the vast majority of the people. Related to this is the idea that Islam is the only authentic source of popular thought and culture, and that the entry of the popular masses into politics puts Islam on the political agenda. The Iraqi example is a clear reminder of the superficiality of these positions, which are based on a retrospective reading of history from the viewpoint of the Iranian Revolution and the developments which followed it.

Superimposed on the political forms outlined above is the politics of conspiracy, where army officers rule supreme. Batatu demonstrates clearly that officers were recruited predominantly from a narrow social-regional base, the Sunni Arabs of the northwest, their political sympathies firmly to the right and in favour of some form of pan-Arabism, with a good measure of Islam thrown in. The Free Officers were composed primarily of these elements, and if the 1958 *coup d'état* had reflected their orientations accurately it would have been an altogether different affair. The enigmatic Qasim, in a super-conspiracy, diverted control into his own hands, and whether from social–ideological sympathies or from a strategy of self-interest, he

thwarted the nationalist officers with the aid of the Communist Party
and its popular organization, at least for a time. The Communist
Party, in turn, became involved in the politics of conspiracy and
established a solid base within the armed forces during the Qasim
years, but for a complex variety of reasons it seemed to lack the will
for winning that game, a failure which was to cost it dear.

## Communalism and Nationhood

'Communalism', social organization and solidarity on the basis of
particularistic identification of tribe, village, religion, ethnicity or
region, was the dominant social pattern in Ottoman times and
survived the processes of modernity (but in crucially different forms)
until the present. For Christians and Jews, this principle of corporate
organization was formally enshrined in the so-called 'millet' system
and its adaptations in the successor states. But it is commonly
recognized that corporate communal organization was also general
among Muslims. Religion, was perhaps the most important marker
of identity: superimposed on the particular local community,
however isolated, was the consciousness of a universal 'sacral
community'[3] of faith. For the Sunni Muslim, however lowly his
particular status might have been, his sacral community was co-
extensive with the political entity of the Ottoman Empire. By the
same token, the Shi'i was excluded from this (theoretical) sphere of
primacy and, though Muslim, marginalized. But, unlike the Christian
or the Jew, he still had a (theoretical) claim to this primacy, which
had illegitimately been assumed by usurpers. However quiescent the
Shi'i community may have been (and they were quiescent, for the
most part, in the later history of the Ottoman Empire), this remained
an implicit issue between Muslim communities. In Baghdad, it was
spatially represented in the juxtaposition of al-A'dhamiyyah and al-
Kadhimiyyah across the river Tigris, the first identified by the title of
*al-imam al-a'dham*, Abu-Hanifa, whose *madhhab* was that of the
Ottoman establishment, the second by the shrines of the Shi'i Imam
of that name. This juxtaposition plays an important part in the
modern history of Iraq, especially in the 1950s and 1960s.

'Communalism' may be considered an 'ideal type' model for social
solidarity and consciousness which, during the nineteenth century,
came to co-exist with another ideal type, that of nationality or
nationalism. The French Revolution model of political community,

initially the domain of particular sectors of the Ottoman intelligentsia (at first, in the middle decades of the nineteenth century, conceiving the whole of the Ottoman entity as a nation-sate, later, towards the end of the century, operating at the level of particular ethnic or regional nationalisms), was then diffused through the socio-economic and techno-cultural processes of modernity to much wider sectors of society, and more fully generalized under the political and educational systems of successor nation-states.

Examples of political action and affiliation based on communalist interests and solidarities are common in Iraq as elsewhere, usually disguised under some modern ideological label, though the salience of political Islam in recent years has legitimized open communalism, whether Muslim or Christian, primarily in Lebanon, but also in Egypt. However, communal background can also enter into the construction of forms and orientations of politics within the national model of political community. These are the examples which will concern us primarily.

For Christian and Jewish minorities, the political choices are as follows. The 'traditional' option, followed by many religious leaders and their followers, is to maximize communal interests of security (ever an important consideration) and economic opportunity. This is best pursued through quietly supporting existing authority and seeking connections of patronage and mutual interest with government personnel at different levels. This attitude seeks the maintenance of communal identity and separateness (in which religious leaders have a vested interest), while at the same time furthering communal interests within the national entity. Understandably, many members of the intelligentsia and modern businessmen are dissatisfied with this kind of mentality and seek closer personal as well as communal integration into mainstream national life. To facilitate this process, a national life must be constructed which allows such integration, that is to say, one in which communal identities and solidarities are not the determinants of participation. Wealthy businessmen and prominent professionals may find individual paths to such participation and integration, although, at least for Jews, this has always been hazardous and uncertain.

More typically, however, the rejection of traditional models and authorities led politically-conscious members of these communities to the adoption of some form of oppositional politics, active or passive, usually in the form of support for the Communists or the National Democrats. It should be clear that such an identification does not follow from the pursuit of particular communal interests or of personal interests for the members of a disadvantaged community, but from an ideological pursuit of an integrated national community. For sectors of the Syrian Christian communities from the nineteenth century, similar preoccupations with the construction of a secular national community led them into the path of Arab or Syrian nationalism. In Iraq, as we have seen, Arab nationalism was seen by many as divisive of the Iraqi national community. The National Democrats and the Communist Party were the main Iraqist forces. In addition the secularist and internationalist emphases of Communist ideology may have been particularly attractive in a situation in which religious solidarities and discrimination on the basis of religious affiliation were prevalent and considered as major reactionary forces obstructing the creation of a modern nation.

There was, however, another option open for members of these religious minorities: the European option. This was the search for wider horizons by means of identification with Europe; the idea that the minorities had more in common with the Western world than with the Arab, and the search for personal salvation in eventual migration to Europe or to North America. For many Jews, Israel fulfilled a similar function as an imagined strip of Europe in the Middle East. In the case of Lebanon, this sort of attitude did not confine itself to migration, but sought to make the country itself an extension of Europe. This option was not open to Iraqis.

For the Kurds, communalism meant traditional tribal and sufi leadership and models of social organization, both explicitly rejected by most of the modern intelligentsia. In reality, however, there were many instances of mixed patterns of tribal and national leaderships, including that of Mullah Mustafa himself. In terms of the national model, political Kurds had to reconcile Kurdish and Iraqi identifications, for outright separatism was not a realistic option and adopted only by some nationalists under particular conditions. The endemic wars were mostly for 'rights' and 'autonomy'. In practice, 'autonomy' was difficult to define or to implement, more so under dictatorial regimes under whose rule it is difficult for an Iraqi to enjoy liberty, let alone autonomy. This dilemma was grasped by many political Kurds, who realized that Kurdish rights could be implemented only in a democratic country, thus orienting their efforts to Iraqi rather than to merely Kurdish solutions. Within Iraqi politics, Arab nationalist options were, for obvious reasons, ruled out for Kurds, which narrowed the choice to Kurdish or Iraqist parties, some embracing both. Of the Iraqist parties, the Communist Party proved to be the dominant option for Kurds.

For the Shi'a (at least the urban Shi'a), communalism meant social and political organization of towns or urban quarters under the leadership of religious leaders and families of notables. These leaders participated in national politics with the objective of safeguarding communal and personal interests. At that level they were involved, mostly in subordinate positions, in the manoeuvrings of establishment politics under the monarchy. The intelligentsia, sectors of businessmen and the more politically conscious members of the working class were, for the most part, dissatisfied with these forms of leadership and of politics and were themselves attracted to the opposition parties. It would be a mistake to identify Shi'i political activism with any one party or tendency. Shi'i individuals would appear to have been widely spread across the whole spectrum of Iraqi politics, at least as leaders (composition of rank and file membership is more difficult to establish). As Batatu argues, identification of modern political Shi'a with Communism and the left is not justified in numerical terms; their representation in the Communist Party in the 1950s was proportionately lower than that in the population at large. We should also note that prominent leaders of the nationalist movements also comprise Shi'a, notably Muhammad Mahdi Kubba of the Independence Party and Fuad al-Rikabi of the Baath Party. Paradoxically there were hardly any Shi'a in the leadership of the National Democrats. It would seem that Shi'i participation in ideological (as against traditional) politics does not present any common position or world view.

On the other hand, in situations of confrontation between the Communists and the nationalists in the Qasim period, as well as in the resistance to the Baathist coup of 1963, the Shi'i cities and the Shi'i quarters of Baghdad were firmly identified with the Communists and provided shelter for Communist fugitives. This is due to the fact that Communist networks and shelters were deeply entrenched in these locations, and nationalist organization weak or absent (which was characteristic of nationalist organization at the popular level universally).

We may conclude that, although at the level of leadership of political parties Shi'is were widely represented, at the level of popular support and organization Shi'i areas were more likely to be identified with the Communists. This, of course, does not mean that a majority of the inhabitants were Communist sympathizers, but it does indicate that they did not actively eject the Communists or inform on them.

We may speculate that these areas maintained traditions of political dissent, intellectual ferment, secrecy and dissimulation, and that their spatial construction (reputedly Najaf contained a network of hidden cellars and underground passages) facilitated such activities. That is to say, Shi'i towns and quarters were characterized by a political culture of dissent and secrecy which had a certain affinity with Communist organization.

It may be noted here that Batatu favours an explanation of the affinity of Shi'i locations and the Communist Party in terms of class: Shi'i areas are also among the poorest in Baghdad.[4] This explanation may be plausible for poor districts such as 'Aqd al-Akrad, but is not so convincing in relation to traditional Shi'i centres such as Najaf and al-Kadhimiyyah. As Batatu demonstrates elsewhere, Communist organization in these areas included the children of some of the most notable religious and wealthy families, while, it may be supposed, the poorer inhabitants were less likely to be involved in organized activity of any kind, though they may have participated in demonstrations and active resistance.

For urban Sunni communities, we may hypothesize a special relationship between the communal and the national models, identifying, as they did, with the dominance of the (theoretical) sacral community of Ottoman Sunnism. Their communal leaders were also political leaders, first in Ottoman times, and then under the successor nation-state. Their identification with the wider universe of Sunni–Ottoman Islam can be seen as conducive to an equally wide identification with the Arab nation (also predominantly Sunni), at least in theory. At the same time, comprising as they do the main political elites, the Sunnis also contributed leaders and cadres to the whole spectrum of politics, traditional and ideological, establishment and opposition. Batatu shows that the majority of successive Central Committees of the Communist Party in the 1950s were composed of Sunni Arabs.[5] This picture, however, has to be qualified. Urban Sunnis were also, perhaps, the most widely differentiated in terms of class, status and region of both individuals and communities. The army officers who were to be the most influential in the course of political development, for instance, were from predominantly petty bourgeois (small business and landholding) backgrounds from the towns of the north-west, and later from particular clans within that region. Sunni intelligentsia from Baghdad and other major cities tended to have wider outlooks and horizons, and commitments to a variety of political tendencies and ideologies.

## Class and Community in Politics

Marxist and some other classical social theories have tended to
conceptualize 'class' as a set of relationships, interests and solidarities
formed at the level of socio-economic relations and 'given' to the
political level. That is to say, classes as subjects of political action
arrive at the political arena ready-made and there act out their
economic and social interests in conflict with each other. In fact,
some reductionist versions of Marxism conceive of the state and
politics as no more nor less than the pattern of class struggles.
Awareness of the importance of communal solidarities in politics
leads to a modification of this picture into one in which two axes of
social solidarity, the 'vertical' and the 'horizontal', intersect or
coincide. This is an equally reductionist picture, because here, too,
social solidarities formed elsewhere are given to the political field. In
fact, the political field itself plays a crucial part in the formation of
political forces and socio-economic interests. Batatu, in his prelimin-
ary theoretical remarks, poses the problem in terms of social
solidarities of class and community, but is clearly uneasy about the
reductionist implications. He qualifies these formulations by widening
the conception of class beyond the conventional criteria of Marxism
and similar social theory. The substantive analyses in the book
demonstrate clearly the crucial role of the political field in shaping
political forces, whether on the basis of class or community or any
other criteria.

Class considerations enter into modern Iraqi politics in some
obvious ways. The most obvious, perhaps, is that of the coalition of
dominant economic interests in the establishment under the monarchy.
Some 'modern' bourgeois elements, however, such as certain
industrialists, aligned themselves with the National Democratic Party
and were among its leading elements. The general social-democratic
programme of that party coincided with their class interests only
according to a particular political *construction* of those interests. The
least politically class-conscious sectors were the common people,
whether peasants or urban poor, for the most part unorganized, and
under crisis situations inclined to follow religious, communal or
demagogic leaderships. The exception were those sections of the
working class and peasants who were organized by the Communist
Party. The formation of the Communist Party itself (admirably
followed and analysed in Batatu's book) was the product of
particular political conjunctures in which cadres drawn from the

intelligentsia, the petty bourgeoisie and the working class played important parts, inspired by international examples and sometimes guided and aided by elements of the international Communist movement. Its *raison d'être* was to be the party of the peasant and the worker (*al-kadihun*) and it proceeded to fulfil this aim with remarkable success (at least in comparison to its counterparts in other countries in the region) under difficult circumstances in which the sectors of these constituencies that it could reach were limited. It achieved its greatest successes in this respect under the favourable conditions of the earlier Qasim period. The class politics of the lower classes were constructed by the Communist Party in accordance with its ideology and the prevalent political conditions.

Instances of class politics can also be seen in sporadic episodes, based on opportunistic affiliations rather than regular organization. The best example is that of the affinity of elements of the propertied classes to the nationalist bandwagon during the period of the 'red tide' in 1959; fearful of a Communist victory, they supported the only other credible force, the nationalists.

We have seen in the previous section that political affiliation on the basis of community was varied. We distinguished between traditional communalist action (based on communal interests) and political affiliations to modern ideological parties which may be conditioned by world views arising from communal experience or perspectives. We also saw that this left a wide range of choices, and that the choices actually made are often difficult to account for in terms of communal affiliation as such. I may add that under the later Baath regime of recent years, communalism of a different sort is encouraged by state patronage and the elimination of ideological opposition. This point will become clearer after a consideration of the evolution of the political field.

## The State and the Political Field

The modern Iraqi state at its inception was a 'weak' formation, structurally and institutionally 'external' to the society over which it was imposed.[6] The socio-economic and cultural processes of modernity under the nation-state increased the institutional penetration of state into society (by means of economic intervention, education, conscription and policing) but to only a very limited extent ('tribes' were still allowed their own customary law under the monarchy and the scope and forms of application of formal law elsewhere were rather limited). In these respects, it may be argued, the Iraqi state was no different from many other 'Third World' states. Nevertheless, it was much less advanced than other countries in the region, notably Egypt, in which the interpenetration of state and society had proceeded from the time of Muhammad Ali, and under much more favourable conditions of a homogeneous and governable population.

The strategy of a weak state is to rule by repression, which the incipient Iraqi state did. However, the capacity of the monarchical regime for effective repression was limited by a number of factors. The elites and the armed forces which constituted its power base were divided; divisions complicated by the requirements and intrigues of the British imperial masters. These divisions surfaced occasionally in this nominally constitutional-parliamentary regime, which also allowed some expression to oppositional political forces. The security services did not command sufficient resources and loyalties for more effective and systematic repression (compared to that which has followed in recent years), thus allowing an oppositional political field to develop and function, now openly, now secretly. The monarchical regime fostered and encouraged traditional communalist and tribal politics and incorporated the leaders of these forces into the regime, but could not prevent the development of ideological and class politics.

The monarchical regime can be contrasted with the Baath regime of more recent years. Although initially based on ideological politics and popular agitation, the Baath Party never commanded a wide popular base. It came to power via conspiratorial politics, then proceeded to eliminate its rivals and all possible bases of opposition. However, savage repression was not sufficiently effective in eliminating the deeply-rooted Communist Party organization, and only the subterfuge of the national 'front' in the 1970s succeeded in discrediting it, dissolving (voluntarily) the party's popular organizations and exposing its secret apparatuses. Having eliminated its rivals, the regime then turned upon itself, and, in a series of purges, progressively narrowed its ruling elites to particular clans and families. The party then becomes a vehicle of loyalty to the ruling clique, and the ideology a symbol of that loyalty. This process was, of course, considerably facilitated by the spectacular growth in oil revenue in the 1970s, allowing the expansion and equipment of the security and surveillance apparatuses on the one hand, and the extension of state and party patronage on the other.

Does the Baath regime have any more organic interconnections with the society it governs than the monarchical regime did? Is it any less 'external'? This is a question difficult to answer without systematic study. All I can say is that if such organic relationships had been established, the regime would not need the extent of repression that it continues to use. Certainly the regime is much more effective than its predecessors in subordinating and policing the society under its control. It is also more able to buy loyalty through patronage. And this is an important factor in relation to the question of 'communalism'.

The Baath regime rules in a situation in which the power of the traditional elites (landlords, merchants, tribal and religious leaders, in so far as they survive) have been eliminated or firmly subordinated to the state (except when these happen to be members of the ruling clans). At the same time, state patronage proceeds on particularistic bases of kinship, religious and regional networks. This, together with constant feelings of threat and insecurity, encourages the formation and maintenance of particularistic solidarities on the bases of kinship and religion, with leaders and patrons negotiating privileges with government departments and personnel. That is to say, communalism is reconstructed, not necessarily in terms of historical continuities with traditional formations, but on bases favoured by the current situation. The 'orientalist' picture of 'Islamic' societies as communalistic, religious and impervious to modern ideologies has actually been realized as a modern phenomenon under totalitarian regimes in Iraq and elsewhere.

Sandwiched between the two regimes sketched above, the Qasim period presents a very different picture, perhaps unique in the modern history of the Middle East. As Batatu makes clear,[7] the 1958 Revolution was a great deal more than a military *coup d'état*. Organized political groups were briefed beforehand and assumed active roles in the support for the Revolution. Vast crowds of the popular classes poured into the streets to demonstrate support and voice their demands. More to the point, political parties and their conflicts played a crucial role in determining the direction of the Revolution. Qasim's weakness *vis-à-vis* his military colleagues forced him to rely increasingly on civilian political forces, mostly Communists and National Democrats. Later his attempted balancing act between the Communists and the nationalists continued to foster the expression and organization of ideological politics. In short, under Qasim, the political field was wide open, in spite of sporadic repressions.

Under the conditions of the Qasim regime, ideological and class politics came to the fore. The organization of political constituencies at popular levels proceeded apace, a process from which the Communists gained the most, but which also led to the organizational elaboration of the nationalist forces and the emergence of the Baath Party as the ideological and political leader of that front. By the same token, traditional communalist forces and politics were on the retreat, their interests and constituencies threatened by the land reforms and by the dominance of class politics challenging traditional privileges. As we have seen, for fear of Communists, they supported nationalist forces. The religious minorities, on the other hand, fearing pan-Arabism and its association with Sunni Islam, tended to support the Communists. That is to say, traditional and communalist interests could function politically only through support for the ideological parties, whether or not they subscribed to their ideologies. The Mosul events of 1959 (superbly analysed in Chapter 44 of Batatu's *Old Social Classes*) illustrate these processes very well.

For these reasons, the Qasim regime is the nearest that Iraq came to populist politics, involving the mobilization and organization of the masses by ideological political forces. The government may still have been institutionally 'external' to society, but was coming nearer to the people politically. This is the most 'national' period in Iraqi history, when the fragmented society most closely approached a common national purpose, albeit in a situation of basic conflict. The conflict itself, however, was fuelled to a greater degree than hitherto by national and class objectives which subordinated communalistic factions. Could this situation have lasted?

### Notes

1. Hanna Batatu, *The Old Social Classes and the Revolutionary Movements of Iraq* (Princeton, 1978), p. 36.
2. Ibid., p. 832.
3. Benedict Anderson, *Imagined Communities* (London, 1983) uses the term 'sacral community' to contrast with the imagined community of the nation.
4. Batatu, *Old Social Classes*, pp. 983–85.
5. Ibid., p. 856, Table 42–7.
6. I have elaborated the concepts and issues used here regarding the relation of state to society in the Middle East in an essay on the subject in my *Islam, the People and the State: Essays on Political Ideas and Movements* (London, 1989), pp. 121–82.
7. Batatu, *Old Social Classes*, pp. 805–07.

# 12

# The Old Social Classes Revisited

## HANNA BATATU

When I began working on *The Old Social Classes* in the late 1950s, I was irresistibly drawn to the literature on revolution. I do not know precisely why, but probably my Palestinian background explains it. The disruptions of the lives and world of many Palestinians made them, so to speak, natural rebels. In Iraq the time was one of troubles and unusual ideological and emotional ferment. The spirit of revolution was in the air. Moreover, what happened in Iraq in 1958 and 1959, and later in 1963 – awe-inspiring and terrible events whose course I watched closely and with intense interest – confirmed me in the view that it is in moments of great upheaval that societies are best studied. It seemed, indeed, that at no other moment did Iraqi society bare itself as much or disclose more of its secrets.

In brief, I developed a craving particularly for books on the Russian, French and English revolutions. As I delved into them it struck me how different images of the same revolution, and especially of the Bolshevik Revolution, emerged from accounts by different historians. There was also at that time a debate in progress in British periodicals on the social origins of the English Civil War of the 1640s, which was carried on with extraordinary vehemence. Outstanding historians – R. H. Tawney, H. R. Trevor-Roper, J. H. Hexter, Lawrence Stone, among others – mobilizing different facts and varying types of evidence, could not agree whether the revolution against King Charles I was led by a rising, profit-calculating, landed gentry, by a decaying landed gentry unconnected with the royal court and deprived of its largess, or by some other social force. The issue was never resolved. I also read a fascinating book on that famous product of the French Revolution, Napoleon. In *Napoleon: For and Against*, Pieter Geyl, a Dutch historian, showed how the interpretation of Napoleon differed from generation to generation and from one historical period to another, depending upon the background and the political and social beliefs of the historian and the literary figures of the time. He clinched his observations with a statement that remained vivid in my memory. 'History', he said, 'is an argument without end.'[1]

All of this was on my mind when I was writing *The Old Social Classes*. At no point was I under the illusion that my book was anything more than *one possible* interpretation of *some* aspects of Iraqi reality. This is why I underlined at the beginning 'the tentative nature' of my inquiry.[2]

I was also conscious of my intellectual predilections. 'In any historical work one does', I warned the reader in the preface, 'there is history but there is also always something of oneself. This is unavoidable. If only unwittingly, one bares one's own narrowness of experience and one's intellectual and temperamental inadequacies.' I did not hide my temperamental bias, but I tried hard to keep it under control. That my sympathies were engaged on the side of the poor and the powerless was easily perceptible. However, I did not, at least consciously, arrange the facts to suit my sympathies.

I had and continue to have another temperamental disposition. I seem unable to analyse matters in terms of realpolitik – it is simply contrary to my nature. Intellectually I was attracted by the dynamism and relevance of many of Karl Marx's ideas, some elements of which essentially date back to Aristotle, but I did not accept all of Marx's concepts and those I accepted I did not accept uncritically. Nor did I use them in an *a priori* or mechanical fashion. I also found some of Max Weber's categories of thought helpful in reading the historical situation. Weber, in fact, systematized many elements relating to the phenomenon of class that had been already articulated by Marx. But, of course, in many other aspects the two thinkers were a world apart. Whereas Weber, for example, ascribed to his concepts a value-free quality (a debatable assertion), Marx's concepts are avowedly not only descriptive and explanatory but also critical, value-charged and action-oriented.

At any rate, my book does not reflect merely the emphasis on structural history which I owe to Marx, but also some elements of British empiricism, especially its scrupulous regard for facts and its distrust of large generalizations. There is, I think, a mirroring in my book of the tension between these two intellectual traditions. The large amount of facts that I accumulated on one aspect or another of Iraqi society pointed not infrequently in many different directions and had a paralysing effect on me. This is why I often qualified or limited my statements in some way and, on the whole, avoided broad generalizations and confined my analysis to a low or middle level of generality.

One other point needs to be emphasized. I originally intended to publish a book merely on the old social classes and the Communist movement of Iraq. This is why in Volume II and in many of the chapters in Volume III the accent of the discussion is on the Communists. Subsequently I gained access to documents relating to the Free Officers and to the Baath Party and was afforded the opportunity to meet with many of their leaders. Eventually nearly half of Volume III was devoted to these movements and the political order that they established. I therefore felt justified in altering the title of my book accordingly. I duly warned my readers in the Preface (xxi) that the history of the Communists formed the original nucleus of Volumes II and III and is represented on a scale larger than the history of the Free Officers and the Baathists, but many reviewers at that time and later missed this warning and formed the impression that I had exaggerated the role of the Communists. I must add, however, that I was always convinced, and remain so today, that in the 1950s the Communists had a more profound influence on the intelligentsia and the labouring people than had either the Baathists or the Free Officers.

\*    \*    \*    \*    \*

Although the authors of the various chapters of the present book deal directly or indirectly with one aspect or another of the Iraqi Revolution of July 1958, they raise different and disparate issues. It is best, therefore, to consider each of their interpretations separately. I follow the sequence of the chapters.

Norman Daniel draws interesting comparisons between the Iraqi Revolution and revolutions in other historical settings, but sets himself the main task of recapturing 'the state of mind' of Iraqis on around 14 July and in the immediate aftermath of the Revolution. He writes colourfully and sometimes in a manner resembling that of poets, who tend to be more suggestive than logically lucid but often see beneath the surface.

I do not share Daniel's view that the reference to 'the lessening influence of Islam' by the British Ambassador Sir John Troutbeck was 'a misjudgement' or 'a monumental error'. I think that Daniel is here reading history backwards in the light of the revival of Islamism after the Arab defeat of 1967 and the deepening of this trend in the wake of the Iranian Revolution. In the middle of the 1950s the prominent Najafi Imam Ayatullah Muhammad al-Husayn Kashif al-Ghita' himself bemoaned the weakening of the religious sense of the people.[3]

Wm. Roger Louis adds much to our knowledge of the British view of the Iraqi scene in the decade before the Revolution. He discusses in depth the opinions of the United Kingdom's last two ambassadors to Iraq's monarchy, Sir John Troutbeck and Sir Michael Wright.

With regard to the causes of the Revolution, Louis discerns a clash between me, on the one hand, and Sir Michael Wright and Michael Ionides, a British economic expert, on the other. He draws a contrast between Wright's and Ionides' 'deliberate political interpretation' and my 'overarching emphasis' on structural changes and dislocations. In my opinion, there are in history hidden processes and surface events and these are interrelated. Hidden processes are noiseless, almost indiscernible. By contrast surface events are sometimes drab, sometimes spectacular and tempestuous, but at all times plainly evident. By dint of function and preoccupation, a diplomatic envoy or a foreign expert, unless he is deeply familiar with the history of the country in which he serves, is more likely to be sensitive to surface events than to hidden processes. We know to what conclusion Michael Wright's 'deliberate political interpretation' led him: 'For it is quite certain', he wrote on 22 April 1958 – less than three months before the Revolution – 'that, today, a revolutionary situation does not exist.'[4] It is almost an echoing of Nuri Said's boast at the end of 1956 that 'dar al-sayyid ma'muna' ('The house of the master is secure'), which Abdul-Salaam Yousif has occasion to mention in his chapter.[5] This on the one hand.

On the other hand, while in the conclusion (1113–1116) and other parts of my book (465–82 and 805–07) the analysis was in terms of structural or long-range causes, in my chapter on the Revolution (765–67) I delineated in some detail the various short-term factors that were instrumental in generating the mood of revolt in the army and that led the Free Officers to strike their blow on 14 July. Most of these factors were of a political rather than of an economic nature. Clearly, both short-term and long-term factors were at play and the structural explanation and the short-range explanation are not mutually exclusive but complement one another.

Nicholas G. Thacher and Frederick W. Axelgard throw much light upon the policy of the US government towards Iraq in the 1950s. Both bring into focus the undue weight Washington gave to British concerns and the attendant adverse consequences. It is not without interest that, as Thacher points out, Dulles, Nuri and working-level State Department functionaries were aware of the perils and drawbacks for Iraq's monarchy inherent in its involvement in a Western-sponsored military system, but this did not deter American officials from exerting, in the words of Axelgard, 'consistent pressure' on Nuri to 'hustle' him (Nuri's own graphic metaphor) into a NATO-style organization.[6] Thacher is of the opinion that the interests of the American government would have been better served by 'a system of quiet assurances' similar to the one it used to shore up the Saudi monarchy.[7] For his part, Axelgard thinks that events in Iraq might have taken a different turn if the United States had distanced itself from the British and pursued an independent line more in tune with local political realities. At any rate, it is clear that American policy showed little sensitivity to Arab popular opinion or to the dominant Iraqi desire to steer clear of outside entanglements and the contentions of the cold war. The declassified American documents upon which Axelgard relied appear also to point to the absence of any long-term approach to the Middle East and to reflect what George F. Kennan called a 'diplomacy by dilettantism'.[8]

The amoral nature of international power politics is amply illuminated in Joe Stork's searching contribution to the understanding of the behaviour of the great powers in the region. The Soviet government sacrificed the revolutionary interests of Iraq's Communists whenever they conflicted with the interests of the Soviet state. The USSR's pro-Israeli orientation in 1947–48, when the Palestine question was at its highest crisis point, and its cautionary advice to the Iraqi Communists in 1959, when the flow of people toward their party was at its fullest, increased the ICP's vulnerability to the devastating blows that eventually fell upon them.

Stork discerns a similarity in the reactions of the US government to the Iraqi Revolution of 1958 and to the Iranian Revolution of 1979. It viewed both revolutions as expressions of a trend inimical to Western interests and inclining towards 'chaos', and countered them in a similar way – with a military intervention at some other points in the region. In the pursuit of its interest in an 'unfettered access' to

Middle Eastern oil at 'acceptable prices', it pitted Iran against Iraq oil nationalism in the 1960s and 1970s as it had pitted Iraq and other Arab states against Iranian oil nationalism in the early 1950s. In the 1980s the workings of the balance-of-power diplomacy and Saddam Hussein's weakness led to his curious enmeshment with the superpowers and his role as an instrument for the containment of the Iranian revolution.

But this summary does not do enough justice to Stork's arguments, which are as complex as they are balanced. He warns against too hasty a view of Iraq as a mere pawn on the international chessboard and reminds us that the dynamics of internal forces, such as those at work in Iraq in 1958–59 or in Iran in 1979, may have a role in shaping regional and international power constellations.

Rashid Khalidi rightly sees in the Iraqi Revolution more than an Iraqi phenomenon. It bore distinctive Iraqi traits but had also an Arab or regional meaning. The great Arab family, if split into jealous and discordant units, forms a definite 'sub-system' of the international order. Within this sub-system there is 'a common discourse' flowing largely from the common language that it shares. If only on this account, and also because Iraq was a link in the British imperial power chain and one of the larger and wealthier of the Arab states, the Iraqi Revolution was bound to reverberate in the region. Khalidi looks at its impact primarily in the light of the ensuing open clash between the particularist and pan-Arab trends. The clash assumed regional dimensions, weakened both the Communists and the pan-Arabists, poisoned the relations between the Arabs and the Soviet Union and paved the ground for the shift to the right that came to characterize Arab politics in the 1970s. In tracing and analysing these after effects of the Revolution, Khalidi provides us with a picture which is as faithful to the facts as it is instructive.

Marion Farouk-Sluglett and Peter Sluglett illuminate the political background and socio-economic context of the 1958 Revolution. In my view, their most interesting contributions are the hypotheses they put forth as bases for further historical inquiry.

Their main provisional supposition is that in Iraq capitalism penetrated rapidly from the middle of the nineteenth century into the realm of trade and commerce, but by the time of the Revolution it had left the 'pre-capitalist' relations of production largely unaffected. If by 'capitalism' is meant an economic system based on the possession of private capital and its use for production and the exchange of goods or a system of society characterized by the dominance of private capitalists, it cannot be denied that the greater part of Iraq's agriculture, in which the majority of the active population was involved, was not *directly* dominated by capital, even though there were in 1958 quite a few large-scale estates managed by merchants on modern capitalist lines, such as the 64,396-acre Latifiyyah, owned by the Chalabi family. At the same time, I am of the opinion that, at least on the agricultural estates of the big shaikhs and the other large landholders, who between them controlled 55.1% of all privately held land in 1958, the 'pre-capitalist' relations of production survived in form rather than in their inner spirit.

It is true that in most of these estates production was not based on wage-labour: the most common cultivators were, as previously, sharecroppers, who tilled the land in family units and were paid in the traditional way, that is, in kind rather than in cash. But the degree of their exploitation intensified. For example, the *murabba'ji* in the Mosul region, who was so-called because formerly he was allowed a quarter of the crop, after the First World War received no more than an eighth.

It is also true that on the whole the major shaikhs were not strictly speaking a business-like class, if only because of their thriftless ways or their concern to maintain their traditional dignity, but they were increasingly driven by the idea of maximizing their income.

A more extortionate treatment of peasants in the matter of crop-sharing was facilitated by the growing practice by shaikhs of hiring sharecroppers from *radd*, or client and weaker, tribes. For instance, the leading families of the Shammar tribe – the Yawers, Farhans and Shallals – who in 1958 owned 444,604 acres (58–59 and 870–71), farmed the land for their own profit, not with Shammarites but with hired labour from extraneous tribes.

Another factor that had the effect of reducing the sharecropper's portion of the farm produce was the rapid growth in the use of pumps: no fewer than 5264 pumps were in use in Iraq in 1957 (150). Investment in pressure pumps was one of the ways by which urban capitalists intruded into landholding, sometimes as partners of shaikhs. Many shaikhs themselves, however, also owned pumps.

Moreover, the expansion of internal and external commerce eroded the subsistence character of the agricultural economy: the shaikhly estate now increasingly produced for a market, and the sharecropper, though he himself merely subsisted, was becoming increasingly a commodity producer. This is suggested by, among other things, the rise of the value of Iraq's export of wheat and barley through the port of Basra from £16,000 (sterling) in 1868 to £612,000 (sterling) in 1908 (241) and of the weight of the average yearly total export of these products from 89,100 tons in 1919–25 to 354,900 tons in 1952–58 (264).

Land itself was also undergoing rapid transformation into a commodity. As early as the 1890s a *jarib* of date-palms, that is, a hectare including one hundred of such palms, was selling in the neighbourhood of Baghdad at almost three times its price in the 1880s (241). During Midhat Pasha's governorship (1869–71) state lands were alienated in *tapu* – a form of conditional but heritable and transferable private tenure – at no more than 4 shillings an acre (240). By 1958 a good rain-fed acre fetched on the average about £3 (sterling), a good irrigated acre about £16 (sterling) and an exceptionally good acre about £81 (sterling) (57).

The spread of private property, in the form of *tapu* and the analogous *lazma* tenure, and its coverage of the bulk of cultivated and cultivable land was also bound to assist the direct or indirect penetration of capitalism into agriculture; in the West agrarian capitalism could not have developed historically without private property as its basis.

It is hard to imagine that all the aforementioned factors did not seriously erode the 'pre-capitalist' agricultural relations of production in Iraq, but the subject bears further research and reflection.

I unreservedly agree with the Slugletts' other major observation: the need for a study in depth of the urban intermediate strata, that is, the small manufacturers, the retailers, the middling wholesale merchants, the owners of service esablishments and the like.

It would be a mistake to draw too sharp a distinction between these elements and the other components of the middle class, that is, the professionals, the bureaucrats and the army officers (For their relative numerical strength, consult Table 59.7, 1126). As I pointed out in my book (1129–30), to make such a distinction would be

tantamount to viewing the various middle-class elements in isolation of the living network of social relationships, that is, to losing sight of such things as informal partnerships or connections between bureaucrats and merchants or the frequent linkages of officials or army officers and tradespeople or proprietors through the family or extended family.

To be more concrete, in the same middle-class family it is often the case that one member is a retailer, another an army officer or a bureaucrat, a third a teacher, and so on. In other words, it is not the individual but the family that constitutes the basic unit of class. This is why I treated 'the business segment of the middle class' (1129) as part of a larger and politically more meaningful whole.

It is no accident that in the first post-revolutionary decade, when the holders of ultimate power were Free Officers, the small-scale traders enjoyed greater facilities than under the monarchy in regard to collaterals and bank credit, and experienced an enhancement in their material situation as the result of the lowering of shop rents by as much as 37% (1129). 'Abd-us-Salam Arif, a Free Officer, who led the republic from 1963 to 1966, and his successor and brother, 'Abd-ur-Rahman, another Free Officer, were sons of a draper. Similarly, the more prominent of their prime ministers, Taher Yahya, also a Free Officer, was the son of a 'alawji, or grain tradesman. To some extent, the Free Officers' movement could be said to have represented, if indirectly, the interests of the small and middle business elements, particularly those of recent rural provenance.

Robert A. Fernea gives us a faithful portrayal of the ideas, values, political practices and social relations prevalent in 1958 before the Revolution in a tribal settlement in the Euphrates region in the neighbourhood of Diwaniyyah. I can only wish that there were more anthropological studies of the kind that Fernea has made or that Shakir Mustapha Salim has provided on Chebayyish.

At first sight it might seem as if my understanding of the shaikhs and that of Fernea diverge markedly. This stems in part from our different uses of the term 'shaikh'. There were in Iraq under the monarchy about 200 tribes and some 3,500 tribal sections. I used the title 'shaikh' to refer exclusively to the chiefs of tribes. In the British and Iraq official records it was also used in this sense. The heads of tribal sections were referred to either as 'sub-shaikhs' or sirkals, because the sirkals, that is, the men directly in charge of cultivation on a shaikhly estate, were often also the heads of tribal sections. I realize that in the countryside the appellation 'shaikh' was widely and sometimes indiscriminately used. To enhance his status, the chief of the smallest tribal sub-section often called himself 'shaikh' and was so addressed by his followers. It would not have been sociologically meaningful for me to lump such a man and a leader of a tribe under the same rubric and treat them as if they belonged to the same social class or status group.

Roger Owen points to an important flaw in my book. He affirms that the state as a cluster of interacting institutions is not present in my study and that there is little discussion, except in an incidental way, of day-to-day class politics or of the role of the British Embassy or the British advisers. I agree fully. I also agree that such a discussion, as should be clear from Owen's own contribution, would have enhanced our understanding of the social structure and of the relative political influence of the various groups and classes, and would have shed much light on the motives behind official policies.

At the same time, in several of its other aspects, the state is present in my book. For example, by analysing the various components of the upper landed class or the social composition of the cabinets or of parliament, I was, in a sense, analysing the social character of the state. Again, the policies of the state in various periods are discussed at some length, but, for the most part, only from the standpoint of their structural effects. It will also be remembered that my main concern and interest was in the indigenous social classes; this is why I impersonalized the British or treated them as an abstraction.

I did not explore the matter of the 'colonial state' because I did not have the necessary data for discussing it meaningfully. For example, the papers of the British Embassy for the 1950s, which Wm. Roger Louis has perused, had not yet been opened to the public. I also could not at that time travel to India where embassy records for earlier periods were kept.

As far as the monarchical state institutions were concerned, I then had the sense that while these institutions counted for something, men and groups counted for much more. Even as late as 1953, Ambassador Sir John Troutbeck, as Louis points out, referred, perhaps not without some overcolouring, to the 'artificiality' of the Iraqi state.[9] The bureaucracy itself was also of modest proportions. All the pensionable government officials, excluding the employees of the railway and of the port of Basra, amounted to only 3,143 in 1920, 9,740 in 1938 and 20,931 in 1958. Today, by contrast, the pensionable bureaucrats number in the hundreds of thousands. Moreover, when Nuri Said rose to the premiership in 1930, he dismissed 'incompetent' officials and filled many of the important places with his own men. He did the same thing when he returned to power in 1939 and other premiers followed suit. Parliament itself had more often than not the characteristic of a rubber-stamp institution. The source of internal policy after 1930, therefore, is not a real problem.

Abdul-Salaam Yousif focuses on the cultural roots and features of the Iraqi Revolution. He shows that this great event had a long incubation period culturally and succeeds in conveying a sense of the importance of Marxism in the unabating work of cultural criticism that preceded its outbreak. From the end of the Second World War Marxism grew increasingly into a widely diffused ideological atmosphere which left its imprint on the rhetoric, imagery and way of thinking even of its opponents and eventually invested the Revolution with intense emotional significance. Abdul-Salaam links its influence in part to the success of its advocates in relating it to indigenous popular traditions. Turning to the cultural effects of the Revolution, he points to 'the democratization of culture' which it initiated, widening, as it did, educational opportunities and cultural access and generating new forms of expression such as the composition of poems or elevated prose in the vernacular. He also draws attention to the use by the Revolution of cultural symbols such as the figure of the 'Imprisoned Thinker' or 'The Monument to Liberty' which had a role in shaping popular perceptions. In the view of Abdul-Salaam, the political culture associated with the Revolution did not survive the rise of the Baath to power: the campaign of repression unleashed against the Marxist intelligentsia and its allies and the flight into exile of no fewer than 700 Iraqi intellectuals contributed to 'the improverishment of Iraqi culture'.[10]

In his closely reasoned chapter essay Sami Zubaida discusses the role in Iraqi politics – particularly in the period preceding and immediately following the 14 July Revolution – of the 'type' of consciousness and solidarity which he identifies as 'communalism' and which is anchored in religion, sect, ethnicity, tribe or region. He also attempts to trace the relationships between this and other forms of loyalty such as those based on class, on Iraqi, Arab or Kurdish nationhood, or on the larger Islamic community. He draws a valid distinction between traditional 'communal' action, which was oriented toward purely 'communal' interests, and political action in the context of the more recent history of Iraq, which was merely conditioned by 'communal' experiences and perspectives. The generalizations that he makes and that flow naturally from this distinction compel assent and are borne out by the historical facts.

I am reluctant to go along all the way with Zubaida's generalization that under the Baathists 'communalism [has been] reconstructed . . . on bases favoured by the current situation.'[11] It is true that the top of the present power structure rests to an important degree on solidarities based on region and kinship. It is also true that the distance between the Kurdish minority and the regime has widened. Saddam Hussein has, however, associated the Shi'is more meaningfully with his regime and extended economic benefits to their areas. I am moreover inclined to the view that the Iraq–Iran war, despite all its negative aspects, has, like the Uprising of 1920 and the Revolution of 1958 – and, probably, the present crisis of 1990 – brought the Sunnis and Shi'is closer together, if only by dint of their common suffering, and assisted the progress of Iraq towards national coherence.

## Notes

1. Pieter Geyl, *Napoleon: For and Against* (London, 1949), pp. 15–18.
2. *The Old Social Classes and the Revolutionary Movements of Iraq* (Princeton, 1978), p. 5. Hereafter page references are given in the text.
3. See my article 'Iraq's Underground Shi'i Movements Characteristics, Causes, and Prospects', *Middle East Journal*, vol. 35, 4 (Autumn 1981), pp. 586–87.
4. See Wm. Roger Louis, 'The British and the Origins of the Iraqi Revolution', p. 52, n. 81 above.
5. See Abdul-Salaam Yousif, 'The Struggle for Cultural Hegemony during the Iraqi Revolution', p. 181, n. 26 above.
6. See Frederick W. Axelgard, 'US Support for the British Position in Pre-Revolutionary Iraq', p. 87, n. 24 above.
7. See Nicholas G. Thacher, 'Reflections on US Foreign Policy towards Iraq in the 1950s', p. 74 above.
8. George F. Kennan, *American Diplomacy, 1900–1950* (New York, 1952), p. 92.
9. See Louis, 'The British and the Origins of the Iraqi State', p. 36 above.
10. See Yousif, 'The Struggle for Cultural Hegemony', pp. 179 and 185 above.
11. Sami Zubaida, 'Community, Class and Minorities in Iraqi Politics', p. 209 above.

# Index